SharePoint 2003 Advanced Concepts

Microsoft Windows Server System Series

Books in the **Microsoft Windows Server System Series** are written and reviewed by the world's leading technical authorities on Microsoft Windows technologies, including principal members of Microsoft's Windows and Server Development Teams. The goal of the series is to provide reliable information that enables administrators, developers, and IT professionals to architect, build, deploy, and manage solutions using the Microsoft Windows Server System. The contents and code of each book are tested against, and comply with, commercially available code. This series should be an invaluable resource for any IT professional or student working in today's Windows environment.

TITLES IN THE SERIES

Paul Bertucci, *Microsoft SQL Server High Availability*, 0-672-32625-6 (Sams)

Peter Blackburn and William R. Vaughn, *Hitchhiker's Guide to SQL Server 2000 Reporting Services*, 0-321-26828-8 (Addison-Wesley)

William Boswell, *Learning Exchange Server 2003*, 0-321-22874-X (Addison-Wesley)

Roberta Bragg, *Windows Server 2003 Security*, 0-321-30501-9 (Addison-Wesley)

Bill English, Olga Londer, Shawn Shell, Todd Bleeker, and Stephen Cawood, *Microsoft Content Management Server 2002: A Complete Guide*, 0-321-19444-6 (Addison-Wesley)

Don Jones, *Managing Windows® with VBScript and WMI*, 0-321-21334-3 (Addison-Wesley)

Sakari Kouti and Mika Seitsonen, *Inside Active Directory, Second Edition: A System Administrator's Guide*, 0-321-22848-0 (Addison-Wesley)

Shyam Pather, *Microsoft SQL Server 2000 Notification Services*, 0-672-32664-7 (Sams)

Jeffrey R. Shapiro and Marcin Policht, *Building High Availability Windows Server™ 2003 Solutions*, 0-321-22878-2 (Addison-Wesley)

For more information please go to www.awprofessional.com/msserverseries

SharePoint 2003 Advanced Concepts

Site Definitions, Custom Templates, and Global Customizations

Jason Nadrowski

Stacy Draper

✦✦Addison-Wesley

**Upper Saddle River, NJ • Boston • Indianapolis
San Francisco • New York • Toronto • Montreal
London • Munich • Paris • Madrid • Capetown
Sydney • Tokyo • Singapore • Mexico City**

Many of the designations used by manufacturers and sellers to distinguish their products are claimed as trademarks. Where those designations appear in this book, and the publisher was aware of a trademark claim, the designations have been printed with initial capital letters or in all capitals.

SharePoint is a registered trademark of Microsoft Corporation.

The authors and publisher have taken care in the preparation of this book, but make no expressed or implied warranty of any kind and assume no responsibility for errors or omissions. No liability is assumed for incidental or consequential damages in connection with or arising out of the use of the information or programs contained herein.

The publisher offers excellent discounts on this book when ordered in quantity for bulk purchases or special sales, which may include electronic versions and/or custom covers and content particular to your business, training goals, marketing focus, and branding interests. For more information, please contact:

U.S. Corporate and Government Sales
(800) 382-3419
corpsales@pearsontechgroup.com

For sales outside the United States please contact:

International Sales
international@pearsoned.com

 This Book Is Safari Enabled

The Safari® Enabled icon on the cover of your favorite technology book means the book is available through Safari Bookshelf. When you buy this book, you get free access to the online edition for 45 days.

Safari Bookshelf is an electronic reference library that lets you easily search thousands of technical books, find code samples, download chapters, and access technical information whenever and wherever you need it.

To gain 45-day Safari Enabled access to this book:

- Go to http://www.awprofessional.com/safarienabled
- Complete the brief registration form
- Enter the coupon code N7CX-5UJE-T1U8-Z6EN-LFG3

If you have difficulty registering on Safari Bookshelf or accessing the online edition, please e-mail customer-service@safaribooksonline.com.

Visit us on the Web: www.awprofessional.com

Library of Congress Cataloging-in-Publication Data
Nadrowski, Jason.
  SharePoint 2003 advanced concepts : site definitions, custom templates, and global
customization / Jason Nadrowski, Stacy Draper.
    p. cm.
  ISBN 0-321-33661-5 (pbk. : alk. paper) 1. Intranets (Computer networks) 2. Web
servers. I. Nadrowski, Jason. II. Title.

TK5105.875.I6D73 2006
004.6'8—dc22

2005034769

ISBN 0-321-33661-5

Text printed in the United States on recycled paper at R.R. Donnelley & Sons, Inc., Crawfordsville, IN.
First printing, March 2006

Contents

Preface

There is a lot to SharePoint Portal Server and Windows SharePoint Services; even so, it is finite. We originally wanted to write a book about everything that Share-Point has to offer. As we were writing, books kept coming out, more and more content was available on the Internet, and we didn't want to write about topics that were covered well elsewhere. What we ended up with is a book jammed full of information that was noticeably absent from the SharePoint community.

The techniques we talk about in this book were born out of necessity. We worked on completely different projects and realized that we were having the same problems. Not readily finding solutions to our problems, we discovered the need for this content. When we approached Addison-Wesley, there were already several books on the market. The publisher wanted to know why our book was going to be a good one. The answer was pretty simple—we have lived and breathed the product and have had to solve real business problems. We've been in the trenches with the product and know it intimately. We know what works and what doesn't work in the real world. We're not a couple of authors who have friends or went to college with folks in the product group. We are hands-on architects/programmers who know the product and how to will it to our ways.

To keep things interesting for both the reader and for us, we wrote in a way that will expose you, the reader, to many of the inner workings of SharePoint without becoming a boring reference manual. You'll see problems that we tried to solve and what we did to come up with solutions for those problems. Your problems might not be exactly the same as ours. As a matter of fact, I'm sure the problems won't be identical. But you should find that the problems you encounter with SharePoint in your enterprise can be solved with the solutions we describe. Exposure to these solutions will enable you to explore other areas of SharePoint otherwise hidden from view.

The SharePoint product family seems to touch everything in the Microsoft world. The SharePoint product line relies on servers such as the Windows Server 2003 and SQL Server and leans heavily on Active Directory, ASP.NET, and even a lot of JavaScript. From the user interface side, the Office products make an appearance. All these technologies make SharePoint a tough animal to deal with in terms of a technical tool set. Working with SharePoint sometimes takes relying on a small army of highly skilled folks to pull off a successful implementation or modification—point being, the technologies that are used are many. This certainly shouldn't be your first technology book and probably shouldn't even be the first SharePoint book you own. This book is for people who have wrestled with SharePoint and have tried to make SharePoint behave in a way that it probably wasn't originally designed to do. The person who will benefit most from a book like this might be saying something like, "If I could just make it do this one thing, then everything else would just fall together!"

Organization of This Book

We organized the content of the book into the following chapters.

Chapter 1: Custom Templates

Site templates and list templates are something that end users can work with. They are a great way to empower end users. Sometimes little things can be done to make the SharePoint experience go a long way. This chapter demonstrates the ins and outs of working with site templates and list templates.

Chapter 2: Site Definitions

Site definitions are not the most intuitive thing. In fact, site definitions are quite different from traditional ASPX applications. Chapter 2 explains the use and development of site definitions, while navigating around their more common pitfalls. In this chapter, you'll work with several configuration files. You'll get down to the technical details to make SharePoint a more pliable application.

Chapter 3: Site Definitions: Exploring List Definitions

If it weren't for lists, there wouldn't be much of a SharePoint product at all. Lists are one of those great features found in SharePoint that empower users to create what they need. Even though list definitions are part of site definitions, there is so much to know about lists that it warrants a dedicated chapter. This chapter exposes you to every detail of creating a list definition.

Chapter 4: Customizing and Implementing Property Types in Windows SharePoint Services

Lists are great things. They enable users to create a table of information fairly quickly and present it to other users in a manner that is readily consumable. Of course, there are a couple shortcomings. The first is a lack of a custom property type. The second and most common shortcoming is the need to integrate with other systems. The inability to pull in key information from another system or even another WSS site can be a showstopper. This chapter shows you how to create custom properties—be it for retrieving information stored in another system or for other special functionality.

Chapter 5: Global Customizations

We close the book with a chapter that applies to SharePoint holistically. Customizing themes and help are explained thoroughly. Other common customizations, such as email alerts, and system notifications, such as the site collection retention warning, are also covered. Document libraries are quite powerful as they are, but there is always room for improvement. Detailed information is provided to make documents display and behave differently based on their extensions.

Appendix: Custom_JS.ASPX

The appendix includes a complete listing of the CUSTOM_JS.ASPX file that is discussed in Chapter 4.

Notations

The LCID figures prominently in SharePoint's physical and virtual paths. The LCID for your deployment is based on the particular SharePoint media you have procured. The English version of SharePoint has an LCID of 1033. Because this book was authored in English, we will go out on a limb and presume that most people who read this book have the English version of SharePoint. So, if you are trying to access a path that has 1033 in it, and it doesn't seem to exist, substitute 1033 for your LCID.

Available Language Packs for SharePoint

Language	SharePoint LCID
English	1033
Japanese	1041
German	1031
French	1036
Spanish	3082
Italian	1040
Dutch	1043
Swedish	1053
Danish	1030
Finnish	1035
Norwegian	1044
Portuguese	2070
Brazilian Portuguese	1046
Polish	1045
Turkish	1055
Czech	1029
Hungarian	1038
Greek	1032
Russian	1049
Korean	1042
Simplified Chinese	2052
Traditional Chinese	1028
Arabic	1025
Hebrew	1037
Thai	1054

Acknowledgments

To start off with, we'd like to thank Karen Gettman for facilitating the creation of this book. We'd also like to thank Elizabeth Hurley-Peterson and her assistant Jana Jones for being so great to work with and holding our hands through each step in the process and putting us together with Jim Markham. We are especially grateful for the technical reviews from Goga Kukrika, Eli Robillard, Peter O'Kelly, and Raul Rojas. We are not authors. We are consultants. Taking this step for us was a little difficult—without Jim and our team of reviewers, this book would have never seen the light of day.

We also have to thank our families. Writing a book takes a lot of time. There were plenty of times when our wives were wondering who we actually spent more time with. Thank you for your support.

About the Authors

Jason Nadrowski is managing partner of Information Hub (www.information-hub.com). Jason's focus at the firm is both architecting and managing enterprise technology solutions. Jason has helped a number of Fortune 50 companies architect some of the largest SharePoint implementations. Jason holds the Microsoft certifications MCSD, MCAD, MCDBA, and MCSE. He also holds the PMI's PMP® (Project Management Professional) certification and a number of other accreditations. He graduated from the University of Florida with a Bachelor of Science and a Master of Science in Electrical and Computer Engineering.

Stacy Draper is an independent consultant based in South Florida. Being involved with web development since 1993 has led his life in a very interesting direction. He started out in UNIX and since 1997 has had a strong concentration in Microsoft technologies. Stacy has spoken at conferences large and small and has worked at some well-known and some not well-known companies. In his consulting practice, Wild Wires, LLC, Stacy has always had a practical view and hopes to paint a vivid picture of that view in the pages of this book.

CHAPTER 1

Custom Templates

Custom templates enable a user to define a default layout, functionality, and default content for a newly created site. A parallel can be drawn between a Microsoft Word stationery template and a SharePoint template. For instance, you might have a stationary template for Microsoft Word with your company logo, company colors, office address, and a myriad of other customizations. You can construct a SharePoint template with the same company logo, company colors, and many other customizations. The parallels continue in the application of SharePoint templates as well. Just as you can apply your Microsoft Word template to a new document, you can apply your SharePoint template to a new site.

Two types of custom templates exist: custom *list* templates and custom *site* templates. Custom list templates contain schema and content data for all types of lists. Thus, custom list templates apply to SharePoint lists. They therefore apply to document libraries, picture libraries, links, announcements, custom lists, and many others. Custom site templates apply to SharePoint sites, which could be top-level sites or subsites. Custom site templates contain schema and content data for everything that can be defined on a site, including lists, themes, web part content and layout, as well as many other customizations.

One of the most attractive features of custom templates is the existence of a graphical interface to construct them. This interface exists in the form of the SharePoint web interface as well as Microsoft FrontPage. The simplicity of this interface empowers you to quickly create a default look for your sites and lists that can be applied even more quickly to new sites. This feature avoids the tedious chore of manually performing each customization upon creating a new site. Instead, you click and drag your way to all these customizations.

Understanding Custom Templates

Custom site templates and site definition templates (see Chapter 2, "Site Definitions") appear to the user at site creation as a unified list of choices as shown in Figure 1.1. Custom list and site templates represent a delta or additional customizations to site definition templates. This delta acts as an addition to the base layer to form a two-layer structure. Consequently, custom site and list templates require more server processing than site definition templates.

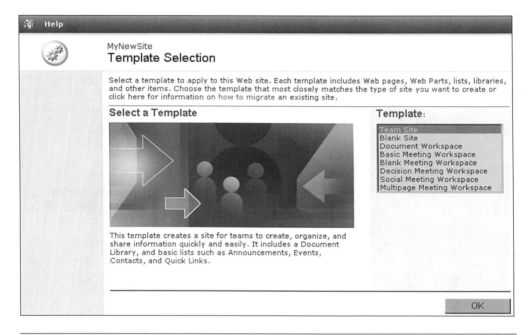

Figure 1.1   Custom template and site definition template selection.

When a user designs a SharePoint list or site, those settings are captured in the database. For instance, a user's customization of a particular site can include applying a site theme, placing web parts, and creating additional list views. All these customizations are stored in the database. The same parallel can be drawn for lists. List customizations—including additional views and stock content—are stored in the database.

SharePoint provides a mechanism to harvest all these customizations to a list or site from the database. That mechanism is a custom template. A custom template is a compilation of customization settings in a single, reusable package. This package defines the delta between the site definition and our site or list customizations.

Custom site and list templates can be created on one server farm and copied to another. A key caveat to successfully rendering the copied template is the existence of the site definition on which the custom template is based. In fact, web parts or any other resources that are referenced in the template must also exist on the new server. If the site definition or other resources that the custom template expects do not exist, the custom template (delta) will have nothing on which to base its changes and will not render. If the site definition is different between server farms, the custom template can render in an unexpected fashion.

Using custom list or site templates is essentially a three-step process. The first step is to customize a list or site as desired. The second step is to save the template to the template gallery. The third and final step is to create a site or list with that template.

It should be noted that there are a few caveats to using custom templates:

- A 10-megabyte limit exists on the total size of a site template.
- Custom templates do not retain the security settings of the site or list from which they were copied.
- Child sites cannot be retained in site templates. You must create any desired child site anew after site creation.

Exploring Custom Site Templates

For the purposes of our conversation, we need a customized site. This site will be customized to serve as the basis for our custom template. We therefore have created a new site based on the *Blank Site* template and customized it through the SharePoint web user interface and Front-Page. The result is shown in Figure 1.2.

Figure 1.2   Customized site on which we want to base our custom site template.

If you are new to SharePoint and are unfamiliar with how to customize a site, either through the SharePoint web interface or through FrontPage, we suggest you refer to one of the many books or articles on the subject because the emphasis in this chapter and this book is on some of the more advanced concepts of custom templates.

Saving a Custom Site Template

The site template is saved through the SharePoint web user interface, which empowers users and avoids the need for administrative intervention. Now that we have a customized site, we are ready to save it as a custom site template for others to reuse. The steps to save the custom site template are enumerated next.

1. Navigate to Site Settings in the newly customized site.
2. Select Site Administration under the Administration section.
3. Select Save Site As Template, which is in the Management and Statistics section (see Figure 1.3).

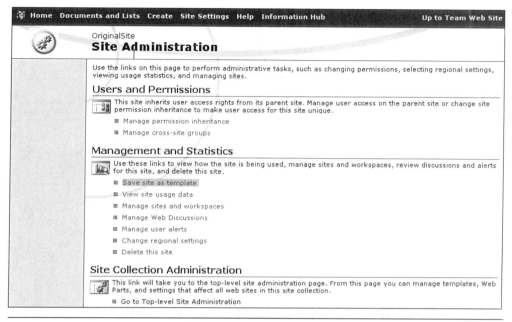

Figure 1.3 Site Administration page with Save Site As Template highlighted.

4. Fill out the Save Site as Template page (see Figure 1.4) as appropriate and then click OK. You can always change the filename, template title, and template description later in the template library. At this time you must decide whether to include the list and library content.

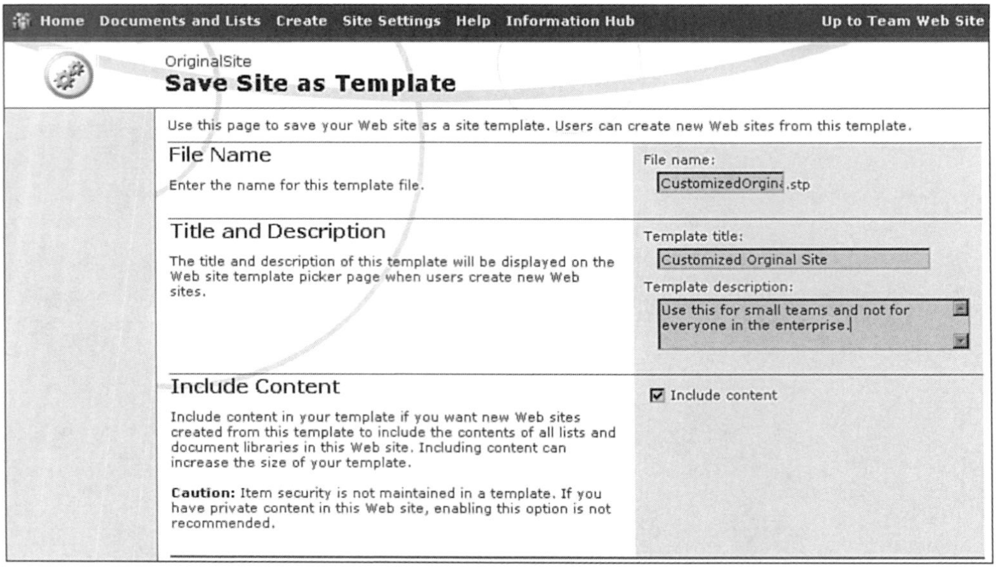

Figure 1.4   Saving a site template.

After completing these steps, the template is now saved to the site template gallery. SharePoint confirms that the operation completed successfully as shown in Figure 1.5, which displays immediately after clicking OK in the Save Site as Template page (refer to Figure 1.4).

Figure 1.5   Successfully saving a site template.

You manage the Site Template Gallery through the *Top-level Site Administration* (see Figure 1.6) page. Because the Site Template Gallery exists at the top-level site of a site collection, the newly created custom template is accessible only from that site collection. This important caveat enables you to isolate custom site templates from other site collections. If you want a site template to be accessible within another site collection, you simply need to upload the desired custom site template to the desired site collection's site template gallery.

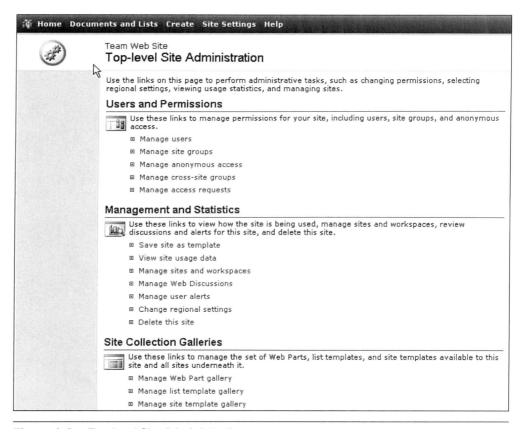

Figure 1.6 Top-level Site Administration.

The *Site Template Gallery* (see Figure 1.7) is simply a customized document library for an entire site collection, which explains why our newly saved template (file) can only be used in the current site collection and not other site collections. It also implies that the template is wholly contained within a single file.

Figure 1.7   Site Template Gallery.

Through the Site Template Gallery, the custom site template file-name, title, and description are all editable. Thus, if you are unhappy with the values you specified for them in Figure 1.4, you can change them.

Applying the Custom Site Template

The next time you create a site, your custom site template appears in the Template Selection web page (see Figure 1.1 and Figure 1.8). In fact, all custom site templates for the current site collection appear in the Template Selection dialog. Notice that the title and the description that we specified while saving the custom template are reflected in the Template Selection web page.

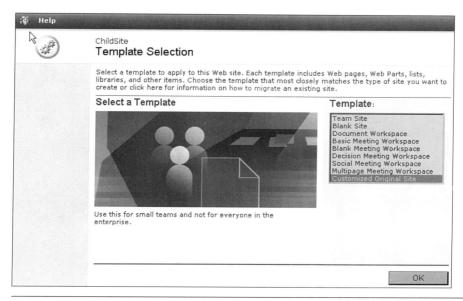

Figure 1.8   Template Selection that includes our newly created Customized Original Site.

After we apply the template to a new site, it looks exactly like the original site from which the template was saved (see Figure 1.9).

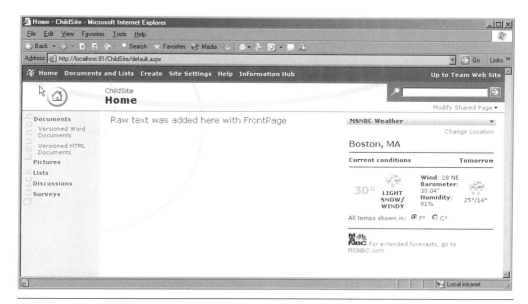

Figure 1.9   ChildSite with Customized Original Site template applied.

The Site Template File

As previously demonstrated, the site template was saved to the Site Template Gallery (document library) as a file. SharePoint saves it to the Site Template Gallery as a file with an STP file extension. This STP file is actually a CAB (Cabinet) formatted file. A CAB file is a compressed collection of files and therefore is similar to a ZIP file. In the case of the custom site template, this collection of files represents the difference between the customization made to the site and the base site definition.

The site template can be copied to a user's local disk through the normal methods afforded by a SharePoint document library. This capability facilitates uploading the site template to another Site Template Gallery and therefore reusing it in another site collection. It also facilitates the extraction and reuse of the custom template's code.

Both the site definition and custom template make extensive use of Collaborative Application Markup Language (CAML). CAML is an XML-based language that SharePoint uses. As such, coding site definitions requires the manual manipulation of several XML files, which leverage CAML. It is sometimes easier to design our site through the graphical user interfaces of SharePoint and FrontPage—as we just did—and then extract those CAML changes. These changes could then be injected into the site definition, which would save a significant amount of manual coding time.

Some of the files contained within the compressed CAB (STP) file are shown in Figure 1.10. Perhaps the most significant file and the only consistently named file within the custom site template is MANIFEST.XML.

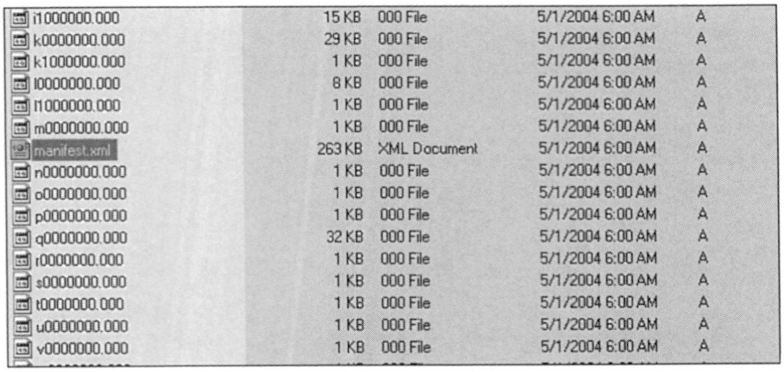

Figure 1.10   STP contents.

The manifest (MANIFEST.XML) is composed of six sections as shown in Listing 1.1. The `MetaInfo` section contains meta data for the site, the `Details` section describes high-level site parameters, the `Structure` section specifies the top navigation and quick launch bar, the `Files` section maps the other files in the CAB as well as virtual files and folders to the site, the `UserLists` section defines the various document or picture libraries and lists, and finally the `WebParts` section defines the placement and settings of web parts throughout the site's web pages.

Listing 1.1   MANIFEST.XML Structure

```
<Web>
    <MetaInfo />
    <Details />
    <Structure />
    <Files />
    <UserLists />
    <WebParts />
</Web>
```

The `Details` section is where the custom template specifies the Site Definition Template on which it is based. This can be seen in Listing 1.2 through the `TemplateID` and `Configuration` elements. We talk more about the Template ID and the Configuration ID in the WEBTEMP.XML section in a later chapter.

Listing 1.2   MANIFEST.XML Details Example

```
<Details>
    <TemplateDescription>Use this for small teams and not for
    everyone in the enterprise.</TemplateDescription>
    <TemplateTitle>Customized Original Site</TemplateTitle>
    <Language>1033</Language>
    <TemplateID>1</TemplateID>
    <Configuration>1</Configuration>
    <Title>OriginalSite</Title>
    <Description />
```

```
    <CalendarType>1</CalendarType>
    <AlternateCSS />
    <CustomJSUrl />
    <AlternateHeader />
    <Subweb>1</Subweb>
    <Locale>1033</Locale>
    <Collation>25</Collation>
    <TimeZone>10</TimeZone>
</Details>
```

Central Template Gallery: Custom Site Templates beyond the Site Collection

The Site Template Gallery is site collection-specific. However, you can make a custom site template universally available to all site collections. SharePoint has a central template gallery that is shared for your entire server farm—which could consist of only one server. Unfortunately, SharePoint only exposes access to it through the stsadm.exe utility and does not provide a set of web pages to manage it as it does with the site template gallery.

However, using the StsAdm Windows GUI (www.microsoft.com/sharepoint/downloads/components/detail.asp?a1=443) does make this a bit more palatable. If you were previously unfamiliar with it, it is simply a wrapper for the stsadm.exe command line program.

Table 1.1 highlights the central template gallery operations. Most of the operations are straightforward. However, CreateSite needs some explanation.

Table 1.1   StsAdm.exe Central Template Gallery Operations

Operation	Description
AddTemplate	Adds a template.
CreateSite	Creates a site. You can optionally apply a template from the central template gallery.
DeleteTemplate	Deletes a template.
EnumTemplates	Lists the templates.

The `SiteTemplate` suboption of `CreateSite` requires that you look up the name of the site template through the `EnumTemplates` operation first. The way to list the templates in the custom template gallery is shown in Listing 1.3.

Listing 1.3 STSADM.EXE Syntax to Enumerate the Global Templates

```
C:>stsadm.exe -o EnumTemplates

Customized Original Site - Language: 1033 - Site Template:
_GLOBAL_#1 - Template Id: 1 Use this for small teams and
not for everyone in the enterprise.
```

Enumerating the templates is the only way to determine the dynamically generated name of custom templates added to the central template gallery. In Listing 1.3, we can see that the Central Template Gallery contains only one template, which has been named GLOBAL_#1. This name can be used with the optional parameter `SiteTemplate` in the `CreateSite` operation. The syntax for the `CreateSite` operation is shown in Listing 1.4.

Listing 1.4 STSADM.EXE Syntax to Create a Site with a Global Template

```
stsadm.exe -o createsite
           -url http://moose/sites/sitecollection2
           -ownerlogin InformationHub\JNadrowski
           -owneremail Jason@InformationHub.com
           -sitetemplate _GLOBAL_#1
```

Exploring Custom List Templates

Custom list templates are very similar to custom site templates except that they are narrower in scope. With list templates, you can create your own custom list types to complement the existing list types such as document libraries, announcements, and links.

NOTE: Because a significant functionality overlap exists between custom site templates and custom list templates, we will try to minimize redundant explanations. As such, we will only cover the saving of a custom list template and the subsequent creation of a list based on that newly created custom list template. We will not detail the internals of the list template file. Instead, we refer you to the earlier section, "The Site Template File."

As we did in our explanation of custom site templates, we will create a customized list. In the following scenario we customize a document library.

Saving a Custom List Template

The list template is saved through the SharePoint web user interface, which empowers users and avoids the need for administrative intervention. Now that we have a customized list, we are ready to save it as a custom list template for others to reuse. The following steps demonstrate how to save the custom list template.

1. Select Save Document Library As Template, as shown in Figure 1.11.

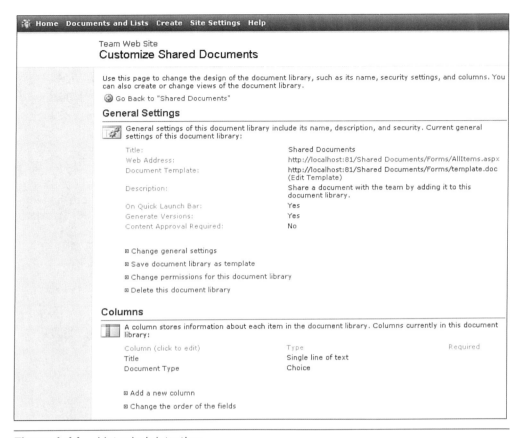

Figure 1.11 List administration.

2. Fill out the Save As Template page (see Figure 1.12) as appropriate and then click OK. You can always change the filename, template title, and template description later in the template library. At this time you must decide whether to include the list content.

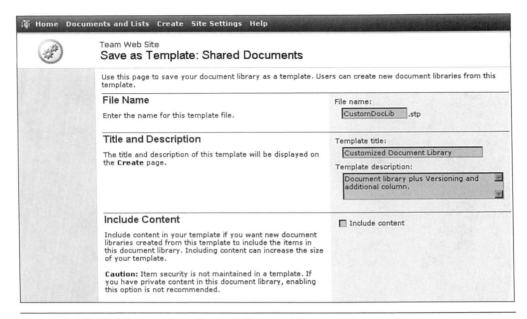

Figure 1.12   Saving a custom list template.

After completing the previous steps, the template is now saved. Share-Point confirms that the operation completed successfully as shown in Figure 1.13, which immediately displays after clicking OK in the Save As Template page.

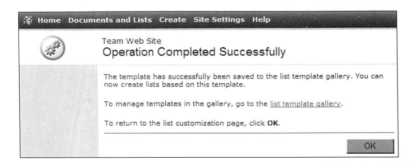

Figure 1.13   Successfully saving a list template.

You manage the List Template Gallery through the *Top-level Site Administration* (refer to Figure 1.6) page just as you manage the other site collection galleries. Because the List Template Gallery exists at the top-level site, the newly created custom template is only accessible from that site collection. This important caveat enables you to isolate custom list templates from other site collections. If you want to make a list template accessible within another site collection, you simply need to upload the desired custom list template to the desired site collection's list template gallery.

The List Template Gallery (see Figure 1.14) is also a customized document library for an entire site collection, which explains why our newly saved template (file) can only be used in the current site collection and not other site collections. It also implies that the template is wholly contained within a single file.

Figure 1.14   List Template Gallery.

Through the List Template Gallery, the custom list template filename, title, and description are all editable. Thus, if you are unhappy with the values you specified for them in Figure 1.12, you can change them.

Applying the Custom List Template

The next time you create a list or library, your new list template will appear on the CREATE.ASPX page. In our example, Customized Document Library appears as a choice (see Figure 1.15). In fact, all custom list templates for the current site collection will also appear on that page. Notice that the title and the description that we specified while saving the custom template are reflected on the CREATE.ASPX web page.

Figure 1.15 Create Page (CREATE.ASPX).

Ghosted and Unghosted Pages

If you explore a SharePoint web site (virtual server) through the IIS MMC, you notice that neither the team sites nor portal areas are visible. However, when you navigate your browser to a team site web page or portal web page, it is rendered. That page is rendered because Share-Point answers the request before IIS is given a chance to look for a physical file mapped to the requested URL.

When SharePoint answers the request for a URL, it looks up the page (URL) in the database. It first examines the Sites table in the configuration database to determine the site collection and consequently the content database to which the page belongs. Next, SharePoint queries the Docs table in the specified content database.

If the returned row from the Docs table has a null Content column, the file is rendered by the file specified in the SetupPath column. This path points to a physical file on the SharePoint front end web server's hard disk. This page is therefore considered a ghosted page because its entry in the Docs table is a pointer or a ghost of a physical file. Because this file exists on the server's hard disk, the ASP.NET parser is used to render the page.

In contrast, if the returned row from the `Docs` table has a non-null `Content` column and therefore a null `SetupPath`, the page is rendered from the data in the `Content` column. This page is considered unghosted because it is the reverse of a ghosted page. It does not contain a pointer to a physical file. Because there is only a virtual file to parse and no physical file, the ASP.NET parser cannot be used. SharePoint uses its own SafeMode parser.

The benefits and drawbacks to ghosted and unghosted pages can be boiled down to the differences between the ASP.NET and SharePoint SafeMode parsers. The ASP.NET parser compiles a page into an assembly the first time it is rendered. On subsequent page executions, the compilation step is skipped because an assembly exists. This results in faster page execution. In contrast, the SafeMode parser does not compile a page into an assembly. It always parses the page anew to form an object tree structure and then executes against that structure. In this regard it is similar to how ASP (the predecessor to ASP.NET) works. The SafeMode parser not only works differently from the ASP.NET parser but also operates under different rules. These rules effectively make unghosted pages execute slower than comparable ghosted pages. The SafeMode parser works differently from the ASP.NET parser in the following ways:

1. The page will not be compiled. Therefore, all compile directives will be ignored.
2. Inline code cannot be run. It will cause an error, and the page will not execute. The only dynamic code allowed is server-side controls that are marked safe (`SafeControls`, trusted controls, etc.).
3. The page cannot be executed on a single threaded apartment (STA) thread. Therefore, the `Page` directive's `AspCompat` attribute cannot be used.
4. Session state is either on for all pages or off for all pages. The `Page` directive's `EnableSessionState` cannot be used to selectively turn on session state for some pages, while disabling it for others.

Now that we understand the functional differences between the parsers, the question becomes what actions make a page ghosted or unghosted? In answering that question, we must talk a little about site definitions (see Chapter 2 for more details). Site definitions consist of physical files that reside on the front end web server's hard disk. When creating a new site, the user can choose a template from one of the front end web server's site definitions. Upon choosing one of these site definition templates, the ASPX pages of the selected template are ghosted and therefore mapped to the physical files on the server's hard disk. Pages become unghosted if the file has been updated using FrontPage 2003 or web folders or if the document library fields have been modified. In addition, all files uploaded to SharePoint are by definition unghosted because there is no physical file on the server's hard disk to reference.

When you understand what types of pages are unghosted (uploaded pages, pages modified with FrontPage, etc.), it should make more sense why the SafeMode parser is more restrictive and therefore slower than the ASP.NET parser. Among other things, the SafeMode parser restricts the user's ability to run malicious server-side code on the front end web server.

It is worth noting that custom site templates are based on site definitions. Therefore, a custom site template duplicates the same ghosting and unghosting found in the site from which it was copied. Thus, all new sites created with this custom site template have the same ghosted and unghosted pages as the original—at the time the template was created. Of course changes to the original site do not cascade to sites using this template.

However, ghosted pages reflect updates made to the physical file to which they are mapped. You could therefore make small formatting changes to these web pages and cascade the changes to sites using them. You would need to be careful not to remove certain resources—such as web part zones—from the page. Modifying or removing resources can result in a loss of functionality. Cascading changes to unghosted pages is generally not practical and almost always a nightmare.

Summary

Custom site and list templates are an easy way for non-technical users to create a reusable site or list definition. They are created by making a copy of a customized list or site. After being created, they seamlessly appear within the SharePoint web user interface and appear as built-in list types or site types. In addition, custom templates have the following properties:

- The templates represent a delta between a site definition (see Chapter 2) and a customized list or site. As such, they put an additional burden on the server.
- Custome site templates can be migrated from one site collection to another or globally installed for all site collections in a farm.
- Custom templates contain no security settings from the list or site from which they were copied.
- A 10-megabyte limit exists on the total size of a template.
- The site template exists as a single file stored in a cabinet (CAB) format within a template library.
- The code within a site template can be extracted and reused in site definitions.
- Ghosted web pages are interpreted with the ASP.NET parser. They exist in the SharePoint database as a pointer to a physical file on the front end web server. They are compiled into an assembly the first time they are executed and run from that compiled assembly thereafter.
- Unghosted web pages are interpreted by the SharePoint SafeMode parser. Their executable code exists entirely within the database and not on the physical disk. They are not compiled. They run slower than a comparable ghosted page.

CHAPTER 2

Site Definitions

Site definition templates, like custom templates (Chapter 1), define the look and function of a site. A site definition is simply a collection of one or more site definition templates in a single package. SharePoint aggregates templates in this way to group similarly themed templates to facilitate component reuse.

Site definitions are primarily composed of presentation (ASPX) and configuration (XML) files. The most significant configuration files are ONET.XML and WEBTEMP.XML. ONET.XML defines the templates and their construction within the site definition. WEBTEMP.XML defines all the site definition templates accessible to a SharePoint user. These and other significant site definition configuration files are listed in Table 2.1.

Table 2.1   Site Definition Configuration Files

File	Description
BASE.XML	Defines the schema and views for the base set of lists—lists of lists, documents, and user information. This file is not technically part of a site definition but is referenced by it. This file should not be modified.
FLDTYPES.XML	Used during site and list creation to define how field types are rendered. This file is not technically part of a site definition but is referenced by it. This file should not be modified.
ONET.XML	Defines the templates and their construction within the site definition.
SCHEMA.XML	Each list/library is defined within its own folder within a site definition. Each list/library definition has one SCHEMA.XML file that defines its schema and its display.

continues

Table 2.1   Site Definition Configuration Files (continued)

File	Description
STDVIEW.XML	Defines the base view from which list/library views are constructed.
VWSTYLES.XML	Defines the various view styles with which a list/library can be formatted. The most common view style is a row style. However, VWSTYLES.XML can be used to display your list's information in a thumbnail view or any other style desired.
WEBTEMP.XML	Defines all the site definition templates exposed by SharePoint to the user.

As implied by the configuration files referenced in Table 2.1, site definitions provide more flexibility than the custom site templates discussed in Chapter 1. However, with this finer level of control comes a greater amount of effort required to construct a site definition.

By default, site definitions are stored in the following location: C:\Program Files\Common Files\Microsoft Shared\web server extensions\60\TEMPLATE\<LCID>, where <LCID> is 1033 for the English version of SharePoint.

The default WSS installation contains three folders in that directory: MPS, STS, and XML. MPS holds the default meeting workspace site definition templates, STS holds the other default site definition templates, and XML holds several configuration files.

Creating a new site definition is rather straightforward. The process begins by making a copy of an existing site definition—usually one of the Microsoft-provided site definitions. Although possible, the option of creating one from scratch is extremely unappetizing. The developer then modifies the configuration and presentation files appropriately. The developer must also add a configuration file to the XML folder (C:\Program Files\Common Files\Microsoft Shared\web server extensions\60\TEMPLATE\1033\XML) to inform SharePoint of the additional site definition.

This chapter focuses on the SharePoint's interaction with WEBTEMP.XML and ONET.XML. We walk through an example of creating a new site definition while concentrating our discussion on site definition elements that are affected by WEBTEMP.XML and ONET.XML.

WEBTEMP.XML and Its Derivatives

The default Windows SharePoint Services (WSS) site definition templates (Team Site, Blank Site, Document Workspace, Basic Meeting Workspace, Blank Meeting Workspace, Decision Meeting Workspace, Social Meeting Workspace, and Multipage Meeting Workspace) were listed in Figure 1.1. SharePoint parses WEBTEMP.XML and any other files matching the pattern WEBTEMP*.XML (such as WEBTEMPMyFirstSiteDefinition.XML) to compile the list of available site definitions. The eight default Microsoft site definitions are listed in WEBTEMP.XML.

SharePoint Portal Server also employs the WEBTEMP metaphor for listing its site definition templates. SharePoint Portal Server's WEBTEMP is named WEBTEMPSPS.XML. It references the home, topics, news, site directory, my site, contents, and a few other templates. These site definition templates work in exactly the same way that Windows SharePoint Services site definition templates function. Thus, when you understand how to customize WSS site definitions, you will also understand how to customize SharePoint Portal Site definitions. The only caveat to Portal Area Templates (site definitions) is that the folder name housing your Portal Site definition must begin with SPS.

WEBTEMP.XML and its derivatives are found in the XML configuration folder C:\Program Files\Common Files\Microsoft Shared\web server extensions\60\TEMPLATE\1033\XML.

The default WSS WEBTEMP.XML is shown in Listing 2.1. It is composed of CAML defined elements. Each `Template` element maps to a particular site definition folder. The `Configuration` element represents a particular template (flavor) for that site definition. Both nodes are described more fully in Table 2.2 and Table 2.3.

Listing 2.1   WSS Default WEBTEMP.XML

```
<Templates xmlns:ows="Microsoft SharePoint">
  <Template Name="STS" ID="1">
    <Configuration ID="0" Title="Team Site" Hidden="FALSE"
      ImageUrl="/_layouts/images/stsprev.png"
      Description="This template creates a site for teams to create,
                organize, and share information quickly and easily.
                It includes a Document Library, and basic lists
                such as Announcements, Events, Contacts, and Quick
                Links.">
```

```
  </Configuration>
  <Configuration ID="1" Title="Blank Site" Hidden="FALSE"
    ImageUrl="/_layouts/images/stsprev.png"
    Description="This template creates a Windows SharePoint
                 Services-enabled Web site with a blank home page.
                 You can use a Windows SharePoint Services-compatible
                 Web page editor to add interactive lists or any
                 other Windows SharePoint Services features.">
  </Configuration>
  <Configuration ID="2" Title="Document Workspace" Hidden="FALSE"
    ImageUrl="/_layouts/images/dwsprev.png"
    Description="This template creates a site for colleagues to
                 work together on documents. It provides a document
                 library for storing the primary document and
                 supporting files, a Task list for assigning to-do
                 items, and a Links list for resources related to
                 the document.">
  </Configuration>
 </Template>
 .
 .
 .
```

Table 2.2 `<Template>` Attributes

Attribute	Required	Type	Description
ID	Yes	Integer	This specifies a unique key for the site definition. Every template key must be unique among all the keys specified in WEBTEMP.XML and WEBTEMP°.xml. To avoid conflict with site definitions provided by Microsoft, the key must be greater than 10,000.
Name	Yes	Text	The folder name for the site definition. The folder is expected to exist at the same level as STS, MPS, and XML.

Table 2.3 `<Configuration>` Attributes

Attribute	Required	Type	Description
Description	No	Text	Specifies the description of the site definition template that appears immediately below the `ImageUrl` of the Template Selection (TemplatePick.aspx) page.
Hidden	No	Boolean	Determines whether the site definition template should be hidden from the Template Selection options.
ID	Yes	Integer	This represents a key unique to all its siblings in a particular `<Template>` element. As described in the next section, it is then matched to the `ID` specified in ONET.XML to determine the template within the site definition.
ImageUrl	No	Text	This is the image that is shown on the Template Section page. This appears above the description.
Name	No	Text	Internally referenced name of the site definition template.
Title	No	Text	The title of the site definition template to be shown in the selection box on the Template Selection page.
Type	No	Text	Identifies the configuration with a specific site definition.

The WEBTEMP*.XML mechanism provides a way to add separate customizations without affecting any existing site definitions. Additionally, it is a good practice to name your WEBTEMP file with respect to your site definition—such as WEBTEMPMyFirstSiteDefinition.XML.

Creating a New Site Definition

Creating a new site definition is as simple as copying a folder and creating a new WEBTEMP file. Create the file WEBTEMPMyFirstSiteDefinition.XML in the folder C:\Program Files\Common Files\Microsoft Shared\web server extensions\60\TEMPLATE\1033\XML (see Figure 2.1). Copy the contents of Listing 2.2 into this newly created file.

Listing 2.2   WebTempMyFirstSiteDefinition.XML Contents

```
<?xml version="1.0" encoding="utf-8"?>
<Templates xmlns:ows="Microsoft SharePoint">
  <Template Name="MyFirstSiteDefinition" ID="10001">
    <Configuration ID="10"
      Title="My First Site Definition Team Site"
      Hidden="FALSE"
      ImageUrl="/_layouts/images/stsprev.png"
      Description="This is my first site definition.">
    </Configuration>
  </Template>
</Templates>
```

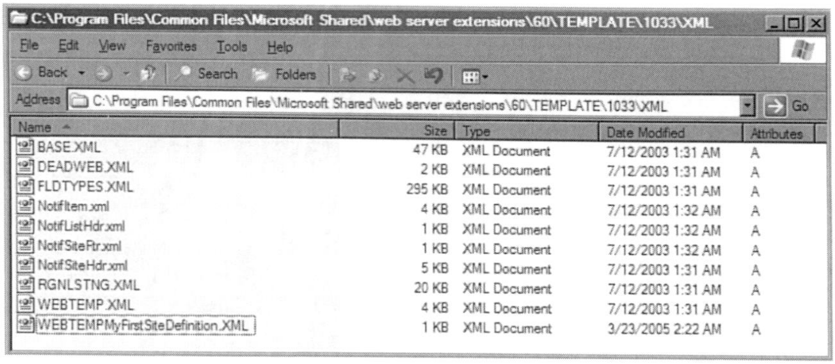

Figure 2.1   XML folder Explorer view.

The CAML definitions for the `Template` and `Configuration` elements are defined in the previous tables. The `Name` attribute within the `Template` node (`Template/@Name`) specifies the folder where the site definition can be found. `Template/@ID` specifies the flavor of the site definition—more specifically, it specifies the site definition template. The various site definition templates are defined within the ONET.XML file packaged within the site definition.

The next step in creating a custom site definition is to make a copy of a site definition after which you want to pattern yours. In our example, we want to pattern our site definition after the team site. Therefore, copy the STS folder and name it `MyFirstSiteDefinition`. Remember, both folders are children of C:\Program Files\Common Files\Microsoft Shared\web server extensions\60\TEMPLATE\1033 (see Figure 2.2).

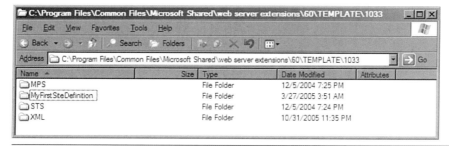

Figure 2.2 1033 Explorer view.

The first time a SharePoint page is requested, the application pool creates an instance of SharePoint, and site definitions are read. To see new site definitions, you must force a restart of SharePoint by running IISReset.EXE or rebooting the server. The new site definitions will appear the next time you apply a template to a site (see Figure 2.3).

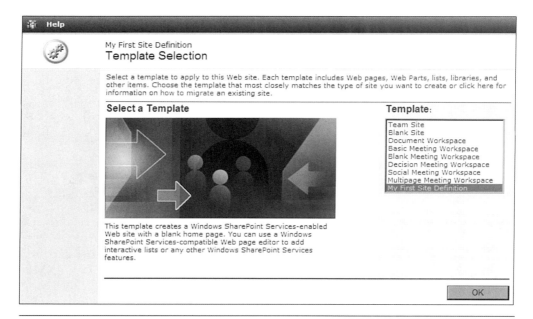

Figure 2.3 New site definition templates appear after creating the WEBTEMP file.

ONET.XML: Defining the Site Definition

Our site definition folder, MyFirstSiteDefinition, contains several resources that can be strung together to form various site definition templates. ONET.XML's main function is to glue these and other resources together to define one or more site definition templates. In our example, it exists on the physical file system in the C:\Program Files\Common Files\Microsoft Shared\web server extensions\60\TEMPLATE\1033\ MyFirstSiteDefinition\XML folder (see Figure 2.4).

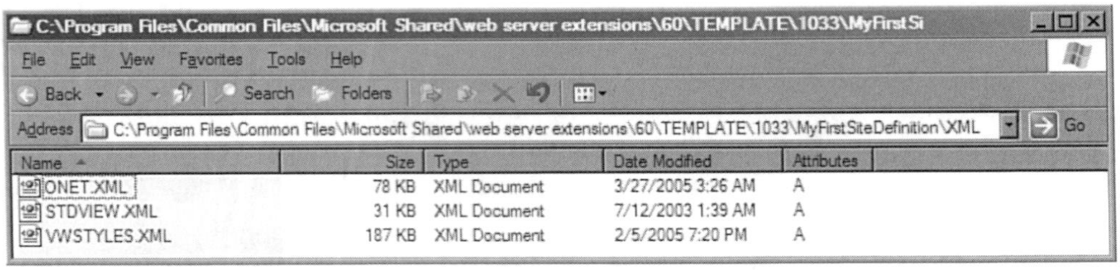

Figure 2.4   Site definition XML Explorer view.

As shown in Listing 2.3, ONET.XML is composed of one `Project` element, which in turn is composed of `NavBars`, `ListTemplates`, `DocumentTemplates`, `BaseTypes`, `Configurations`, and `Modules` elements. Each element has an extensive sub-element structure, which we detail in the following sections.

Listing 2.3   ONET.XML Structure

```
<Project>
  <NavBars/>
  <ListTemplates/>
  <DocumentTemplates/>
  <BaseTypes/>
  <Configurations/>
  <Modules/>
</Project>
```

`<Project>`: Defining Settings That Apply throughout the Site Definition Template

The `Project` element exists at the top level and is used to define properties that are universal to the site. The allowable attributes are described in Table 2.4. The most popular attributes include `AlternateCSS`, `AlternateHeader`, and `CustomJSUrl`.

Table 2.4 `<Project>` Attributes

Attribute	Required	Type	Description
AlternateCSS	No	Text	Specifies an alternate CSS file to be used that overrides the default styles specified in OWS°.CSS, which is located in the C:\Program Files\Common Files\Microsoft Shared\web server extensions\60\TEMPLATE\LAYOUTS\1033\STYLES folder. The specified CSS must exist in the C:\Program Files\Common Files\Microsoft Shared\web server extensions\60\TEMPLATE\LAYOUTS\1033\STYLES folder.
AlternateHeader	No	Text	Specifies an alternate header for the SharePoint site definition. The page must exist in the C:\Microsoft Shared\web server extensions\60\TEMPLATE\LAYOUTS\1033 folder.
CustomJSUrl	No	Text	Defines a custom JavaScript file to be included with all the files associated with the site definition. The script must exist in the C:\Microsoft Shared\web server extensions\60\TEMPLATE\LAYOUTS\1033 folder.
DisableWeb DesignFeatures	No	Text	Disables specified Microsoft FrontPage editing features. Values are semicolon delimited and can be any collection of the following: `wdfbackup`, `wdfrestore`, `wdfpackageimport`, `wdfpackageexport`, `wdfthemeweb`, `wdfthemepage`, `wdfnavigationbars`, `wdfnavigationview`, `wdfpublishview`, `wdfpublishselectedfile`, `wdfopensite`, `wdfnewsubsite`.

continues

Table 2.4   `<Project>` Attributes (continued)

Attribute	Required	Type	Description
ListDir	Yes	Text	According to the documentation, this specifies the folder where new lists are to be implemented. However, this has no real effect.
Title	Yes	Text	Defines the default name for the SharePoint site.

AlternateCSS: Using a Custom CSS

`AlternateCSS` is used to override the default SharePoint styles located in C:\Program Files\Common Files\Microsoft Shared\web server extensions\60\TEMPLATE\LAYOUTS\1033\STYLES. It provides a quick and simple way to affect these styles throughout all pages in the site. However, it must reside in the C:\Program Files\Common Files\ Microsoft Shared\web server extensions\60\TEMPLATE\LAYOUTS\ 1033\STYLES folder.

Overriding various cascading style sheet styles is more powerful than it might first appear because almost every HTML element within Share-Point has a style associated with it. These style-specified elements include text, toolbars, icons, watermarks, tabs, and many other things. The CSS primarily facilitates changing the formatting or image associated with these elements.

AlternateHeader: Creating Your Own Header across All Site Definition Pages

The `AlternateHeader` attribute allows the substitution of the standard SharePoint header—the top navigation menu bar. This alternate header is typically an ASPX page and must be located in the C:\Microsoft Shared\web server extensions\60\TEMPLATE\LAYOUTS\1033 folder.

Fortunately, all the site's administration pages have ASP.NET code built in to render the custom header if it has been specified. By site administration pages, I mean all the pages that are mapped to the _layouts (C:\Microsoft Shared\web server extensions\60\TEMPLATE\ LAYOUTS) virtual directory for the IIS web site. These include the list creation pages, site settings, site administration, and other administration pages.

The snippet in Listing 2.4 is taken from the CREATE.ASPX page and is representative of all the alternate header code written by Microsoft. By retrieving the context of the web site and then retrieving the `AlternateHeader` property, it can determine whether an `AlternateHeader` was specified through the `<Project>` element. If an alternate header was specified, it will be executed instead of painting the standard header.

Listing 2.4   Alternate Header Snippet Taken from CREATE.ASPX

```
<%
  string alternateHeader =
          SPControl.GetContextWeb(Context).AlternateHeader;
  if (alternateHeader == null || alternateHeader == "")
  {
%>
<TR>
  <TD COLSPAN=3 WIDTH=100%>
  <!--Top bar-->
  <table class="ms-bannerframe" border="0" cellspacing="0"
         cellpadding="0"
         width="100%">
   <tr>
    <td nowrap valign="middle"><img ID=onetidHeadbnnr0 alt="Logo"
        src="/_layouts/images/logo.gif"></td>
     <td class=ms-banner width=99% nowrap ID="HBN100"
      valign="middle">
        <!--webbot Bot="Navigation" startspan-->
        <SharePoint:Navigation LinkBarId="1002" runat="server"/>
     </td>
    <td class=ms-banner>  </td>
    <td nowrap class=ms-banner style="padding-right: 7px">
        <SharePoint:PortalConnection runat="server" />
    </td>
   </tr>
  </table>
  </TD>
 </TR>
<%
  }
  else
  {
    Server.Execute(alternateHeader);
  }
%>
```

Unfortunately, this code is not included in any of the Microsoft-provided site definitions. As such, `AlternateHeader` is designed primarily to customize only the header of administration pages, and not content pages. If you are going to pattern your site definition after Microsoft's site definition templates, you will need to modify every page you want to expose. Considering that there are about 100 pages in the STS site definition folder, it would require a non-trivial amount of time to modify each page—even if you were only pasting code from the clipboard and saving.

More unfortunately, almost every ASPX page within the Microsoft-provided site definition templates has a different HTML structure. Thus, you cannot simply replace the top few lines of an ASPX page with your new and improved alternate header code and move on. You must tediously work this code into each page of your site definition.

For the moment, let's ignore the fact that the site definitions do not have the alternate header code embedded within them. Instead, let's go through the much simpler exercise of setting up an alternate header for the SharePoint administrative pages.

The first step is to add the `AlternateHeader` attribute to the `Project` element within ONET.XML. That change is shown in Listing 2.5.

Listing 2.5   ONET.XML `Project` Element Referencing an Alternate Header

```
<Project Title="Team Web Site" ListDir="Lists"
        xmlns:ows="Microsoft SharePoint"
        AlternateHeader="MyFirstSiteDefinition_Header.aspx">
```

The second step is to create an alternate header page that is located in the C:\Microsoft Shared\web server extensions\60\TEMPLATE\ LAYOUTS\1033 folder. The name of the file should match the previously mentioned `Project` element's `AlternateHeader` attribute. That code is detailed in Listing 2.6.

Listing 2.6   MyFirstSiteDefinition_Header.ASPX Alternate Header Definition

```
<%@ Register Tagprefix="SharePoint"
Namespace="Microsoft.SharePoint.WebControls"
```

```
Assembly="Microsoft.SharePoint, Version=11.0.0.0, Culture=neutral,
PublicKeyToken=71e9bce111e9429c" %>

<TR>
  <TD COLSPAN=3 WIDTH=100%>
  <!--Top bar-->
  <table border="0" cellspacing="0" cellpadding="0" width="100%">
    <tr>
      <td nowrap valign="middle" bgcolor="#1863bd">
        <img ID=onetidHeadbnnr0 alt="Logo"
            src="/_layouts/images/InformationHubLogo.png">
      </td>
    </tr>
  </table>
  <table class="ms-bannerframe" height="25pt" border="0"
   cellspacing="0"
   cellpadding="0" width="100%">
    <td class=ms-banner width=99% nowrap ID="HBN100"
     valign="middle">
        
      <!--webbot Bot="Navigation" startspan-->
      <SharePoint:Navigation LinkBarId="1002" runat="server"/>
    </td>
    <td class=ms-banner> </td>
    <td nowrap class=ms-banner style="padding-right: 7px">
      <SharePoint:PortalConnection runat="server" />
    </td>
  </tr>
  </table>
  </TD>
</TR>
```

To support the alternate header we just authored, we need to copy the InformationHubLogo.png image file to the C:\Program Files\Common Files\Microsoft Shared\web server extensions\60\TEMPLATE\ IMAGES folder.

After executing an IISReset and creating a new site with the modified site definition template, we see the result of our alternate header work as shown in Figure 2.5. The code we implemented for the alternate header was very simple. It displayed an Information Hub logo bar above the menu. However, it need not have been so simple. It could have used DHTML drop-down menus or just about any other HTML elements that the client browser can understand.

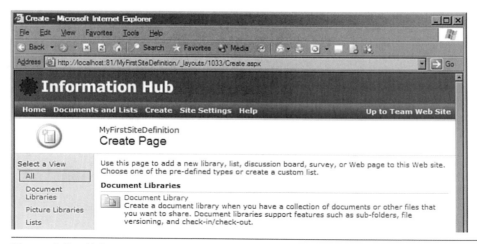

Figure 2.5 Using an alternate header.

Overriding SharePoint JavaScript Functions with `CustomJSUrl`

Another noteworthy attribute of the `Project` element is `CustomJSUrl`. `CustomJSUrl` provides a quick way to add a JavaScript file to every page in the site definition. One of its more interesting uses is to override specific functions within OWS.JS—affectionately known as SharePoint's client-side API. This technique takes the form of rewriting the selected OWS.JS functions in a custom JavaScript file. Although this method will result in two valid functions with the same name, the functions in the custom JavaScript file will be run instead of those within OWS.JS.

Of course, this override is a function of JavaScript and is not dependent on using `CustomJSUrl`. Therefore, you could replicate this functionality several ways. Instead of using `CustomJSUrl`, you could manually edit a SharePoint ASPX page or use the Content Editor web part on that page. Both methods enable you to inject a JavaScript function.

Adding Menu Items to the Drop-Down List Menus

In the following example, we add a menu item to the DHTML drop-down menus for SharePoint libraries and lists. When selected, this menu item will send an email link to the selected list or library item. The resulting document library menu is shown in Figure 2.6 and is representative of the list, picture library, and form library menus.

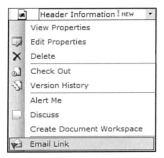

Figure 2.6   Email Link menu item added to document library.

Of the various ways to accomplish this task, the easiest is to use the `CustomJSUrl` attribute. The modified `Project` element in `MyFirst-SiteDefinition` is shown in Listing 2.7.

Listing 2.7   ONET.XML Project Element Referencing a `CustomJSUrl`

```
<Project Title="Team Web Site" ListDir="Lists"
    xmlns:ows="Microsoft SharePoint"
    AlternateHeader="MyFirstSiteDefinition_Header.aspx"
    CustomJSUrl="_layouts/[%=System.Threading.Thread.CurrentThread.
CurrentUICulture.LCID%]/OWS_MyFirstSiteDefinition.JS">
```

The first thing you might notice is that the `[%` and `%]` symbols delineates .NET code and appears to function as the `<%` and `%>` symbols do in ASP.NET. If you are like me, you might immediately think that you could use the full ASPX object model within ONET.XML. Unfortunately, that is not the case. Only the simplest ASPX code is allowed. Furthermore, this code's results are cached within the ASPX application and reused until that application has shut down. In the previous case, the code inserts the locale identifier (LCID). If you are using the default English version of SharePoint, your LCID should be 1033. Currently, Microsoft has defined over 200 LCIDs, which are documented on Microsoft's Global Development and Computing Portal (http://www.microsoft.com/globaldev/reference/lcid-all.mspx).

The next tasks involve adding a menu item to the DHTML drop-down menu. Adding a menu item simply requires invoking the `CAMOpt` function (see Listing 2.8). However, that function must be passed the appropriate parameters and called from the appropriate place.

Listing 2.8   SharePoint `CAMOpt` JavaScript Function Declaration

```
CAMOpt(m, strDisplayText, strAction, strImagePath);
```

> `CAMOpt` takes four parameters: the menu object, the display text string, the action string, and the image path string. The menu object defines the entire DHTML menu. The display text will be displayed in the menu. The action is a JavaScript action that will be performed when the item is selected. The image path specifies an icon for the menu item.
>
> In our example, we will use the `A` tag's `HREF` attribute to enable emailing. Thus, `strAction` could use JavaScript's `window` object to create an email message as shown in Listing 2.9.

Listing 2.9   Example Use of `CAMOpt`'s `strAction` Parameter

```
// Mimic <a
//   href="mailto:jason@informationhub.com?subject=TestA&body=TestB">
strAction = 'window.navigate
          (
          "mailto:jason@informationhub.com?subject=TestA&body=TestB"
             )';
```

> The `strAction` parameter need not trigger client-side applications. It could also interact with SharePoint or other server applications. For instance, we could have called a custom ASPX page through `window.navigate`. This custom page could have taken subject, body, and other querystring parameters to send an email through the SharePoint server's SMTP resources instead of Microsoft Outlook. As such, these drop-down menus offer a tremendous amount of functionality.
>
> Now the question is where to invoke `CAMOpt`. Because we want this functionality in both document libraries and lists, we need to extend the `AddDocLibMenuItems` and `AddListMenuItems` functions. It should come as no surprise that `AddDocLibMenuItems` adds items to the menu for document libraries and `AddListMenuItems` adds items to the menu for lists.
>
> We need to copy the `AddDocLibMenuItems` and `AddListMenuItems` functions from OWS.JS to OWS_MyFirstSiteDefinition.JS. Both of

these JavaScript files reside in the C:\Microsoft Shared\web server extensions\60\TEMPLATE\LAYOUTS\1033 folder.

The only change to the `AddListMenuItems` and `AddDocLibMenu-Items` functions is to call `AddEmailLinkToMenu` immediately before exiting the function. `AddEmailLinkToMenu` is a function that we will need to write. The insertion of `AddEmailLinkToMenu` is shown in Listing 2.10.

Listing 2.10 Modified `AddListMenuItems` and `AddDocLibMenuItems` JavaScript Functions

```
function AddListMenuItems(m, ctx)
{
.
.
.


    AddEmailLinkToMenu (m, ctx);
}

function AddDocLibMenuItems(m, ctx)
{
.
.
.


    AddEmailLinkToMenu (m, ctx);
}
```

Ultimately, `AddEmailLinkToMenu` (see Listing 2.11) appends an Email Link item to the menu using `CAMOpt`. However, the bulk of the work is determining the URL for the item and then formatting that information in a JavaScript statement that creates a new prepopulated mail message.

The more interesting aspects of this function include the use of `ctx`, `CAMSep`, and `itemTable`. The `ctx` object retrieves the virtual path to SharePoint's images directory, which maps to C:\Program Files\Common Files\Microsoft Shared\web server extensions\60\TEMPLATE\IMAGES. `CAMSep` is a function that appends a separator to the end of the menu. The `itemTable` object defines the table row of the selected library or list item.

Listing 2.11   `AddEmailLinkToMenu` JavaScript Function Definition

```
function AddEmailLinkToMenu(m, ctx)
{
  var strDisplayText = "Email Link";
  var strAction = "";
  var strImagePath = ctx.imagesPath + "SendTo.gif";
  var strURL = "";

  //Using regular expressions, find the URL of the item
  var strItemHTML = itemTable.innerHTML;
  var regexURL = /href="([^"]*)"/;
  var mURL = regexURL.exec(strItemHTML);
  if(mURL != null)
    strURL = mURL[1];

  //Encode white space with %20
  var regexEncode = / /;
  strURL = strURL.replace(regexEncode, "%20") ;

  //Only add menu item if a valid URL exists
  if (strURL != "")
  {
    strSubject = "Please review " + strURL;
    strMessage = "Please review the following item: " + strURL;
    strAction = 'window.navigate("mailto: ?subject='
      + escape(strSubject) + '&body=' + escape(strMessage) + '")';

    //Add Separator
    CAMSep(m);

    //Add Menu Item
    CAMOpt(m, strDisplayText, strAction, strImagePath);
  }
}
```

An example `itemTable.innerHTML` is shown in Listing 2.12. Although this was taken from a document library, it is representative of all lists and libraries. In the `AddEmailLinkToMenu` function, we used regular expressions to find the A tag's HREF attribute. The URL referenced by HREF was passed into the email message.

Listing 2.12   Example Value of `itemTable.innerHTML` from a Document Library

```
<TABLE class=ms-selectedtitle onmouseover=OnItem(this) height="100%"
       cellSpacing=0 SourceUrl="" COUId="" FSObjType="0"
       DocIcon="icgen.gif||" FileType="dat" HTMLType=""
       FileDirRef="MyFirstSiteDefinition/DL"
       ServerUrl="/MyFirstSiteDefinition/DL/Header Information.dat"
       ItemId="2" CTXName="ctx1">
  <TBODY>
    <TR>
      <TD class=ms-vb width="100%">
       <A onfocus=OnLink(this)
        onclick="DispDocItemEx(this,'FALSE','FALSE','FALSE','')"
        href="http://Moose:81/MyFirstSiteDefinition/DL/
        HeaderFile.dat">
          HeaderFile
       </A>
       <IMG alt=New src="/_layouts/1033/images/new.gif"/>
      </TD>
      <TD class=ms-menuimagecell style="VISIBILITY: visible">
        <IMG style="VISIBILITY: visible" alt=Edit
            src="/_layouts/images/downarrw.gif" width=13/>
      </TD>
    </TR>
  </TBODY>
</TABLE>
```

Defining and Rendering Navigation with the `<NavBars>`

`NavBars` specify the navigation bars that are rendered by the SharePoint Navigation web control. Listing 2.13 details the top navigation bar defined in ONET.XML. The results of this listing are shown in Figure 2.7.

Listing 2.13   Default ONET.XML Top Navigation Bar

```
<Project Title="Team Web Site" ListDir="Lists"
        xmlns:ows="Microsoft SharePoint">
  <NavBars>
    <NavBar Name="SharePoint Top Navbar"
```

```
           Separator="   "
           Body="&lt;a ID='onettopnavbar#LABEL_ID#' href='#URL#'
           accesskey='J'&gt;#LABEL#&lt;/a&gt;"
           ID="1002">
    <NavBarLink Name="Documents and Lists"
              Url="_layouts/[%=System.Threading.Thread.
➥ CurrentThread.CurrentUICulture.LCID%]/viewlsts.aspx">
      </NavBarLink>
      <NavBarLink Name="Create"
              Url="_layouts/[%=System.Threading.Thread.
➥ CurrentThread.CurrentUICulture.LCID%]/create.aspx">
      </NavBarLink>
      <NavBarLink Name="Site Settings"
              Url="_layouts/[%=System.Threading.Thread.
➥ CurrentThread.CurrentUICulture.LCID%]/settings.aspx">
      </NavBarLink>
      <NavBarLink Name="Help"
                Url='javascript:HelpWindowKey("NavBarHelpHome")'>
      </NavBarLink>
    </NavBar>
      .
      .
      .
```

Home Documents and Lists Create Site Settings Help

Figure 2.7   Default top navigation defined in ONET.XML.

Navigation links can be added, modified, or deleted by modifying the appropriate NavBars section of ONET.XML. For instance, Listing 2.14 now includes an additional NavBarLink to Information Hub. The resulting navigation bar is shown in Figure 2.8.

Listing 2.14   Modified ONET.XML Top Navigation Bar

```
<Project Title="Team Web Site" ListDir="Lists"
        xmlns:ows="Microsoft SharePoint">
  <NavBars>
    <NavBar Name="SharePoint Top Navbar"
            Separator="   "
```

```
                    Body="&lt;a ID='onettopnavbar#LABEL_ID#' href='#URL#'
                    accesskey='J'&gt;#LABEL#&lt;/a&gt;"
                    ID="1002">
      <NavBarLink Name="Documents and Lists"

Url="_layouts/[%=System.Threading.Thread.CurrentThread.
➥ CurrentUICulture.LCID%]/viewlsts.aspx">
      </NavBarLink>
      <NavBarLink Name="Create"
                    Url="_layouts/[%=System.Threading.Thread.
➥ CurrentThread.CurrentUICulture.LCID%]/create.aspx">
      </NavBarLink>
      <NavBarLink Name="Site Settings"
                    Url="_layouts/[%=System.Threading.Thread.
➥ CurrentThread.CurrentUICulture.LCID%]/settings.aspx">
      </NavBarLink>
      <NavBarLink Name="Information Hub"
                    Url='javascript:void(window.open(
                        "http://www.informationhub.com",
                        "InformationHub"))'>
      </NavBarLink>
      <NavBarLink Name="Help"
                    Url='javascript:HelpWindowKey("NavBarHelpHome")'>
      </NavBarLink>
   </NavBar>
   .
   .
   .
```

Figure 2.8   Modified top navigation defined in ONET.XML.

One of the first things you might have noticed is that Home is not defined in the navigation bar. That is because it is handled in another section of ONET.XML. That link is defined in the `File` section of ONET.XML and is more fully explained later in Table 2.11.

Complex changes to the top navigation are not simple to implement. Although it is tempting to believe that the ASP.NET code embedded within the `NavBarLink` elements could be used as a mechanism for dynamic menus, this is not the case.

As mentioned earlier, the top navigation is rendered with a Share-Point web control. The SharePoint web control retrieves the NavBar element with an ID defined in the LinkBarID. In the case of our site definition, this ID is 1002, so the web control retrieves the navigation as explained previously. Additionally, this ID must also be referenced in the appropriate Modules section—which we cover later in this chapter.

Listing 2.15   SharePoint Navigation Web Control to Render Top Navigation

```
<!--webbot bot="Navigation"
     S-Type="sequence"
     S-Orientation="horizontal"
     S-Rendering="html"
     S-Btn-Nml="<a ID='onettopnavbar#LABEL_ID#' href='#URL#'
                   accesskey='J'>#LABEL#</a>"
     S-Btn-Sel="<a ID='onettopnavbar#LABEL_ID#' href='#URL#'
                   accesskey='J'>#LABEL#</a>"
     S-Btn-Sep="   "
     B-Include-Home="FALSE"
     B-Include-Up="FALSE"
     S-Btn-Nobr="FALSE"
     U-Page="sid:1002"
     S-Target startspan -->
     <SharePoint:Navigation LinkBarId="1002" runat="server"/>
<!--webbot bot="Navigation" endspan -->
```

<ListTemplates>: Specifying the Allowed Lists and Libraries

ListTemplates defines the documents and lists as well as their properties for the site definition. Only the list types specified (through the ListTemplate elements) can be created for the site. For example, the XML specified in Listing 2.16 only enables document libraries to be created. This is further evidenced by Figure 2.9, which shows Document Libraries as the only list type.

Listing 2.16   ONET.XML `ListTemplates` Definition That Allows Only Document Libraries

```
<ListTemplates>
  <ListTemplate Name="doclib" DisplayName="Document Library"
    Type="101" BaseType="1" OnQuickLaunch="TRUE"
    SecurityBits="11"
    Description="Create a document library when you have a
                collection of documents or other files that you
                want to share. Document libraries support features
                such as sub-folders, file versioning, and check-in/
                check-out."
    Image="/_layouts/images/itdl.gif" DocumentTemplate="101">
  </ListTemplate>
</ListTemplates>
```

Although other choices might appear on the page, such as Import Spreadsheet, you can only create list types listed in your `ListTemplates` section. In the current example, if you try to import a spreadsheet, it will fail because Import Spreadsheet is dependent on a `Custom List` type—which isn't specified in ONET.XML.

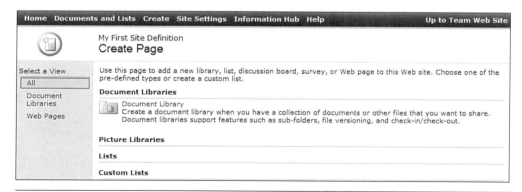

Figure 2.9   List Creation page with only Document Libraries allowed.

When restricting the available list types, be mindful that dependencies on these lists can trigger an error. For instance, both the `Configuration` and `Modules` sections can reference a list type that you have not listed—hence denying its availability. If that happens, SharePoint will not be able to create your site, and the user will be presented with an error. If you truly want to create a default document library, such as Shared Documents, but do not want to allow the user to create other lists, you should consider using the `Hidden` attribute for `ListTemplate`. All the `ListTemplate` attributes are shown in Table 2.5.

Table 2.5   `<ListTemplate>` Attributes

Attribute	Required	Type	Description
BaseType	Yes	Integer	This specifies the schema for the list. That schema is defined in the `BaseTypes` section of ONET.XML.
Catalog	No	Boolean	If TRUE, indicates that the list is of a special catalog type. Thus, the list type is a Site Template Gallery, List Template Gallery, or Web Part Gallery.
Default	No	Boolean	According to the documentation, a TRUE value indicates that new SharePoint sites will include this list. However, it has no effect.
Description	No	Text	Provides a description for the list template that shows up on the Create and ViewLists pages.
DisplayName	Yes	Text	Specifies a friendly name for the list template.
DocumentTemplate	No	Integer	Implemented only for document libraries. This is the default file that is opened when the user clicks the New Document button in the document library's AllItems page.
DontSaveIn Template	No	Boolean	If TRUE, the content of the list will not be saved when creating a custom template.
Hidden	No	Boolean	If TRUE, the list type will not be shown on the Create page, so the user will not be able to create that type of list.

Attribute	Required	Type	Description
HiddenList	No	Boolean	If TRUE, the list instance created from this list template will be hidden from the user.
Image	No	URL	Associates an icon with the list. This icon is only specified on the Create page. The icon on the individual list page (for example, /Lists/Discussions/AllItems.aspx) is actually hard coded in the ASPX and is not affected by changing this value.
MultipleMtgData List	No	Boolean	If TRUE, indicates that the list is within a Meeting Workspace site and contains data for multiple meeting instances.
MustSaveRootFiles	No	Boolean	This is only intended for internal Microsoft use.
Name	Yes	Text	This specifies the internal name for the list template. This should be only alphanumeric text with no spaces or other special characters.
OnQuickLaunch	No	Boolean	If TRUE, the list instance will be placed on the Quick Launch bar if created through the <Configurations> element in ONET.XML.
Path	No	Text	Specifies the name of the site definition that defines the list schema. This would be helpful if you wanted to externally define (in another site template) the schema. The Meeting Workspaces make use of this to reference schemas in the STS site definition.
RootWebOnly	No	Boolean	If TRUE, indicates that the list created only exists at the root web site of the site collection. This is used for special lists, such as a Web Part Gallery, that need to be defined only once and not for each instance of a site.

continues

Table 2.5   `<ListTemplate>` Attributes (continued)

Attribute	Required	Type	Description
SecurityBits	No	Text	For non-document libraries, this specifies the read and write security. This maps to `tp_ReadSecurity` and `tp_WriteSecurity` columns in the `Lists` database table.
Type	No	Integer	Specifies a unique key to identify the list template. This is referenced when creating the list in the `<Configurations>` element. SharePoint defines the following list types: 100-Generic list, 101-Document Library, 102-Survey list, 103-Links list, 104-Announcement list, 105-Contact lists, 106-Event lists, 107-Task lists, 108-Discussion lists, 109-Picture Libraries, 110-Data sources lists, 111-Site Template Gallery, 113-Web Part Gallery, 114-List Template Gallery, 115-XML Form library, 120-Custom grid for a list, 200-Meeting series list, 201-Meeting agenda list, 202-Meeting attendees list, 204-Meeting decisions list, 207-Meeting objectives list, 210-Meeting text box, 211-Meeting things to bring list, 212-Meeting workspace pages list, 1100-Issue tracking list, 2002-Personal document library, and 2003-Private document library. You should not change the values of these types. You should also not create another list template with any number less than 3000.
Unique	Yes	Boolean	If TRUE, a list of this type can only be created at site creation, and not through the Create page or the object model. Therefore, this effectively sets the `Hidden` attribute to TRUE. Like `RootWebOnly`, this attribute is used by the galleries.

Let's examine the use of `Hidden` and `HiddenList`. Let's assume that our site definition will create a document and image library—which will be discussed in the `Configurations` section. If we were also to modify our site definition as specified in Listing 2.17, we would make all instances of document libraries hidden and make the picture library list type hidden. This is evidenced by the screenshots in Figure 2.10, Figure 2.11, and Figure 2.12.

Listing 2.17   ONET.XML `ListTemplate` Definitions

```
<ListTemplate Name="doclib" DisplayName="Document Library"
     HiddenList="TRUE" Type="101" BaseType="1" OnQuickLaunch="TRUE"
     SecurityBits="11"
     Description="Create a document library when you have a
                  collection of documents or other files that you
                  want to share.
                  Document libraries support features such as
                  sub-folders, file versioning, and check-in/
                  check-out."
     Image="/_layouts/images/itdl.gif" DocumentTemplate="101">
</ListTemplate>
<ListTemplate Name="imglib" DisplayName="Picture Library"
     Hidden="TRUE"
     Type="109" BaseType="1" OnQuickLaunch="TRUE" SecurityBits="11"
     Description="Create a picture library when you have pictures
                  you want to share.  Picture libraries provide
                  special features for managing and displaying
                  pictures, such as thumbnails, download options,
                  and a slide show."
     Image="/_layouts/images/itil.gif"
     DocumentTemplate="100">
</ListTemplate>
```

In Figure 2.10, we see that Document Libraries can be created. Furthermore, we see that even though Picture Libraries are a valid list type, they cannot be created through the Create page. This is because the `Hidden` attribute has been set to TRUE for the list template.

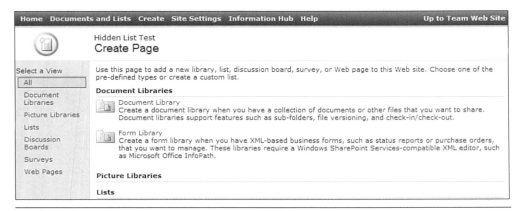

Figure 2.10   The hidden list template of Picture Libraries does not appear on the Create page.

Because the document library list template is set with the `Hidden` list attribute, all instances of that list type will be hidden from the user—but they will exist. Figure 2.11, which shows all documents and lists, is noticeably vacant of our Shared Documents document library. However, it does exist—as shown in Figure 2.12.

Figure 2.11   Shared Documents as a hidden list that does not appear to exist.

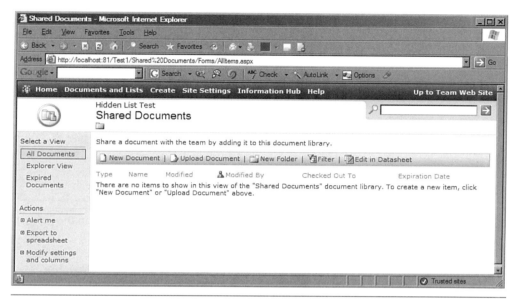

Figure 2.12   Shared Documents as a hidden list that is still navigable.

You might have noticed the `DocumentTemplate` attribute. If you are creating a document library, you should define the document template on which all new documents will be based. You reference this template through the `DocumentTemplate` attribute. The document template that you reference here is defined in the `DocumentTemplates` section.

`<DocumentTemplates>`: Specifying the Default New Document for a Document Library

Have you ever wondered how the New Document button—as shown in Figure 2.13—knows what document to create? How does it know to use a Word, Excel, HTM, or other template? Have you ever wanted to customize that file—perhaps with your organization's standard header? If so, you will be happy to know that all this is controlled through the `DocumentTemplates` element.

If a user creates a new document library, the user specifies the template at the document library's time of creation. However, if it needs to be created at site creation—as part of the site definition—it is mapped to the desired `DocumentTemplate` element. In turn, this `DocumentTemplate` element specifies a template file that resides as a physical file in your site definition folder.

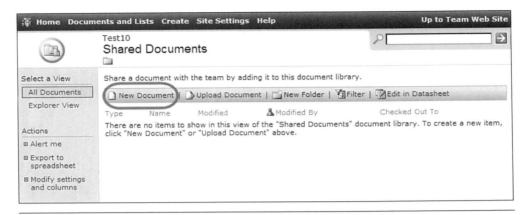

Figure 2.13   Document Library Toolbar.

To specify the default new document for a document library created during site creation, the `ListTemplate/@DocumentTemplate` attribute is mapped to the matching `DocumentTemplate/@Type` attribute. In the `ListTemplates` code snippet shown previously in Listing 2.17, you will notice that the document library's `DocumentTemplate` attribute is specified as 101. In the `DocumentTemplates` element detailed in Listing 2.18, you will notice that the matching element with a type of 101 is a Microsoft Word file. That is how the document library list knows to create a Word document when the user clicks New Document.

Listing 2.18   ONET.XML `DocumentTemplates` Definition

```
<DocumentTemplates>
  <DocumentTemplate  Name="" DisplayName="None" Type="100"
      Default="FALSE" Description="This document library will not
              use templates.">
  </DocumentTemplate>
  <DocumentTemplate  DisplayName="Microsoft Office Word document"
      Type="101" Default="TRUE"
      Description="A blank Microsoft Office Word document.">
    <DocumentTemplateFiles>
      <DocumentTemplateFile Name="doctemp\word\wdtmpl.doc"
          TargetName="Forms/template.doc" Default="TRUE"/>
    </DocumentTemplateFiles>
  </DocumentTemplate>
```

The `DocumentTemplate` element is defined in Table 2.6. All the attributes defined in the table are fairly straightforward. The only attribute that stands out is `Default`. It specifies the default document template to be used when creating a document library. This template is preselected when the user visits the New Document Library page—as shown in Figure 2.14.

Table 2.6   `<DocumentTemplate>` Attributes

Attribute	Required	Type	Description
Default	No	Boolean	If TRUE, this document template is selected as the default in the drop-down menu on the New Document Library page. There should only be one `DocumentTemplate` element with a value of TRUE in all of ONET.XML.
Description	No	Text	Specifies a description for the document template.
DisplayName	Yes	Text	Specifies the display name of the document template.
Name	No	Text	Specifies an internal name for the document template.
Path	No	Text	Specifies the name of the site definition to which the document template belongs. This is helpful if you want to externally define (in another site template) the document template file.
Type	Yes	Integer	A unique ID/Key for the document template. This is what the `ListTemplate's` `DocumentTemplate` references.
XMLForm	No	Boolean	If TRUE, the document template applies to a form library.

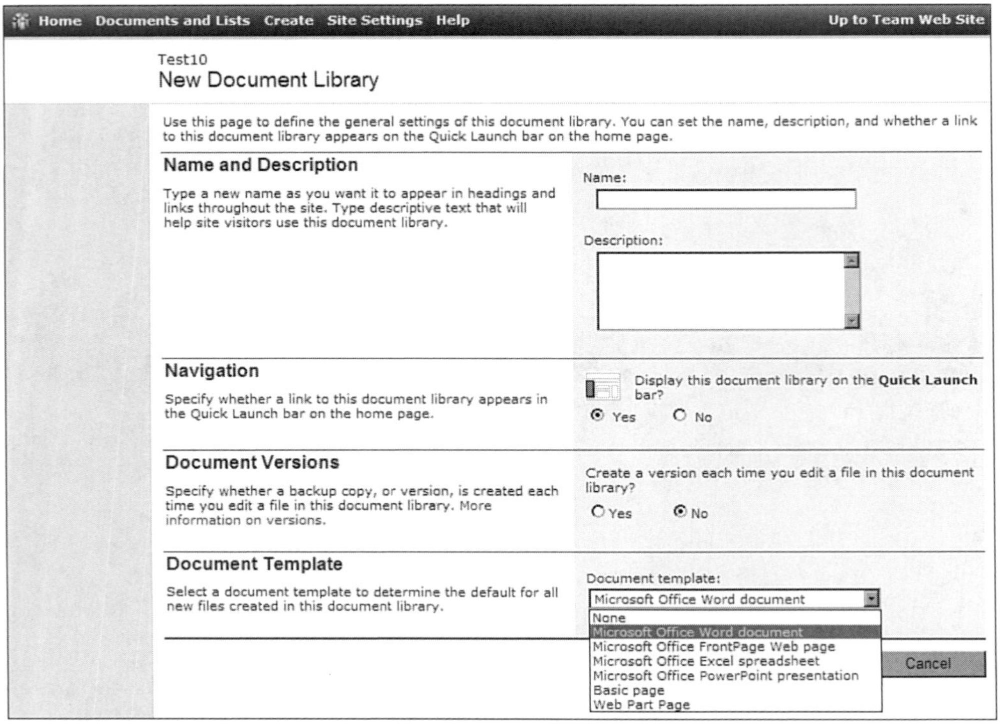

Figure 2.14   Creating a new document library.

The `DocumentTemplateFile` element specifies the actual file to be used. As alluded to earlier, this file could be of any type and could be seeded with some custom content. Such would be the case with a Word document that has the corporate stationary embedded in it.

The `DocumentTemplateFile/@Name` attribute specifies the relative path to the file within the site definition. Listing 2.18 specifies the Word document template as doctemp\word\wdtmpl.doc relative to your site definition folder. In our example, this would map to C:\Program Files\Common Files\Microsoft Shared\web server extensions\60\TEM-PLATE\1033\MyFirstSiteDefinition\doctemp\word\wdtmpl.doc.

Conversely, the `TargetName` attribute creates a hidden virtual path to this file in the document library. In the Word document template case, it is Forms/template.doc. You can verify this by going to any document library that uses this document template, switching to the Explorer view, and navigating into the Forms folder to see template.doc. Thus, when the user clicks the New Document button, the user is actually loading the customized Forms/template.doc file.

Table 2.7   `<DocumentTemplateFile>` Attributes

Attribute	Required	Type	Description
Default	No	Boolean	If TRUE, the document template file will be the default file. Practically speaking, you should have only one file for each DocumentTemplate element. That one file will also be the default file.
Name	Yes	Text	The physical relative path to the file within the site definition.
TargetName	No	Text	The virtual path to the file within the document library.

`<BaseTypes>`: The Foundation for List and Library Definitions

BaseTypes define the schema for the lists and libraries (see Listing 2.19). As mentioned earlier, the list base type is specified through the ListTemplate/@BaseType attribute. This attribute actually references the BaseType/@Type attribute. BaseType attributes are defined in Table 2.8.

Listing 2.19   ONET.XML BaseType Definition

```
<BaseType Title="Document Library" Image="_layouts/images/itdl.gif"
      Type="1">
  <MetaData>
    <Fields>
      <Field ColName="tp_ID" ReadOnly="TRUE" Type="Counter"
            Name="ID" DisplayName="ID"></Field>
      <Field ColName="tp_Created" Hidden="TRUE"
            ReadOnly="TRUE" Type="DateTime" Name="Created"
            DisplayName="Created Date"
            StorageTZ="TRUE"></Field>
      <Field ColName="tp_Author" ReadOnly="TRUE" Type="User"
            List="UserInfo" Name="Author"
            DisplayName="Created By" ></Field>
      <Field ColName="tp_Modified" Hidden="TRUE"
            ReadOnly="TRUE" Type="DateTime" Name="Modified"
            DisplayName="Last Modified"
```

```
           StorageTZ="TRUE"></Field>
<Field ColName="tp_Editor" ReadOnly="TRUE" Type="User"
       List="UserInfo" Name="Editor"
       DisplayName="Modified By" ></Field>
<Field ColName="tp_ModerationStatus" ReadOnly="TRUE"
       Type="ModStat" Name="_ModerationStatus"
       DisplayName="Approval Status" Hidden="TRUE"
       CanToggleHidden="TRUE" Required="FALSE">
  <CHOICES>
    <CHOICE>0;#Approved</CHOICE>
    <CHOICE>1;#Rejected</CHOICE>
    <CHOICE>2;#Pending</CHOICE>
  </CHOICES>
  <Default>0</Default>
</Field>
```

.
.
.

The snippet in Listing 2.19 details part of the schema definition for document libraries. Because the functionality of lists is bound to their schemas, you should never remove field elements. For instance, if you removed the column that stores the name of the person who checked out a file, the built-in functionality for document libraries would suddenly break.

Table 2.8   `<BaseType>` Attributes

Attribute	Required	Type	Description
Image	No	Text	Specifies the URL to an icon representing this list type. Typically, this value will be overwritten by the list (`ListTemplate\@Image`).
Title	No	Text	The title/name for the list schema.
Type	No	Integer	This is a unique ID for the list schema. SharePoint defines five built-in base types: (0) Custom List, (1) Document Library, (2) Not Used, (3) Discussion, (4) Survey, and (5) Issue.

There are five base types in SharePoint. Unfortunately, other base list types cannot be added. However, the custom list type can be augmented to provide the functionality desired. This is done through modifying a SCHEMA.XML, which we cover more fully in Chapter 3.

SCHEMA.XML is designed to extend the functionality of the `Base-Type` element. In fact, the `MetaData` element is used in both ONET.XML and SCHEMA.XML. In ONET.XML, `MetaData` defines the base fields for a list. In SCHEMA.XML, `MetaData` can define additional fields, views, toolbars, forms, and a default description.

It is worth mentioning that the FLDTYPES.XML file defines the allowable `Field` types. Thus, `Field/@Type` must be of a value defined within FLDTYPES.XML. FLDTYPES.XML should not be modified.

We also recommend that you do not modify the `BaseTypes` section in ONET.XML. You should be able to modify SCHEMA.XML to effect any changes that modifying the `BaseType` would accomplish.

`<Configurations>`: Defining the Site Definition Templates

A site definition can contain multiple flavors of templates—which are referred to as site definition templates. In fact, all eight default WSS templates (Team Site, Blank Site, Document Workspace, Basic Meeting Workspace, Blank Meeting Workspace, Decision Meeting Workspace, Social Meeting Workspace, and Multipage Meeting Workspace) are created from only two site definitions. The STS site definition contains Team Site, Blank Site, and Document Workspace definitions. The MPS site definition contains the Basic Meeting Workspace, Blank Meeting Workspace, Decision Meeting Workspace, Social Meeting Workspace, and Multipage Meeting Workspace.

The snippet in Listing 2.20 details a few site definition templates in the MyFirstSiteDefinition site definition that we created earlier. As you might recall, we simply copied the STS site definition and therefore inherited all the templates from STS. So now you are thinking, if I have inherited all these templates defined in ONET.XML, why aren't they showing up on the Template Selection page when I create a new site? Well, the WEBTEMP*.XML file controls what shows up on that page. Thus, you could have multiple site definition templates defined in ONET.XML but only a subset of them exposed—which is the case here.

Listing 2.20   ONET.XML Configuration for Team Site

```xml
<Configurations>
  <Configuration ID="-1" Name="NewWeb"/>
  <Configuration ID="0" Name="Default">
    <Lists>
      <List Title="Shared Documents"
            Url="Shared Documents"
            QuickLaunchUrl="Shared Documents/Forms/AllItems.aspx"
            Type="101" />
      <List Title="General Discussion"
            Url="Lists/General Discussion"
            QuickLaunchUrl="Lists/GeneralDiscussion/AllItems.aspx"
            Type="108" />
      <List Title="Announcements"
            Type="104"
            Url="Lists/Announcements" />
      <List Title="Links"
            Type="103"
            Url="Lists/Links" />
      <List Title="Contacts"
            Url="Lists/Contacts"
            QuickLaunchUrl="Lists/Contacts/AllItems.aspx"
            Type="105" />
      <List Title="Events"
            Type="106"
            Url="Lists/Events" />
      <List Title="Tasks"
            Url="Lists/Tasks"
            QuickLaunchUrl="Lists/Tasks/AllItems.aspx"
            Type="107" />
      <List Title="Site Template Gallery"
            Type="111"
            Url="_catalogs/wt"
            RootWebOnly="TRUE" />
      <List Title="Web Part Gallery"
            Type="113"
            Url="_catalogs/wp"
            RootWebOnly="TRUE" />
      <List Title="List Template Gallery"
            Type="114"
            Url="_catalogs/lt"
            RootWebOnly="TRUE" />
```

```
    </Lists>
    <Modules>
      <Module Name="Default"/>
      <Module Name="WebPartPopulation"/>
    </Modules>
  </Configuration>
  <Configuration ID="1" Name="Blank">
    <Lists>
      <List Title="Site Template Gallery" Type="111"
            Url="_catalogs/wt" RootWebOnly="TRUE" />
      <List Title="Web Part Gallery" Type="113"
            Url="_catalogs/wp" RootWebOnly="TRUE" />
      <List Title="List Template Gallery" Type="114"
            Url="_catalogs/lt" RootWebOnly="TRUE" />
    </Lists>
    <Modules>
      <Module Name="DefaultBlank"/>
      <Module Name="WebPartPopulation"/>
    </Modules>
  </Configuration>
  .
  .
  .
</Configurations>
```

In our example WEBTEMP*.XML file, we are only referencing the Configuration with an ID of 0 despite the multiple other IDs available in ONET.XML. Irrespective of WEBTEMP*.XML, each Configuration element specified in ONET.XML can define several List and Module elements.

The Module elements define files that are mapped into the site definition template. We will save our discussion of Modules for the next section. Furthermore, we have already defined the Configuration element in our previous discussion on WEBTEMP.XML, so we will not duplicate that discussion here.

The List elements define the various lists that are created when the site definition template is applied. The seven user lists specified in the Lists element for Configuration ID 0 are shown in a newly created site with the template in Figure 2.15. The other three lists specified— Site Template Gallery, Web Part Gallery, and List Template Gallery— are special list types that are not exposed to the user through the

Document and Lists page shown in Figure 2.15. As you might recall from Chapter 1, "Custom Templates," the Site Template Gallery is a document library for storing custom site templates, and the List Template Gallery is a document library for storing custom list templates. The Web Part Gallery stores WebPart DWP files. When you define your own `List` element, you will probably specify at least `QuickLaunchURL`, `RootWebOnly`, `Title`, `Type`, and `Url`. The complete set of List attributes is described in Table 2.9. It is worth noting that SCHEMA.XML can override the settings within ONET.XML. Thus, if you change the value here and are confused about why nothing happened, check SCHEMA.XML to see whether it is overriding your settings.

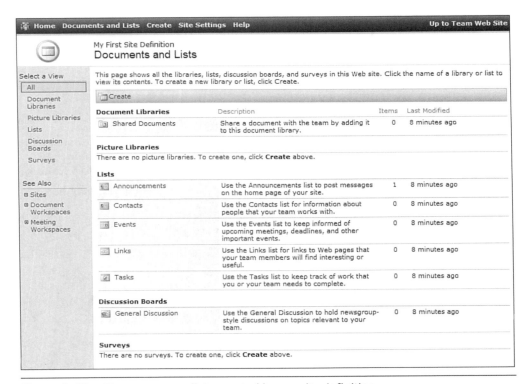

Figure 2.15   The seven user lists created by our site definition.

If we wanted to create additional lists, we would have simply added another `List` element with the appropriate attribute settings. If we want to limit the lists that are created, we would remove the undesired `List` elements.

Table 2.9 `<List>` Attributes

Attribute	Required	Type	Description
BaseType	No	Integer	This specifies the schema for the list. That schema is defined in the `BaseTypes` section of ONET.XML.
Default	No	Boolean	If TRUE, the list will be created at site creation, and if FALSE, it will not be created at site creation. However, the list is created regardless of the setting.
Direction	No	Integer	This specifies the direction of the reading order for the list. 0 is left to right, and 1 is right to left. Contrary to Microsoft documentation, it is required in neither ONET.XML nor SCHEMA.XML.
DisableAttachments	No	Boolean	If TRUE, attachments cannot be added to the list.
EventSinkAssembly	No	Text	This specifies the strong named assembly that hooks into SharePoint's event model for the document library.
EventSinkClass	No	Text	This specifies the class within the `EventSinkAssembly` that will respond to the SharePoint events.
EventSinkData	No	Text	Specifies an arbitrary string that is passed to your custom event handler. It is left to the discretion of your custom handler to handle events differently depending on the value of this string.

continues

Table 2.9   `<List>` Attributes (continued)

Attribute	Required	Type	Description
Name	No	Text	Specifies the internal name for the list.
OrderedList	No	Boolean	If TRUE, asks an additional question in the Edit View page: "Allow users to order items in this view?"
PrivateList	No	Boolean	If TRUE, does not inherit permissions of the site and allows only the web designer role to access the list.
QuickLaunchUrl	No	Text	If specified, the list will be featured on the Quick Launch bar of the site's home page with the specified URL.
RootWebOnly	No	Boolean	If TRUE, the list should only exist at the root site collection level, and there should not be separate instances for each site.
ThumbnailSize	No	Integer	This defines the pixel width of thumbnails in picture libraries.
Title	Yes	Text	Specifies the name that the user sees for this list.
Type	Yes	Integer	Specifies the list template that should be used to create this list. This is specified by referencing the `ListTemplate/@Type` attribute. SharePoint's default types are covered in Table 2.5.
Url	No	URL	This specifies the virtual path of the site for which the list will be created.
URLEncode	No	Boolean	If TRUE, the URL will be encoded.
VersioningEnabled	No	Boolean	If TRUE, Versioning will be enabled by default.
WebImageHeight	No	Integer	When the list is a picture library, this specifies the pixel height for an image in the library.
WebImageWidth	No	Integer	When the list is a picture library, this specifies the pixel width for an image in the library.

If the `QuickLaunchURL` attribute has been specified, the specified URL is listed on the Quick Launch bar on the site's home page. You can specify any URL—including one that does not link to the list. However, the Quick Launch URL can be reset to the correct one. This will happen if the user modifies the list's general settings to display it on the Quick Launch bar—as shown in Figure 2.16. This action will erase the URL you have specified as part of the `List` attribute and will replace it with the default All Items view.

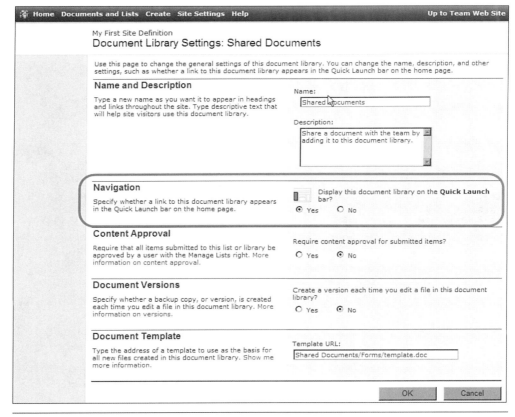

Figure 2.16 Quick Launch settings on the List General Settings page.

The `RootWebOnly` attribute specifies that the list should not actually exist at the site level. Instead, it should exist at the root web of the site collection, and there should not be an instance at every site. A good example of a list that should exist only at the root web is the Web Part Gallery list. Obviously, you don't need to duplicate this list at every site. With that said, this attribute presumes that the root web list specified already exists. Thus, make sure the list exists before you use this setting.

Lastly, URL specifies the virtual path to link to your list. If the Contacts list URL was modified from Lists to MyLists, as shown in Listing 2.21, then the virtual path to the Contacts list would change. Therefore, the URL to the list would be /MyFirstSiteDef/ MyLists/ MyContacts/AllItems.aspx, which is shown in Figure 2.17.

Listing 2.21 ONET.XML List Definition

```
<List Title="Contacts" Url="MyLists/MyContacts"
QuickLaunchUrl="MyLists/MyContacts/AllItems.aspx" Type="105" />
```

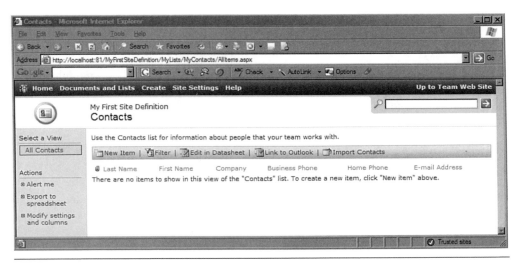

Figure 2.17 The URL changes in List are reflected here.

`<Modules>`: **Grouping Elements of a Site Definition Together to Use within Configurations**

`Modules` are simply functional file groups. As explained in the previous section, when you select a specific site definition template, you are actually selecting a specific `Configuration` element in ONET.XML. That `Configuration` element inevitably specifies several modules. The files specified in those modules are then deployed to the newly created site. `Module` attributes are defined in Table 2.10.

Table 2.10 `<Module>` Attributes

Attribute	Required	Type	Description
List	No	Integer	Specifies the list type as defined in the `ListTemplates` section earlier in ONET.XML.
Name	Yes	Text	Defines an identifier by which the module can be referenced.
Path	No	Text	Specifies the physical relative folder path from which to retrieve the file.
RootWebOnly	No	Boolean	If TRUE, this signifies that the modules are installed at the top-level web site (of the site collection).
Url	No	Text	Specifies the virtual relative folder path in which to place the file.

Module Basics

The module in Listing 2.22 defines two pictures to be included with a site definition. Although the `Name`, `Url`, and `Path` attributes all have a value, they each have a different function.

Listing 2.22   ONET.XML Simple Module Definition

```
<Module Name="Images" Path="images" Url="images">
      <File Url="InformationHub.png" />
      <File Url="JasonNadrowski.jpg" />
</Module>
```

The `Name` attribute specifies an identifier that can be used to reference this specific module. This would be used to reference this module from the `Configuration` section in ONET.XML as we discussed in the previous section. `Name` could be something very cryptic because it is never exposed to the user.

The `Path` attribute specifies a folder relative to the site definition template's physical path. As shown in the Explorer screenshot in Figure 2.18, the `images` path is a child folder of the MyFirstSiteDefinition site definition and exists on the server's local physical hard drive.

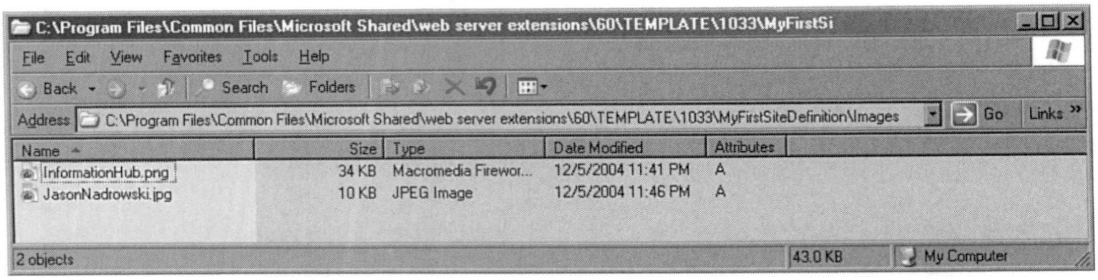

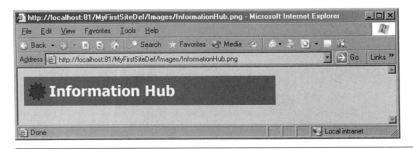

Figure 2.18   Physical path as defined by the `Path` attribute.

Conversely, the `Url` attribute specifies a virtual path relative to an instance of the site. In the example shown in Figure 2.19, the image is mapped from the database to images virtual folder. Keep in mind that this is not an absolute path. It is a virtual path off an instance of the site definition template. Therefore, you will need to think a little more carefully when referencing these images from your various pages within the site definition because the image might or might not be available on /MyFirstSiteDef/Images/InformationHub.png or /MyFirstSiteDef/Subsite1/Images/InformationHub.png.

Figure 2.19   Virtual path as defined by the `Url` attribute.

Both the `Path` and `Url` attributes can support a syntax of a multiple-level folder structure. For instance, a `Url` value of "images/information-hub/2005" could just as easily have been specified in Listing 2.22.

Fortunately, there is no need to build a multiple-level virtual path with multiple parent modules (for example, `Url="images"`, `Url="images/informationhub"`) as you would with a physical folder structure. The module files are actually mapped in the database, and their entire path is stored with them. The somewhat negative aspect of this is that you cannot browse their parent folders. When you try to browse to the images folder, you get a 404 error (see Figure 2.20), which gives the user the impression that there are no other child items here—which is not the case. In our current scenario, there are two images within the images folder (JasonNadrowski.jpg and InformationHub.png).

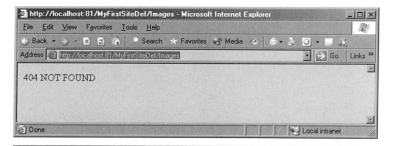

Figure 2.20   Images parent folder does not exist even though it contains pictures.

From a best practice standpoint, you should match your physical path to the virtual `Url` as we have done with images. Making your virtual and physical paths the same helps to minimize confusion when someone new looks at the site definition or when you revisit it.

The `File` element is the only child element that a module can have. The `File` element is described in Table 2.11.

Table 2.11 `<File>` Attributes

Attribute	Required	Type	Description
Name	No	Text	Defines an identifier by which the `File` element can be referenced.
NavBarHome	No	Boolean	If `TRUE`, the file will be referenced by the navigation bar home link.
Type	No	Text	If `Ghostable`, the file will be cached. If `GhostableInLibrary`, the file will be cached as part of a list whose base type is Document Library.
Url	Yes	Text	Specifies the relative physical path on the server's disk in relation to the `Module`'s `Path` attribute.

In Listing 2.22, we only use the `File` element's `Url` attribute. This attribute name is a bit confusing because it is more in line with the `Module`'s `Path` attribute than with the module's `Url` attribute. It defines the physical path relative to the module's `Path` attribute. We had simply specified the filenames with no path in the file's `Url` attribute because they resided within the images folder.

Specifying `true` for the `NavBarHome` attribute signifies that Home on the top navigation bar (see Figure 2.21) will be linked to the `File` element. Because that navigation bar is used throughout the entire site, it is invalid to have more than one link for Home. Although you can have multiple `File` elements that have their `NavBarHome` attribute set to `TRUE` within all of ONET.XML, you can only have one `File` element with its `NavBarHome` attribute set to `TRUE` within a single `Configuration` element.

Home   Documents and Lists   Create   Site Settings   Help

Figure 2.21 Top navigation bar.

SharePoint will cache most file types (GIF, JPG, PNG, etc.) when referenced with the `File` element, but ASPX files will not be cached. Thus, changes to an ASPX file will be immediately reflected in a site without an IISReset. However, changes to other file types, such as a JPG file, will not be reflected until SharePoint is restarted through an IISReset.

Advanced Module Concepts: Views, WebParts, and Navigation Bars

Now let's look at a little more intricate use of the `Module` element. The code snippet in Listing 2.23 details a `Module` for deploying the DEFAULT.ASPX file. In this listing, the `File` element has three additional child elements: `NavBarPage`, `AllUsersWebPart`, and `View`.

Listing 2.23   ONET.XML Complex Module Definition

```
<Module Name="Default" Url="" Path="">
  <File Url="default.aspx" NavBarHome="True">
    <View List="104" BaseViewID="0" WebPartZoneID="Left"/>
    <View List="106" BaseViewID="0" WebPartZoneID="Left"
        WebPartOrder="2"/>
    <AllUsersWebPart WebPartZoneID="Right" WebPartOrder="1">
      <![CDATA[
        <WebPart
           xmlns="http://schemas.microsoft.com/WebPart/v2"
           xmlns:iwp="http://schemas.microsoft.com/WebPart/v2/
➡ Image">
          <Assembly>
            Microsoft.SharePoint, Version=11.0.0.0,
            Culture=neutral, PublicKeyToken=71e9bce111e9429c
          </Assembly>
          <TypeName>
            Microsoft.SharePoint.WebPartPages.ImageWebPart
          </TypeName>
          <FrameType>None</FrameType>
          <Title>Site Image</Title>
          <iwp:ImageLink>/_layouts/images/homepage.gif</
➡ iwp:ImageLink>
        </WebPart>
      ]>
    </AllUsersWebPart>
    <View List="103" BaseViewID="0" WebPartZoneID="Right"
        WebPartOrder="2"/>
    <NavBarPage Name="Home" ID="1002" Position="Start"></NavBarPage>
    <NavBarPage Name="Home" ID="0" Position="Start">
```

```
      </NavBarPage>
    </File>
  </Module>
```

The `NavBarPage` element interacts with the navigation bar that we defined in the `NavBars` section. You might recall that although we defined navigation items for Documents and Lists, Create, Site Settings, and Help, we didn't define a Home element. You can add items to the top navigation bar in the `Module`.

The first `NavBarPage` element—with an `ID` of 1002—binds DEFAULT.ASPX to the top navigation bar we defined within the `NavBars` section. It is no coincidence that the `ID` of the `NavBarPage` element (Listing 2.23) matches the `ID` of the `NavBar` element (Listing 2.13). If it didn't, SharePoint would become confused.

The second `NavBarPage` element—with an `ID` of 0—adds Home to the top navigation bar. Additional `Modules` could be added to the top navigation bar, just as DEFAULT.ASPX was mapped to home, with the aid of `NavBarPage`. Those additional modules would need a unique `ID` for their `NavBarPage` element and their position. Their placement on the navigation bar would be controlled by the `Position` attribute. `Position` can be `Start`, `End`, or a number.

`AllUsersWebPart` enables you to place a named web part on the web part page. In our example, we place the Image web part on the web part page. We just as easily could have placed the Members, Announcements, or any other custom web parts on the page. Initial configuration data for these web parts is usually passed through a child `CData` element. In our case, we specify the web part, its frame type, title, and an initial image. Keep in mind that the user could drastically modify these initial settings in the future.

The `WebPartZoneID` and `WebPartOrder` attributes are valid in both `AllUsersWebPart` and `View` elements. These attributes control the placement of the web parts. The `WebPartZoneID` places the web part in a named zone, and the `WebPartOrder` specifies the order of the web part within a zone. In our example detailed in Listing 2.24, DEFAULT.ASPX has two zones defined—`Left` and `Right`.

Listing 2.24   DEFAULT.ASPX Web Part Zone Declarations

```
<tr>
  <!-- Middle column -->
  <td valign="top" width="70%">
    <WebPartPages:WebPartZone runat="server"
➡ FrameType="TitleBarOnly" ID="Left" Title="loc:Left" />
     
  </td>
  <td> </td>
  <!-- Right column -->
  <td valign="top" width="30%">
    <WebPartPages:WebPartZone runat="server"
➡ FrameType="TitleBarOnly" ID="Right" Title="loc:Right" />
     
  </td>
  <td> </td>
<tr>
```

The `View` element is very similar to the `AllUsersWebPart`. Instead of a named web part, the `View` element displays the contents of a list or library. This makes a lot of sense if you recall how web parts are added to a page through the GUI. As shown in Figure 2.22, the web part list that you select from includes not only web parts but also the lists and libraries of a site. In Figure 2.22, these lists include Announcements, Contacts, Events, General Discussion, and Links. Actually, these lists use the same web part class but with different connections to the underlying data source. The Announcements web part connects to the Announcements list, the Contacts web part connects to the Contacts list, and so on. This is exactly the same metaphor that the `AllUsersWebPart` and `View` elements use.

Figure 2.22   Web Part List showcasing views of lists.

In Listing 2.23, the `View` elements reference a `List` attribute and a `BaseViewID` attribute of 0. The `List` attributes reference 104 and 106. These `List` values were defined in the `Configuration` section of ONET.XML and correspond to Announcements and Events, respectively. Thus, a view of Announcements and Events will be added to the DEFAULT.ASPX page. The `BaseViewID` is the initial view selected for the web part. Those view `ID`s are initially defined within SCHEMA.XML. Figure 2.23 shows the initial views for an event list that originated from SCHEMA.XML. Through `BaseViewID`, the initial view of the Events list could be set to All Events, Calendar, or Current Events. Of course, this could always be changed through the GUI after the site has been created.

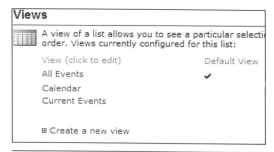

Figure 2.23   Example Event List views.

Only a subset of `View` element attributes is used within ONET.XML. SCHEMA.XML, which we describe later, more fully utilizes the `View` attributes. Table 2.12 describes all the `View` element attributes.

Table 2.12 `<View>` Attributes

Attribute	Required	Type	Description
AggregateView	No	Boolean	If TRUE, indicates that the view is a merge forms view. This pertains to an XML Form library.
BaseViewID	No	Boolean	Specifies the view to use when referenced from ONET.XML. When used in SCHEMA.XML, defines an identifier for the view.
DefaultView	No	Text	If TRUE, indicates that this is the default view.
DisplayName	No	Boolean	This is the name of the view as shown in the Quick Launch view.
Editor	No	Text	Specifies the editing tool used to create the view. Valid choices are `SharePoint Team Services`, `FrontPage`, and `Custom`.
FailIfEmpty	No	Boolean	If TRUE, a view that returns no items will return an HTTP error code. If FALSE, `<ViewEmpty><![CDATA[<I> There are no items in this view.</I>]]></ViewEmpty>` will be returned. This only applies if you are interacting with the view through the SharePoint API. There will be no noticeable difference when looking at the view through the AllItems.aspx or similar page.
FileDialog	No	Boolean	If TRUE, the view is marked as the one to be displayed from the Microsoft Office application suite. One can test its results through the URL http://MyWSSServer/Subweb1/_vti_bin/owssvr.dll?location=MyDocLibraryName&dialogview=FileSave.

continues

Table 2.12   `<View>` Attributes (continued)

Attribute	Required	Type	Description
FPModified	No	Boolean	If TRUE, the view has been modified by FrontPage and therefore can no longer be customized by the SharePoint web user interface.
FreeForm	No	Boolean	If TRUE, more flexibility is allowed for formatting the various fields of a list.
Hidden	No	Boolean	If TRUE, the view is not displayed through the SharePoint web user interface. For example, the Microsoft Office views discussed in the `FileDialog` attribute are hidden.
List	No	Integer	Specifies the list type defined within ONET.XML.
Name	No	Text	Specifies a unique name for the view. However, the value of the `DisplayName` attribute is what is exposed to users.
OrderedView	No	Boolean	If TRUE, specifies that the view is ordered.
Path	No	Text	Specifies the filename for the view. This is primarily used with `FileDialog` views and is in lieu of specifying this file with the `Url` attribute.
ReadOnly	No	Boolean	If TRUE, the view cannot be modified. This is helpful if you never want users modifying the view through the web user interface.
RecurrenceRowset	No	Boolean	If TRUE, recurring events will be expanded in the view. This is only applicable to the events list.
RowLimit	No	Integer	Specifies the maximum number of items to show per page. Valid values include an integer or None. If None is specified, all records are returned with no paging.

Attribute	Required	Type	Description
Scope	No	Text	This only applies to libraries. Valid values include `FilesOnly`, `Recursive`, and `RecursiveAll`. If `FilesOnly`, display the files of the current folder. If `Recursive`, display all files so that they appear at the root level. If `RecursiveAll`, show all files and subfolders so that they appear at the root level. If left unspecified (the default), the files and subfolders of the current folder will be displayed.
Threaded	No	Boolean	If `TRUE`, items will be threaded. The best example of this is within the discussion board list.
Type	No	Text	Specifies the view rendering. Valid choices include `HTML`, `Chart`, and `Pivot`.
Url	No	Url	Binds a URL of the list or library view file to a view. This is akin to the `Path` attribute.
WebPartOrder	No	Integer	The order in which the view web part will be placed within an already specified zone.
WebPartZoneID	No	Text	The zone in which the view web part will be placed.

DEFAULT.ASPX: The Site's Home Page

The cornerstone of any SharePoint site is its home page. Although the `Module` section of ONET.XML enables you to set the home page to anything, DEFAULT.ASPX should be the name of your site definition's home page. As discussed previously, the SharePoint site definition templates place this file in the root of the site definition folder (for example, C:\Program Files\Common Files\Microsoft Shared\web server extensions\60\TEMPLATE\1033\STS).

DEFAULT.ASPX can be modified to your heart's desire. Additional web part zones could be added, icons could be changed, the Quick Launch could be removed, and the list goes on.

To help facilitate your own modifications, let's spend some time deconstructing STS's DEFAULT.ASPX. A typical instance of DEFAULT.ASPX from the STS site definition is shown in Figure 2.24. The major elements include the top blue navigation bar, the bar immediately under navigation bar, the Quick Launch, and the Left and Right web part zones.

Figure 2.24   DEFAULT.ASPX Design view.

Top Navigation Bar

The code that generates the top blue bar is shown in Listing 2.25. The code generates a three-column HTML table row. The first column is a SharePoint team logo. The second column represents the navigation bar we discussed in ONET.XML's `NavBars` section. The last column is a connection to the parent site, or the portal if the site is the topmost site in the site collection. The content of second and third columns is dynamically generated by web controls from the `Microsoft.SharePoint.WebControls` namespace.

Listing 2.25 DEFAULT.ASPX Top Bar

```
<td nowrap valign="middle">
  <img ID=onetidHeadbnnr0 alt="Logo" src="/_layouts/images/logo.gif">
</td>
<td class=ms-banner width=99% nowrap ID="HBN100" valign="middle">
  <!--
    webbot
      bot="Navigation"
      S-Type="sequence"
      S-Orientation="horizontal"
      S-Rendering="html"
      S-Btn-Nml="<a ID='onettopnavbar#LABEL_ID#' href='#URL#'
        accesskey='J'>#LABEL#</a>"
      S-Btn-Sel="<a ID='onettopnavbar#LABEL_ID#' href='#URL#'
        accesskey='J'>#LABEL#</a>"
      S-Btn-Sep="   "
      B-Include-Home="FALSE"
      B-Include-Up="FALSE"
      S-Btn-Nobr="FALSE"
      U-Page="sid:1002"
      S-Target startspan
  -->
    <SharePoint:Navigation LinkBarId="1002" runat="server"/>
  <!--
    webbot
      bot="Navigation"
      endspan
  -->
</td>
<td class=ms-banner>  </td>
<td nowrap class=ms-banner style="padding-right: 7px">
  <SharePoint:PortalConnection runat="server" />
</td>
```

Logo, Site Title, Search Box, and SharePoint Modify Page Link

Immediately underneath the top blue bar is a row that contains the home logo, site title and location, search box, and modify shared/personal page link. That code is shown in Listing 2.26.

What might be surprising to learn is that neither the circular home logo nor the "Home" page title is dynamically defined. They are simply coded as static links. Thus, it is very straightforward to reference another URL for the home icon or change the page title to something else.

The only things that are dynamically defined within that row are the site's description, the search box, the modify shared/personal page link, and the authentication button. These dynamic generations are powered by web controls from the `Microsoft.SharePoint.WebControls` and `Microsoft.SharePoint.WebPartPages` namespaces.

As you build your own site definition templates, you should consider upgrading Windows SharePoint Services' weak search support. WSS only enables you to search the current site. It does not search subsites or parent sites. Because it does not declare this weakness, users usually do not realize that content might exist in a subsite even though it did not show up in the search results.

Although this weakness is being solved in the next version of Share-Point, Microsoft has released an upgraded search box as an interim solution. Specifically, Anthony Petro's MSDN article "Creating a Site Context Search Box that Uses SharePoint Portal Server Search Results" includes an updated search box that can be integrated into DEFAULT.ASPX or any other site definition page. Anthony's search web part enables the user to select the context (site, site collection, or all content indexed by SharePoint Portal Server) of his or her search and uses SharePoint Portal Server to generate the results. The web part posts the search query along with its context to SharePoint Portal Server's search page through the querystring. The next version of Share-Point will expand on this idea.

Listing 2.26   DEFAULT.ASPX Logo, Title, Search Box, Settings Link, and Authentication Button

```
<td align=center nowrap style="padding-top: 4px" width="132"
    height="46">
  <img ID=onetidtpweb1 src="/_layouts/images/home.gif" alt="Icon"
      height="49" width="49">
</td>
<td>
  <IMG SRC="/_layouts/images/blank.gif" width=22 height=1 alt="">
</td>
<td nowrap width="100%" style="padding-top: 0px">
```

```
  <table cellpadding=0 cellspacing=0>
    <tr>
      <td nowrap class="ms-titlearea">
        <SharePoint:ProjectProperty Property="Title"
➥ runat="server"/>
      </td>
    </tr>
    <tr>
      <td ID=onetidPageTitle class="ms-pagetitle">
        Home<!-- -->
      </td>
    </tr>
  </table>
</td>
<td align=right valign=top>
  <table cellpadding=0 cellspacing=0 height=100%>
    <tr>
      <SharePoint:ViewSearchForm ID="L_SearchView"
        Prompt="Search this site"
        Go="Go"
        Action="searchresults.aspx"
        runat="server"/>
    </tr>
    <tr style="padding-right:1px">
      <td colspan=5 nowrap style="padding-bottom: 3px; padding-top:
                                  1px; vertical-align: bottom"
        align=right class="ms-vb">
        <span class='ms-SPLink'>
          <span class='ms-HoverCellInActive'
              onmouseover="this.className='ms-HoverCellActive'";
              onmouseout="this.className='ms-HoverCellInActive'">
            <WebPartPages:SettingsLink runat="server"/>
          </span>
        </span>
        <WebPartPages:AuthenticationButton runat="server"/>  
      </td>
    </tr>
  </table>
</td>
```

Quick Launch Bar

One would expect the Quick Launch bar to be a single web part. However, it is composed of several web parts, one for each list type.

The code snippet in Listing 2.27 provides a window into how the Documents section of Quick Launch is generated, and it is representative of the other sections. The Documents text is statically defined and links to VIEWLSTS.ASPX with a querystring parameter. The querystring parameter filters the page for document libraries.

Listing 2.27   DEFAULT.ASPX QuickLaunch

```
<TR>
  <TD class="ms-navheader">
    <A HREF="_layouts/<%

=System.Threading.Thread.CurrentThread.CurrentUICulture.LCID
        %>/viewlsts.aspx?BaseType=1">
      Documents
      </A>
  </TD>
</TR>
<TR>
  <TD style="height: 6px">
    <!--
      webbot bot="Navigation"
              S-Btn-Nobr="FALSE"
              S-Type="sequence"
              S-Rendering="html"
              S-Orientation="Vertical"
              B-Include-Home="FALSE"
              B-Include-Up="FALSE"
              U-Page="sid:1004"
              S-Bar-Pfx="<table border=0 cellpadding=4
cellspacing=0>"
              S-Bar-Sfx="</table>"
              S-Btn-Nml="<tr><td><table border=0 cellpadding=0
                      cellspacing=0><tr><td><img
                      src='_layouts/images/blank.gif'
                      ID='100' alt='Icon' border=0> </td>
                      <td valign=top><a
ID=onetleftnavbar#LABEL_ID#
```

```
                        href='#URL#'>#LABEL#</td></tr></table></td>
                        </tr>"
              S-Target TAG="BODY"
              startspan
    -->
      <SharePoint:Navigation LinkBarId="1004" runat="server"/>
    <!--
      webbot bot="Navigation"
              endspan
    -->
  </TD>
</TR>
```

The site's document libraries are enumerated immediately below the static `Documents` text. This dynamic generation is made possible through the `Microsoft.SharePoint.WebControls.Navigation` web control class. The site's document library instances are formatted with regard to a `NavBar` defined within ONET.XML. In the current case, `Documents` links back to the `NavBar` with an `ID` of 1004. The `Documents NavBar` is detailed in Listing 2.28.

Listing 2.28   Documents NavBar

```
<NavBar Name="Documents"
        Prefix="&lt;table border=0 cellpadding=4 cellspacing=0&gt;"
        Body="&lt;tr&gt;&lt;td&gt;&lt;table border=0 cellpadding=0
            cellspacing=0&gt;&lt;tr&gt;&lt;td&gt;&lt;img
            src='/_layouts/images/blank.gif' ID='100' alt='Icon'
            border=0&gt; &lt;/td&gt;&lt;td
            valign=top&gt;&lt;a ID=onetleftnavbar#LABEL_ID#
            href='#URL#'&gt;#LABEL#&lt;/td&gt;&lt;/tr&gt;&lt;
            /table&gt;&lt;/td&gt;&lt;/tr&gt;"
        Suffix="&lt;/table&gt;" ID="1004">
</NavBar>
```

Site Description and Web Part Zones

The last elements are the description property and web part zones as shown in Listing 2.29.

The description is generated from the `ProjectProperty` class with a `Property` attribute set to `Description`. Recall that the site's title was rendered in the same fashion except for the `Property` attribute being set to `Title`.

Listing 2.29   DEFAULT.ASPX Description and Web Part Zones

```
<form runat="server">
  <table style="margin-top: 4px" cellpadding="3" cellspacing="0"
         border="0" width="100%">
    <tr>
      <td class="ms-descriptiontext" valign="top" colspan=4>
        <SharePoint:ProjectProperty Property="Description"
                                    runat="server"/>
      </td>
    </tr>
    <tr>
      <!-- Middle column -->
      <td valign="top" width="70%">
        <WebPartPages:WebPartZone runat="server"
                                  FrameType="TitleBarOnly"
                                  ID="Left"
                                  Title="loc:Left" />
         
      </td>
      <td> </td>
      <!-- Right column -->
      <td valign="top" width="30%">
        <WebPartPages:WebPartZone runat="server"
                                  FrameType="TitleBarOnly"
                                  ID="Right"
                                  Title="loc:Right" />
         
      </td>
      <td> </td>
    </tr>
  </table>
   
  <!-- FooterBanner closes the TD, TR, TABLE, BODY, And HTML regions
       opened above -->
   
</form>
```

DEFAULT.ASPX has two web part zones. In our example, we have Left and Right web part zones. Both web parts have their `FrameType`, `ID`, and `Title` attributes specified. These and other attributes are defined in Table 2.13.

Table 2.13 `WebPartZone` Properties

Attribute	Required	Type	Description
AllowCustomization	No	Boolean	If `TRUE`, the shared page view of this web part zone can be modified.
AllowPersonalization	No	Boolean	If `TRUE`, the personal view of this web part zone can be modified.
ContainerWidth	No	Text	Specifies any valid CSS width value (for example, 50px) for the zone. Note that this is considered a hint and is not guaranteed to be honored.
FrameType	No	Text	Specifies the default frame type for web parts added to this zone. Valid frame types include `Default`, `None`, `Standard`, and `TitleBarOnly`.
ID	Yes	Text	Specifies an `ID` that will be referenced by ONET.XML to add web parts to the specified web part zone.
LockLayout	No	Text	If `FALSE`, web parts within this zone can be added, deleted, resized, and moved.
Orientation	No	Text	Specifies the direction web parts will be placed in the zone. Valid values include `Horizontal` and `Vertical`.
Title	No	Text	Specifies a friendly name for the web part zone.

As you start to experiment with adding web part zones to your pages, you will discover that `WebPart` and `WebPartZone` controls must live in a `runat='server'` `HtmlForm`. You will therefore have to move the `form` tag to surround all `WebPart` and `WebPartZone` controls. Depending on where you place the opening and closing `form` tag, you can run into a somewhat confusing error: ***The Controls collection cannot be modified because the control contains code blocks (that is, <% . . . %>)***. ASP.NET complains because ASPX code blocks (`<% . . . %>`) cannot exist within a `form` tag that is run at the server. Assuming you didn't put any additional ASPX code blocks into your DEFAULT.ASPX page, the only ASPX code blocks are from Quick Launch. Quick Launch uses the code blocks to determine the LCID of the SharePoint server. This value is then embedded within a dynamically generated URL. Your options now include building a custom web control to render the LCID, removing the Quick Launch from the home page, hard coding the LCID into the site definition, using client-side JavaScript, or some hybrid. Whichever option you choose, it should be relatively easy to navigate around this issue.

Maintaining and Debugging Site Definitions

Although we will talk more about site definitions in upcoming chapters, now is a good time to take a step back and give some general insight into maintaining and debugging them. As you work with site definitions, you will inevitably run across technology restrictions, business restrictions, and maintenance and debugging issues. Over the next few pages, we address some of the more common site definition issues and their resolutions.

Overcoming Site Definition Limitations

Although site definitions have a customization option for just about everything, they have limitations. Those shortcomings include: (1) themes cannot be specified, (2) security settings cannot be set explicitly, and (3) limitations exist in prepopulating document library content. However, all these shortcomings can be overcome either by leveraging other site definition customization or using the SharePoint API shortly after site creation to overcome these issues programmatically.

For instance, the `Artic` theme can be applied programmatically to a newly created site as part of a custom provisioning process, or a custom CSS that is functionally equivalent to the `Artic` theme can be applied through `AlternateCSS`. In the case of restricting access to a document library, a custom application can be run after the site is created to initialize a set of permissions, or the list could be marked as a private list or hidden. Finally, content could be uploaded to a newly created site with an application that uses WebDAV, or it could be added through the site definition in a similar manner to the way that hidden views and forms are added to a library. In the latter case, the content would not appear as an element in the document library but rather would exist just as Forms/ALLITEMS.ASPX does.

In all these cases and the cases that you encounter, there is always a way around the limitation. In general, try to think of a creative way to implement the functionality within the site definition first and a programmatic solution second.

Restricting Functionality in the Enterprise

Custom templates provide an easy way for business users to create their own templates. Although sites based on custom templates are slightly slower than those based on site definition templates and provide less functionality, they provide an enormous opportunity for empowering business users. Many large companies wrestle with allowing or disallowing customizations through custom templates or other means. The ROI on empowerment is always countered by its costs, which include administration, maintenance, user support, and additional server resource consumption.

In general, many enterprises selectively lock down user functionality on universal SharePoint offerings and prefer to open up functionality on specialty server farms. This approach helps to minimize costs so that only a few server farms bear increased costs of operation.

Restricting functionality in SharePoint can take many forms. The three primary vehicles include:

- **SharePoint configuration change**. An example would be disallowing FrontPage modifications to site definition templates. This is accomplished through the Project's `DisableWebDesignFeatures` attribute in ONET.XML.

- **Modifying file permission**. One scenario would be to disallow access to saving or uploading templates. This can be done by removing all file permission ACLs from SAVETMPL.ASPX, the *WEBTEMP* folder and its files, and the *LISTTEMP* folder and its files. It would then be prudent to grant access only to domain administrators or local Windows server administrators on these resources.
- **Removing choices**. For instance, if web pages were discouraged from being stored in the document library, CREATE.ASPX could be modified so that the links for creating a Basic Page or a Web Part Page were removed.

Site Definition Maintenance

After the template is deployed, additional changes should not be made. Instead, the template should be versioned, and a new updated template should run side-by-side with the old template.

However, there can be cases where changes must be made to an existing site definition template. Potential scenarios include adding static links to the site's home page or changes to a document library in response to an edict handed down from on high. In cases such as these, we feel it is important to highlight that it can be done—accompanied by the strong recommendation for versioned templates.

Although it is technically possible to upgrade all aspects of a deployed site definition, it is virtually impossible from a practical standpoint. Deployed site definitions rely on both physical files (the site definition files) and data within the database. This data includes not only content formatted in accordance with the site definition's various XML configurations, but also deltas from the views (additional views, modified existing views, and so on) and schemas (modified existing columns, new columns, deleted columns, and so on). Thus, modifications to deployed site definitions can require changing the underlying data. The most difficult changes to deployed site definition templates are the ones that require changing the underlying data in the database.

In the first scenario, the links need to be added to the DEFAULT.ASPX page. This would require simply making changes to that ASPX page, and it represents a very easy change with no database implications. The scenario of extending a Document Library schema is a bit more complicated.

Although it would be possible to make changes in place—modify the document library's schema and then run a SQL script on the database to update it with regard to the new schema—a much simpler alternative exists. Trying to update an existing list definition's SCHEMA.XML and then develop and run a SQL script to update a production database is not fun or easy. The alternative is to hide the creation of the old document library and then create a new document library with the extended schema. This technique would not preclude the use of the existing old document libraries. Furthermore, only the new document libraries could be created.

If you are using a custom assembly with your versioned site definition templates, an updated custom assembly might need to be used with the new site definition template. Most likely you cannot simply upgrade the assembly in place because its new functionality might not be compatible with the older site definition template. Although there are many ways to do this task, it is preferable to run multiple assemblies that share the same class name but differ by version. As shown in Listing 2.30, you can use `dependentAssembly` within SharePoint's WEB.CONFIG to accomplish this job.

Listing 2.30 Example Use of `dependentAssembly` in WEB.CONFIG

```
<configuration>
  <runtime>
    <assemblyBinding xmlns="urn:schemas-microsoft-com:asm.v1">
      <dependentAssembly>
        <assemblyIdentity name="com.InformationHub.SPS"
                          publicKeyToken="1234567890abcdef"
                          culture="neutral" />

        <codeBase version="1.0.0.0"
           href="file://C:/Web/bin/1.0.0.0/com.InformationHub.SPS"/>
        <codeBase version="1.1.0.0"
           href="file://C:/Web/bin/1.1.0.0/com.InformationHub.SPS"/>
        <codeBase version="1.2.0.0"
           href="file://C:/Web/bin/1.2.0.0/com.InformationHub.SPS"/>

      </dependentAssembly>
    </assemblyBinding>
  </runtime>
/<configuration>
```

Debugging

Mistakes happen. .NET provides great debugging functionality for errors within ASPX pages and web parts. Unfortunately, this rich debugging support does not necessarily translate to site definitions. When an error exists in a site definition, you will usually receive a very general error message that does not give you insight into what was specifically wrong. This generic error is shown in Figure 2.25. The purpose of this section's discussion is to give some insight into where the problem might be happening, given the terse clues from SharePoint.

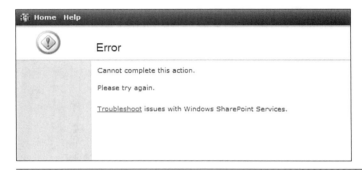

Figure 2.25   Error in site definition.

When applying a site definition template to a newly created site, a problem in WEBTEMP°.XML, ONET.XML, or the list definitions SCHEMA.XML could trigger the generic errors shown in Figure 2.25, Figure 2.26, and Figure 2.27.

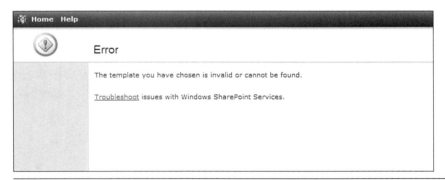

Figure 2.26   Error in site definition because the template was invalid.

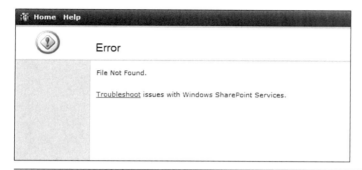

Figure 2.27 Error in site definition because a file was not found.

Tracking Down the Problem

When you receive one of the errors shown in Figure 2.25, Figure 2.26, and Figure 2.27, click the Home link to examine the home page. Examining the home page will help direct us to the problem.

If you are again prompted to apply a template, then the problem is with the site definition's WEBTEMP*.XML file. Most likely the problem is that your `Template's ID` conflicts with another WEBTEMP*.XML `Template`, or the `Name` specified does not match the folder name of your site definition.

If your site's home page looks partially deployed, similar to Figure 2.28, then the problem is most likely with ONET.XML. Because you could deploy part of the template, your WEBTEMP*.XML must be okay.

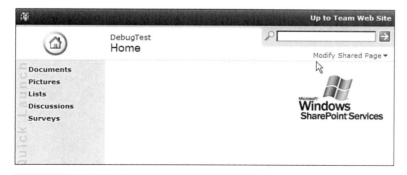

Figure 2.28 Partially deployed site definition without top navigation links.

If you receive a 404 NOT FOUND error, then the problem could be in WEBTEMP°.XML, ONET.XML, or any SCHEMA.XML file.

Keep in mind that problems in SCHEMA.XML might not necessarily trigger one of these errors. These errors are only visible when viewing the affected page in the list. Such a failure is shown in Figure 2.29.

Figure 2.29   SCHEMA.XML error.

After narrowing down the error's possible locations and triple checking that the problem is not with WEBTEMP.XML, you might still be at a loss. In those situations, I find it best to selectively remove List and Module elements from the selected site definition template Configuration in ONET.XML. After making the changes, be sure to execute an IISReset.EXE and then create the site anew.

In fact, it is always safest to create a new site when trying to work through an error. It is tempting to only create a new instance of a list within an existing site when trying to debug a problem with a list definition. Although this method can be quicker than creating a new site and then going through the process of checking the changes, there are cases when your changes do not appear to fix the problem in an existing broken site. Thus, you could be spinning your wheels and be thoroughly frustrated even though the site definition template problem was resolved but didn't appear so because the underlying site instance was broken.

Summary

Site definition templates provide a default look and function to a newly created site. They function very similarly to custom site templates, except that they provide significantly more customizations and are more complicated to author.

Site definitions are a collection of site definition templates in a single package. They exist as physical files on the SharePoint server's hard disk. For instance, the STS site definition contains the Team Site, Blank Site, and Document Workspace site definition templates. By default, it is installed in the C:\Program Files\Common Files\Microsoft Shared\web server extensions\60\TEMPLATE\1033\XML\STS folder.

All files that take the form WEBTEMP*.XML, which are found in the C:\Program Files\Common Files\Microsoft Shared\web server extensions\60\TEMPLATE\1033\XML folder, are parsed by SharePoint to determine which site definition templates are presented as choices to users. These WEBTEMP files provide the physical folder and the specific configuration identifier defined within ONET.XML of a site definition template.

There is one ONET.XML per site definition, and it is physically located within the site definitions folder. ONET.XML defines the major elements of the site definition and defines which of these elements are used for the various site definition templates. This methodology fosters reuse between the site definition templates within a single site definition.

The major elements within ONET.XML include `NavBars`, `ListTemplates`, `DocumentTemplates`, `BaseTypes`, `Configurations`, and `Modules`. `NavBars` defines various navigation bars. `ListTemplates` defines the general function and properties of lists and libraries. `DocumentTemplates` defines the default document created when a user clicks a document library's new toolbar button. `BaseTypes` defines list and library schemas. `Configurations` define the site definition templates and their composition. `Modules` define functional file groups.

Rendering a site definition requires the interaction of multiple layers—WEBTEMP files, ONET.XML, various SCHEMA.XML files, data from the SharePoint database, and several other components. A single problem in the chain will cause an error, which has a direct affect on the complexity of debugging and maintaining site definitions. We concluded this chapter with some debugging and maintenance best practices for SharePoint site definitions.

CHAPTER 3

Site Definitions: Exploring List Definitions

In this chapter, we build on Chapter 2, "Site Definitions," by focusing on lists and libraries defined within site definitions. Libraries are a type of list and therefore are defined the exact same way as lists. As we discussed in Chapter 2, ONET.XML defines the lists available in a site. However, it does not provide a mechanism to describe list views, default list data, and many other attributes. These are specified inside the list definition.

List definitions are packaged as child folders within the site definition. Thus, the document library list definition exists in one child folder, whereas the announcement list exists within another child folder.

The key XML configuration file of the list definition is SCHEMA.XML. SCHEMA.XML is akin to the site definition's ONET.XML in that there is only one per list definition and it binds all the various parts of the list definition together.

Introducing the Major Components

The lists and libraries for a particular site definition are defined in two places: ONET.XML and the LISTS folder. ONET.XML provides the hooks for lists, whereas the content within the LISTS folder provides the list definition. Because we have already explored ONET.XML in Chapter 2, we will focus our attention on the LISTS folder. The LISTS folder is shown in Figure 3.1. Each subfolder defines the functionality of a particular list type. ANNOUNCE defines announcements, DOCLIB defines document libraries, and WEBTEMP defines custom site templates. SharePoint's list definitions are more fully described in Table 3.1.

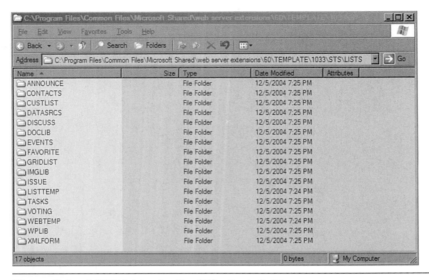

Figure 3.1   LISTS folder for the STS site definition.

Table 3.1   LISTS Folder Descriptions

Folder	Description
AGENDA	Defined within the MPS site definition. This defines a list of agenda items.
ANNOUNCE	Defined within the STS site definition. This defines a list of announcement items.
CONTACTS	Defined within the STS site definition. This defines a list of people contact items.
CUSTLIST	Defined within the STS site definition. This defines a custom list of items.
DATASRCS	Defined within the STS site definition. This defines data sources for the web.
DECISION	Defined within the MPS site definition. This defines a list of decision items.
DISCUSS	Defined within the STS site definition. This defines a list of discussion board items.
DOCLIB	Defined within the STS site definition. This defines the document library.

Folder	Description
EVENTS	Defined within the STS site definition. This defines a list of events items.
FAVORITE	Defined within the STS site definition. This defines a list of link items.
GRIDLIST	Defined within the STS site definition. This defines a custom list of items in a datasheet view.
IMGLIB	Defined within the STS site definition. This defines the picture library.
ISSUE	Defined within the STS site definition. This defines a list of issue items that can be prioritized and tracked.
LISTTEMP	Defined within the STS site definition. This defines the List Template Gallery.
MEETINGS	Defined within the MPS site definition. This defines a list of meetings attached to this workspace.
OBJECTIV	Defined within the MPS site definition. This defines a list of meeting objectives.
PEOPLE	Defined within the MPS site definition. This defines a list of meeting workspace users.
TASKS	Defined within the STS site definition. This defines a list of task items.
TEXTBOX	Defined within the MPS site definition. This defines a "text box" list of custom text items.
THGBRING	Defined within the MPS site definition. This defines a list of things to bring.
VOTING	Defined within the STS site definition. This defines a list of survey items.
WEBTEMP	Defined within the STS site definition. This defines the Site Template Gallery.
WKSPGLIB	Defined within the MPS site definition. This defines a list of meeting workspace pages.
WPLIB	Defined within the STS site definition. This defines the Web Part Gallery.
XMLFORM	Defined within the STS site definition. This defines the form library.

The commonality between lists and libraries is that each definition has one SCHEMA.XML file and many other supporting files. SCHEMA.XML defines the initial views, forms, toolbar, and special fields. The other files support the SharePoint web user interface and dialogs that appear in Microsoft Office applications. The DOCLIB folder files, which include SCHEMA.XML, are shown in Figure 3.2.

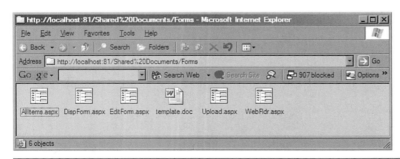

Figure 3.2   DOCLIB folder for the STS site definition.

In the case of a document library, these other files drive the web user interface. The ASPX files listed in Figure 3.2 are copied to the virtual Forms folder shown in Figure 3.3. These ASPX files provide the SharePoint web user interface for the document library. The templated.doc file was copied to the Forms folder through the `Document-Templates` section of ONET.XML.

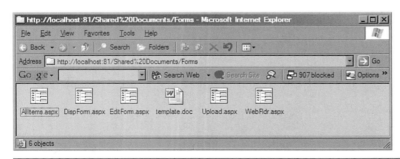

Figure 3.3   Document library virtual Forms folder.

One of the publicized drawbacks of site definition templates when compared to custom templates is that lists and libraries cannot be pre-populated with content. However, that is not completely true. As you can see in Figure 3.3, the Forms folder was prepopulated with several files. The process that copied those files to the Forms folder can be amended to copy additional files to any location within the document library. The drawback is that all these files appear hidden within all views of the document library except the Explorer view.

The only files we have yet to discuss are EDITDLG.HTM and FILEDLG.HTM. Microsoft Office applications use these files to assist in the file saving process when the repository is a document library. FILEDLG.HTM rendered through Microsoft Word is shown in Figure 3.4. EDITDLG.HTM rendered through Microsoft Word is shown in Figure 3.5.

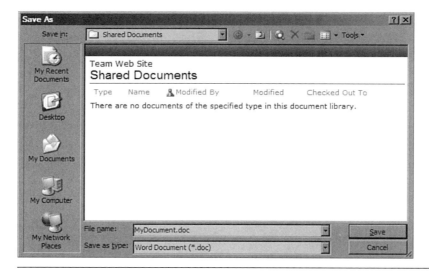

Figure 3.4   Document library FILEDLG.HTM.

EDITDLG.HTM is displayed only when there are library fields (columns) that must be filled out. Thus, we need to create a required column in our document library for Figure 3.5 to render.

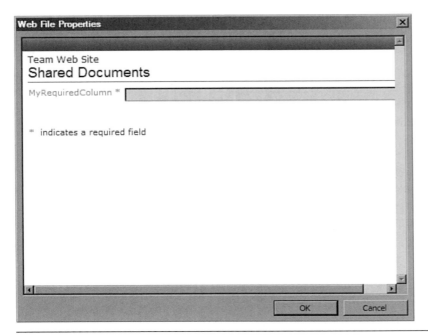

Figure 3.5   Document library EDITDLG.HTM.

FILEDLG.HTM and EDITDLG.HTM are not directly browsable as the ASPX pages were. Because they were designed to be accessed exclusively from Microsoft Office, SharePoint obfuscates access to them. EDITDLG.HTM is accessible through /MySite/_vti_bin/ owssvr.dll?location=MyDocLib/MyDoc.doc&dialogview=SaveForm, while FILEDLG.HTM is accessible through /MySite/_vti_bin/ owssvr.dll?location=MyDocLib&dialogview=FileSave. It should be noted that the FILEDLG.HTM in the Layouts folder—which is a different file from the one in our list definition—is rendered when no location parameter is specified. This is shown in Figure 3.6.

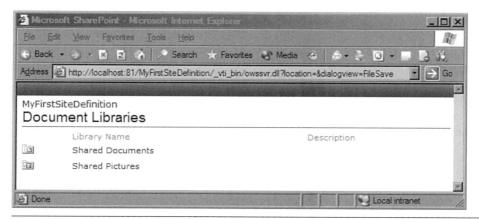

Figure 3.6   FILEDLG.HTM from the Layouts folder.

SCHEMA.XML

The relationship between SCHEMA.XML and the ASPX/HTM files in the list definition is akin to ASPX's code-behind concept. SCHEMA.XML should be thought of as the code-behind, whereas ASPX and HTM files represent the presentation code. In fact, the web part zone in the ASPX page and a web part zone-like component in the HTM file are the receptacles for SCHEMA.XML's CAML execution.

As mentioned previously, ONET.XML overlaps SCHEMA.XML's functionality in some places. In these cases, ONET.XML's settings will override SCHEMA.XML, or vice versa. You therefore need to be aware of these nuances when modifying list definitions and should check both files if the list does not appear as you feel it should.

The structure of SCHEMA.XML is shown in Listing 3.1. The major elements are `List`, `Fields`, `Views`, `Forms`, `DefaultDescription`, and `Toolbar`.

Listing 3.1   SCHEMA.XML Structure

```
<List>
  <MetaData>
    <Fields />
    <Views />
    <Forms />
    <DefaultDescription />
    <Toolbar />
  </MetaData>
</List>
```

`<List>`: Top-Level List Definition Settings

List provides some top-level settings. Many of the List attributes were covered in Table 2.9 during our discussions of ONET.XML. In this section, we will expand on our discussion of the List element. Listing 3.2 shows the default List element for a document library in the STS site definition. As previously mentioned, if these same attributes are specified in ONET.XML, they can take precedence over those specified within SCHEMA.XML.

Listing 3.2   SCHEMA.XML Document Library List Element Declaration

```
<List xmlns:ows="Microsoft SharePoint" Name="Documents"
      Title="Shared Documents" Direction="0" Url="Shared Documents"
      BaseType="1">
```

If our site definition includes the code from Listing 3.2 and Listing 3.3, the values of Title and Url specified in ONET.XML will be used over those specified in SCHEMA.XML.

Listing 3.3   ONET.XML Configuration for Team Site

```
<Configurations>
      <Configuration ID="-1" Name="NewWeb"/>
      <Configuration ID="0" Name="Default">
            <Lists>
```

```
<List Title="Documents"
  Url="Documents"
  QuickLaunchUrl="Documents/Forms/AllItems.aspx"
  Type="101" />
```

The `BaseType` attribute specified in the `List` element refers to a particular base type defined within ONET.XML. Recall that the base types specify a base schema (columns) for the list types. This base schema can be developed once and then applied to the various list types as appropriate. For example, the `BaseType` of 1 is applied document libraries, picture libraries, and form libraries.

Configuring Event Handlers

Some of the more powerful list customizations for document, picture, and form libraries are event sinks. With event sinks, your custom code can hook into SharePoint library events—check in, check out, and so on. Event sinks only apply to libraries and do not apply to other types of lists.

It should be noted that these events are fired after the operation is performed. For example, the delete event is fired after a document is deleted from a document library. The next version of SharePoint will feature events that fire before the operation is performed. However, if you cannot wait until the next version of SharePoint, you might want to consider writing your own HTTP Module to act on requests immediately before SharePoint acts on them.

Assuming you have enabled event handlers for your Virtual Server (see Figure 3.7), SharePoint can pass the document library events to a specified `EventSinkAssembly` and `EventSinkClass`. Additionally, you can specify `EventSinkData` that will be passed with the event information to the specified assembly and class. This capability is useful if you have one generic assembly responding to events from various sources. Your event handler can therefore react appropriately to the event depending on what the associated `EventSinkData` is passed to the handler. Because you can attach only one assembly to each document library in this version of SharePoint, creating a generic assembly to respond to events from different libraries is a good practice to follow.

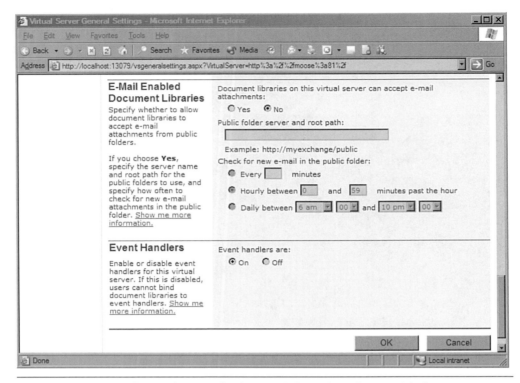

Figure 3.7 Virtual Server General Settings with Event Handlers enabled.

Figure 3.8 shows the advanced settings of a document library. The Advanced Settings page is where you can manually specify a custom event handler through the web user interface. Alternatively, you could use the `List` element's `EventSinkAssembly`, `EventSinkClass`, and `EventSinkData` attributes within the site definition's ONET.XML to avoid this manual task.

Configuring event handlers in a library can be incredibly useful. One scenario underscoring their usefulness would be processing newly uploaded documents in a document library. For instance, a newly uploaded Excel file could be processed to extract data to update an enterprise application.

The page in Figure 3.8 is also where a Microsoft Exchange public folder can be specified. If specified, SharePoint will download its content into the SharePoint document library. Site definitions provide no way to bind a library with an Exchange public folder. However, this does not preclude writing code that interacts with the SharePoint API to configure this setting. This code could be embedded within NEW.ASPX and run immediately after a document library was created.

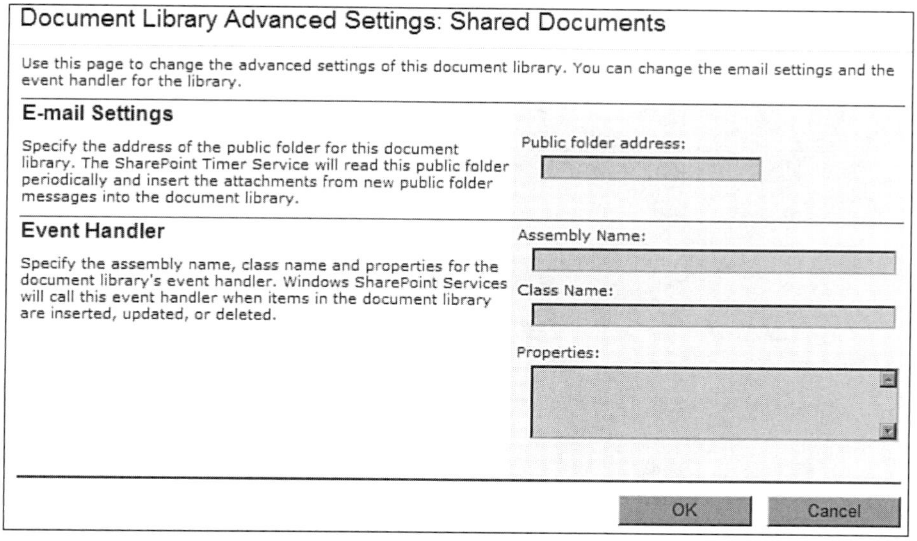

Figure 3.8 Document Library Advanced Settings.

`<Fields>`: Defining Additional Columns over the Base Type

The `Fields` element can define list columns and can define how a list is rendered. In the former case, we use the `Fields` element to add additional fields to what was defined by the base list type. In the latter case, the `Fields` element is embedded within the `Views` and `Forms` elements along with quite a bit of other CAML.

In Listing 3.4, we examine defining the Title and Expiration Date fields in our document library through the `Fields` element. Title is a holdover from the SCHEMA.XML taken from the STS site definition. Expiration Date is something we will be adding to our MyFirstSiteDefinition site definition. It represents a date at which the document content is considered stale and therefore out of date.

Listing 3.4 SCHEMA.XML Adding `Fields` to a Document Library

```
<Fields>
  <Field Type="Text" Name="Title" ShowInNewForm="FALSE"
         ShowInFileDlg="FALSE" DisplayName="Title" Sealed="TRUE"/>
  <Field Type="DateTime" Name="ExpirationDate" ShowInNewForm="TRUE"
         ShowInFileDlg="TRUE" DisplayName="Expiration Date"
         Required="TRUE" Sealed="TRUE">
    <DefaultFormula>
      =DATE(YEAR(Today)+3,MONTH(Today),DAY(Today))
    </DefaultFormula>
  </Field>
</Fields>
```

Because we do not want the `ExpirationDate` element to be removed, we have set the `Sealed` attribute to `TRUE`. The effects are shown in Figure 3.9. As you can see from the figure, sealing the field restricts more than the option to delete the column. The data type, data type formatting, default value, and whether it is required are also inaccessible to the user.

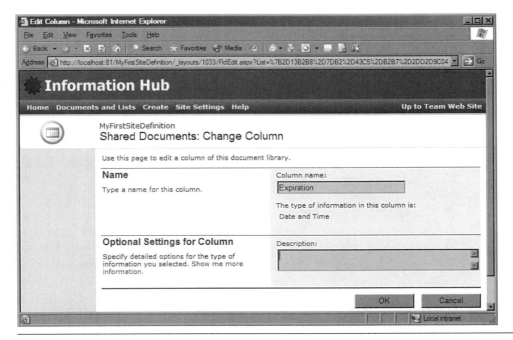

Figure 3.9 FLDEDIT.ASPX Expiration Date as a sealed column.

We have also set the `ShowInNewForm`, `ShowInFileDlg`, and `Required` attributes to `TRUE`. `ShowInNewForm` specifies whether the field should show up in UPLOAD.ASPX. As shown in Figure 3.10, `ShowInNewForm` for Expiration Date was set to `true`, whereas for Title, it was set to `false`. In contrast, `ShowInFileDlg` specifies whether the field should show up in EDITDLG.HTM (refer to Figure 3.5), which is accessible from Microsoft Office applications. The `Required` attribute forces a user to select a non-blank value for that column. The caveat is that this constraint is not enforced when a file is uploaded through the Explorer View. In that case, there is no facility to specify a value, and it will be set to null.

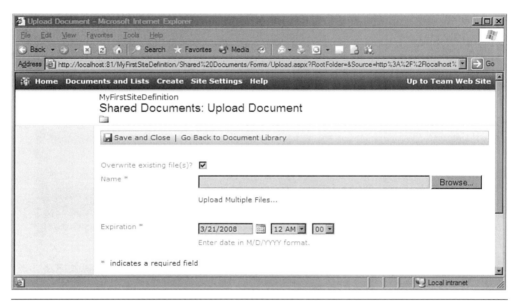

Figure 3.10   UPLOAD.ASPX Expiration Date as a required column.

A default value of three years from today was set for the `ExpirationDate` column. This was done through the `DefaultFormula` element. We used the functions defined within the Formulas and Functions section of SharePoint's online help—which is shown in Figure 3.11. It is interesting to note that these functions are not explicitly defined within the SharePoint CHM help file.

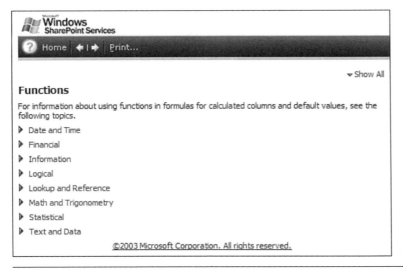

Figure 3.11   SharePoint Help on Functions.

Although we have touched on a number of `Field` attributes, we have merely scratched the surface of its capabilities. The complete list of `Field`'s attributes are summarized in Table 3.2.

Table 3.2   `<Field>` Attributes

Attribute	Required	Type	Description
Aggregation	No	Text	This is used as an aggregate field in an XML form. The possible aggregations include `sum`, `count`, `average`, `min`, `max`, `merge`, `text`, `first`, and `last`.
AllowHyperlink	No	Boolean	If TRUE, hyperlinks can be used.
AllowMultiVote	No	Boolean	If TRUE, multiple responses to a survey are permitted.
AuthoringInfo	No	Text	A hidden description that is primarily used as a way to explain the differences between two columns that have the same display name.

Attribute	Required	Type	Description
BaseType	Yes	Text	This can be set to either `Integer` or `Text`. `Text` is the default.
CanToggleHidden	No	Boolean	If `TRUE`, the column can be hidden through the user interface.
ClassInfo	No	Text	Specifies the CSS class to be applied to this column.
ColName	No	Text	Specifies the content database column in the database table that maps to the field. This is primarily used with base types in ONET.XML.
Commas	No	Boolean	If `TRUE`, commas are used for thousands separators.
Decimals	No	Integer	The number of decimal places to store. For instance, specifying 2 for this attribute will store 1.051 as 1.06.
Description	No	Text	Specifies the description of the field. This will be viewable by users.
Dir	No	Text	This specifies the direction of the text in the field. 0 is left to right, and 1 is right to left. This is very similar to the `Direction` attribute in the `List` element.
DisplayImage	No	Text	Specifies the URL to an icon to be displayed in the column.
DisplayName	No	Text	Specifies a friendly name for the field that will be exposed to users. The value of the `Name` attribute is not exposed to users.
DisplayNameSrcField	No	Text	Links the field to another. This is primarily used in cases where there are two fields with the same display name and if the first field's display name changes, you want this field's display name to appear to match that change.

(continues)

Table 3.2   `<Field>` Attributes (continued)

Attribute	Required	Type	Description
Div	No	Number	Specifies a scale factor by which to divide the value of the field. The value of the column is calculated as Field Value ° `Mult` / `Div`.
FieldRef	No	Text	Specifies another field that can be used as a lookup for this field.
FillInChoice	No	Boolean	If `TRUE`, the user can specify a value for the field.
Filterable	No	Boolean	If `TRUE`, the field can be filtered on.
ForcedDisplay	No	Text	Specifies static text to be used in place of a field's value.
Format	No	Text	Specifies the numeric formatting. For `Date` fields, valid values include `DateOnly`, `DateTime`, `ISO8601`, and `ISO8601Basic`. For `Choice` fields, valid values include `Dropdown` and `RadioButtons`. For `URL` fields, valid values include `Hyperlink` (uses `A` tag) or `Image` (uses `IMG` tag).
FromBaseType	No	Boolean	Deprecated. Use `Sealed`.
HeaderImage	No	Text	Specifies an image that will appear in the field's header.
Hidden	No	Boolean	If `TRUE`, the field is hidden. The column will not be accessible through the SharePoint web user interface. However, it can still be displayed in views if those views were defined through the site definition template.
HTMLEncode	No	Boolean	If `TRUE`, the value of the field is HTML encoded so that it does not conflict with HTML elements on the page.

Attribute	Required	Type	Description
JoinColName	No	Text	Like the `ColName` attribute, this references a database column. This specifies a column to join on in local and foreign lists.
JoinType	No	Text	Specifies the type of SQL join to use with `JoinColName`. Values include `INNER`, `LEFT OUTER`, and `RIGHT OUTER`.
LCID	No	Integer	Specifies the locale identifier for the field if it is different from the LCID of the SharePoint installation.
List	No	Text	Specifies the database table name to join with.
Max	No	Number	Specifies a maximum value for the field.
MaxLength	No	Integer	Specifies a maximum number of characters for the field.
Min	No	Number	Specifies a minimum value for the field.
Mult	No	Number	Specifies a scale factor by which to multiply the underlying value of the field. The value of the column is calculated as Field Value ° `Mult` / `Div`.
Name	No	Text	Specifies the internal name of the field.
NegativeFormat	No	Text	Specifies how to indicate negative values. Allowed values include `MinusSign` and `Parens`.
Node	No	Text	Used in XML forms to specify the `XPath` expression.
NoEditFormBreak	No	Boolean	If `TRUE`, line breaks are prevented from being added to the field. This will apply to the view properties and edit properties forms.

(continues)

Table 3.2   `<Field>` Attributes (continued)

Attribute	Required	Type	Description
NumLines	No	Integer	Specifies a hint/recommendation for the number of lines to display for a `TextArea` HTML element.
Percentage	No	Boolean	If TRUE, the value will be displayed as a percentage. Thus, 0.01 will be displayed as 1%.
PIAttribute	No	Text	Used in XML forms to provide attribute details for XML processing instructions.
PITarget	No	Text	Used in XML forms to provide a link to the form's template.
Presence	No	Boolean	If TRUE, the field user presence information is included in the field.
PrimaryKey	No	Boolean	If TRUE, the field is the primary key for the list. This is important for providing a relationship to another list.
ReadOnly	No	Boolean	If TRUE, the field is not editable. It therefore will not be displayed in new and edit forms.
RenderXMLUsingPattern	No	Boolean	This affects the display format of calculated fields. If TRUE, the field is rendered based on its display pattern type instead of the field's true type.
Required	No	Boolean	If TRUE, the web user interface will require that a non-null value be specified. As discussed previously, this can be subverted. For instance, the document library's explorer view will allow null values for extended metadata.
RichText	No	Boolean	If TRUE, the field can contain rich text.

Attribute	Required	Type	Description
Sealed	No	Boolean	If TRUE, the field cannot be changed or deleted.
SeparateLine	No	Boolean	Internal attribute (do not use). If TRUE, rendering is continued on a separate line.
ShowAddressBookButton	No	Boolean	Internal attribute.
ShowField	No	Text	Specifies the field to display when joining to an external list (database table).
ShowInEditForm	No	Boolean	If TRUE, the field will be displayed in the Edit Item page.
ShowInFileDlg	No	Boolean	If TRUE, the field will be displayed in the file dialog that is accessed through Microsoft Office applications.
ShowInNewForm	No	Boolean	If TRUE, the field will be displayed in the New or Upload Item page.
Sortable	No	Boolean	If TRUE, the list can be sorted on this field.
StorageTZ	No	Text	Specifies how the date/time will be serialized to the database.
StripWS	No	Boolean	If TRUE, leading and trailing white spaces are removed from the value.
SuppressNameDisplay	No	Boolean	If TRUE, the user name will not be displayed in the User field.
TextOnly	No	Boolean	If TRUE, the field will contain only string or text values.
Type	No	Text	Specifies the data type of the field. Valid values include Attachments, Boolean, Choice, Computed, Counter, CrossProjectLink, Currency, DateTime, File, Guid, Integer, Lookup, ModStat, MultiChoice, Note, Number, Recurrence, Text, Threading, URL, and User.

(continues)

Table 3.2   `<Field>` Attributes (continued)

Attribute	Required	Type	Description
URLEncode	No	Boolean	If TRUE, the values in the field are URL Encoded. This is similar to HTMLEncode.
URLEncodeAsUrl	No	Boolean	If TRUE, the value in the field is URL Encoded; however, the forward slashes are not encoded.
Viewable	No	Boolean	If TRUE, the field should be added to the default view.
Xname	No	Text	Internal attribute. Identifies XML form attributes that have been added, deleted, or modified.

`<Fields>`: Advanced Concepts

In the previous section, we concentrated our efforts on a simple example—adding a document expiration field to a document library. In this section, we explain the `Fields` element's link to the database.

Ultimately the individual list fields are stored in the database. The primary table where list items are stored is `UserData`, which is found in every content database. Additional list items can be retrieved from other database tables through database joins. Listing 3.5 showcases some of these joins to other tables.

Listing 3.5   ONET.XML Document Library Base Type Definition

```
<BaseType Title="Document Library" Image="_layouts/images/itdl.gif"
        Type="1">
  <MetaData>
    <Fields>
      <Field ColName="tp_ID" ReadOnly="TRUE" Type="Counter" Name="ID"
          DisplayName="ID"/>
      <Field ColName="tp_Created" Hidden="TRUE" ReadOnly="TRUE"
          Type="DateTime" Name="Created" DisplayName="Created Date"
          StorageTZ="TRUE"/>
```

```
<Field ColName="tp_Author" ReadOnly="TRUE" Type="User"
       List="UserInfo" Name="Author" DisplayName="Created By"/>
<Field ColName="tp_Modified" Hidden="TRUE" ReadOnly="TRUE"
       Type="DateTime" Name="Modified" DisplayName="Last Modified"
       StorageTZ="TRUE"/>
<Field ColName="tp_Editor" ReadOnly="TRUE" Type="User"
       List="UserInfo" Name="Editor" DisplayName="Modified By"/>
<Field ColName="tp_ModerationStatus" ReadOnly="TRUE"
       Type="ModStat" Name="_ModerationStatus"
       DisplayName="Approval Status" Hidden="TRUE"
       CanToggleHidden="TRUE" Required="FALSE">
  <CHOICES>
    <CHOICE>0;#Approved</CHOICE>
    <CHOICE>1;#Rejected</CHOICE>
    <CHOICE>2;#Pending</CHOICE>
  </CHOICES>
  <Default>0</Default>
</Field>
<Field ReadOnly="TRUE" Type="Note" Name="_ModerationComments"
       DisplayName="Approver Comments" Hidden="TRUE"
       CanToggleHidden="TRUE" Sortable="FALSE"/>
<Field Name="FileRef" ReadOnly="TRUE" Hidden="TRUE"
       Type="Lookup"
       DisplayName="URL Path" List="Docs" FieldRef="ID"
       ShowField="FullUrl" JoinColName="DoclibRowId"
       JoinType="INNER"/>
<Field Name="FileDirRef" ReadOnly="TRUE" Hidden="TRUE"
       Type="Lookup" DisplayName="URL Dir Name" List="Docs"
       FieldRef="ID" ShowField="DirName"
       JoinColName="DoclibRowId"
       JoinType="INNER"/>
<Field Name="Last_x0020_Modified" ReadOnly="TRUE"
       DisplayName="Modified" Type="Lookup" List="Docs"
       FieldRef="ID" ShowField="TimeLastModified"
       Format="TRUE"
       JoinColName="DoclibRowId" JoinType="INNER"/>
<Field Name="Created_x0020_Date" ReadOnly="TRUE"
       DisplayName="Created" Type="Lookup" List="Docs"
       FieldRef="ID" ShowField="TimeCreated" Format="TRUE"
       JoinColName="DoclibRowId" JoinType="INNER"/>
```

```
<Field Name="File_x0020_Size" Hidden="TRUE" ReadOnly="TRUE"
    Type="Lookup" DisplayName="File Size" List="Docs"
    FieldRef="ID" ShowField="SizeInKB" Format="TRUE"
    JoinColName="DoclibRowId" JoinType="INNER"/>
```

.
.
.

The entire document library base type is defined within ONET.XML. Listing 3.5 defines only the top portion of this definition. This base type retrieves information from the UserData, UserInfo, and Docs database tables.

The first bold field definition in Listing 3.5 defines the approval status. The ColName attribute specifies that the column will be stored in the tp_ModerationStatus database column. The lack of a List attribute implies that its value will reside in the UserData database table. Furthermore, the three choices—Approved, Rejected, and Pending—will be serialized as 0, 1, and 2, respectively. tp_ModerationStatus has a data type of int, so saving these values as anything other than an integer is not acceptable. If a column name is not specified, SharePoint will choose one for you.

The second bold field definition in Listing 3.5 defines the file size (File_x0020_Size). This definition is a bit more complicated. The field's value is defined in the Docs table and not UserData, Furthermore, the size data retrieved from the Docs table is further computed (see Listing 3.6) to return the size in kilobytes.

The file size field references the Docs table through the List attribute. The field also defines an inner join where Docs.DoclibRowId equals UserData.tp_ID. Docs.Size is selected from the resulting join and returned as the field's value. It was the computation that we alluded to previously that helped map ID to tp_ID and SizeInKB to Size (see Listing 3.6).

This translation needs to happen because the FieldRef and Show-Field attributes reference other field definitions. Let's first search for the ID field defined by FieldRef. This ID field is the first field element defined earlier in Listing 3.5. As specified in its definition, it maps to the tp_ID database field in UserData. The definition for SizeInKB can be found in BASE.XML located in the C:\Program Files\Common Files\Microsoft Shared\web server extensions\60\ TEMPLATE\1033\ XML folder (assuming your LCID is 1033).

The kilobyte size field definition is bolded in Listing 3.6. This translation specifies a database column of size and a scaling division factor of 1024. Thus, DOCS.size will be retrieved and divided by 1024. Furthermore, the user will see this value with a friendly column name of File Size.

Listing 3.6 BASE.XML Docs Database Table Mapping

```
<List Name="Docs" Title="Documents">
  <MetaData>
    <Fields>
      <Field ReadOnly="TRUE" Type="Guid" Name="ID" ColName="Id"
             Sortable="FALSE" DisplayName="ID"></Field>
      <Field Type="Text" Name="FullUrl" ColName="FullUrl"
             TextOnly="TRUE" Sortable="FALSE"
             DisplayName="Name"></Field>
      <Field Type="Text" Name="DirName" ColName="DirName"
             TextOnly="TRUE" Sortable="FALSE"
             DisplayName="Name"></Field>
      <Field Type="Text" Name="LeafName" ColName="LeafName"
             TextOnly="TRUE" Sortable="TRUE"
             DisplayName="Name"></Field>
      <Field Type="Guid" Name="DoclibRowId" ColName="DoclibRowId"
             Sortable="FALSE" DisplayName="Doclib Item ID"></Field>
      <Field Type="Integer" Name="Size" ColName="Size"
             ReadOnly="TRUE"
             Hidden="TRUE" Sortable="TRUE"
             DisplayName="File Size"></Field>
      <Field Type="Integer" Name="SizeInKB" Div="1024"
             ColName="Size"
             ReadOnly="TRUE" Hidden="TRUE" Sortable="TRUE"
             DisplayName="Size (KB)"></Field>
```

.
.

<Views>: Defining List Views

The Views element defines the initial views for the list. You are no doubt familiar with the All Documents and Explorer views of a document library. These, along with three other views, are defined within SCHEMA.XML for the standard document library.

You might recall that in Table 2.12, we enumerated the attributes of the `View` element. The `View` element is the only child element allowed for `Views`. In Listing 3.7, we show the top-level nodes of all the views within a document library. Unfortunately, the `View` definitions are quite large and therefore difficult to dissect in detail. For example, the view definition for ALLITEMS.ASPX spans approximately 1,500 lines.

Listing 3.7   SCHEMA.XML Document Library `Views` Structure

```
<Views>
  <View BaseViewID="0" Type="HTML">
  .
  .
  .
  <View BaseViewID="1" Type="HTML" WebPartZoneID="Main"
        DisplayName="All
        Documents" DefaultView="TRUE" Url="Forms/AllItems.aspx">
  .
  .
  .
  <View BaseViewID="2" Type="HTML" FileDialog="TRUE"
        DisplayName="File
        Dialog View" Hidden="TRUE" Path="filedlg.htm"
        ModerationType="Moderator">
  .
  .
  .
  <View BaseViewID="3" Type="HTML" WebPartZoneID="Main"
        DisplayName="Explorer View" Url="Forms/WebFldr.aspx"
        ReadOnly="TRUE">
  .
  .
  .
  <View BaseViewID="6" Type="HTML">
  .
  .
  .
</Views>
```

By looking at the `Path` and `Url` attributes, you have probably surmised that the `View` with a `BaseViewID` of 1 maps to the All Document view, the one with a `BaseViewID` of 2 maps to the dialog rendered from Microsoft Office, as shown previously in Figure 3.4, and finally the `BaseViewID` of 3 maps to the Explorer view.

You've probably also noticed the references to web part zones in these three views. They are rendered within a web part zone on the `Url` or `Path` specified page. This means that anything outside of this web part zone is not modifiable through SCHEMA.XML. In these cases, the ASPX or HTM page must be modified.

Creating an Additional View

Our emphasis in this section will be adding an additional view based on the All Documents view. This view will be entitled Expired Documents.

So now you are probably rolling your eyes and saying, "These views are 1,500+ lines long, and you want me to create one?" Well, it actually is much simpler than it sounds. We can recycle almost everything from the All Documents view and tweak the rest. Alternatively, we could design a custom list template and capture the appropriate CAML code from MANIFEST.XML. Of course you could painstakingly look up all the CAML elements instead of generating a custom list template. However, it is generally far easier to recycle code from MANIFEST.XML.

Let's start by designing our custom list template. Because the Expired Documents view requires an `ExpirationDate` column, we will create one. We need not give it all the properties that our `ExpirationDate` column in Listing 3.4 defined. The column need only be based on a `Date` and `Time` type and could look as simple as Figure 3.12.

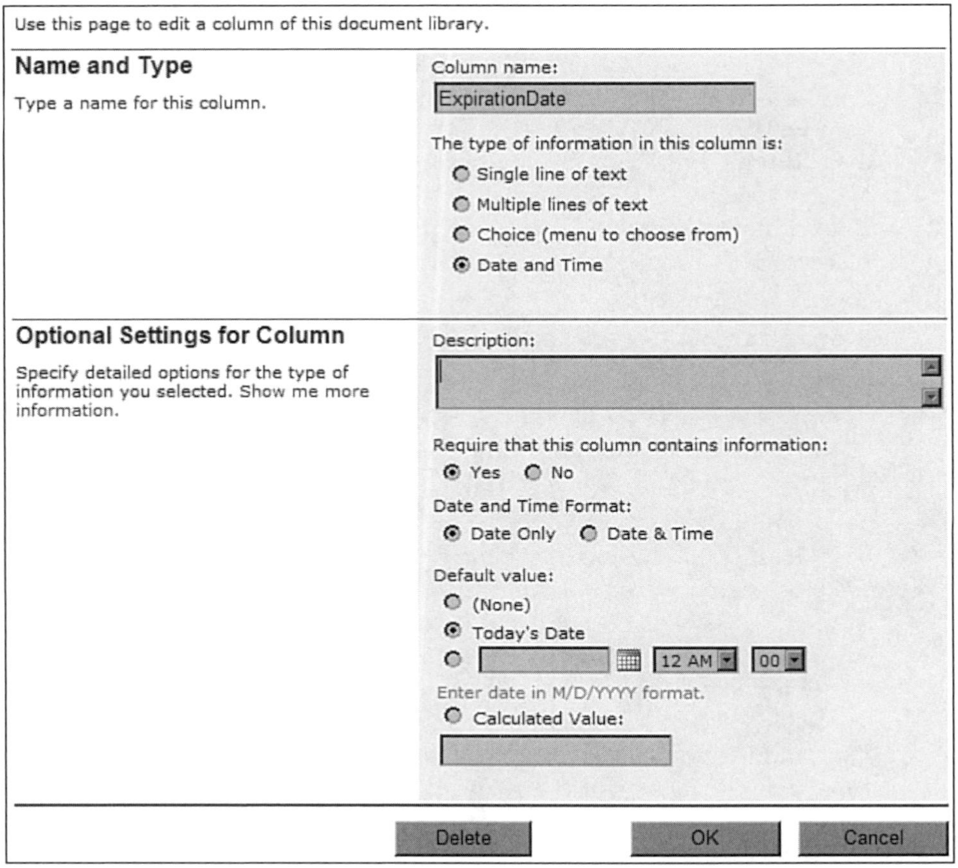

Use this page to edit a column of this document library.

Name and Type

Type a name for this column.

Column name:

ExpirationDate

The type of information in this column is:

- ○ Single line of text
- ○ Multiple lines of text
- ○ Choice (menu to choose from)
- ◉ Date and Time

Optional Settings for Column

Specify detailed options for the type of information you selected. Show me more information.

Description:

Require that this column contains information:
- ◉ Yes ○ No

Date and Time Format:
- ◉ Date Only ○ Date & Time

Default value:
- ○ (None)
- ◉ Today's Date
- ○ [   ] 🎬 [12 AM ▼] [00 ▼]

Enter date in M/D/YYYY format.
- ○ Calculated Value:

[   ]

| Delete | | OK | | Cancel |

Figure 3.12   Expiration Date created within a custom list template.

Next, create a standard view for the Expired Documents and fill it out as shown in Figure 3.13. You will need to specify the view name, the sort order, the group by column, the filter, and enable showing documents without folders.

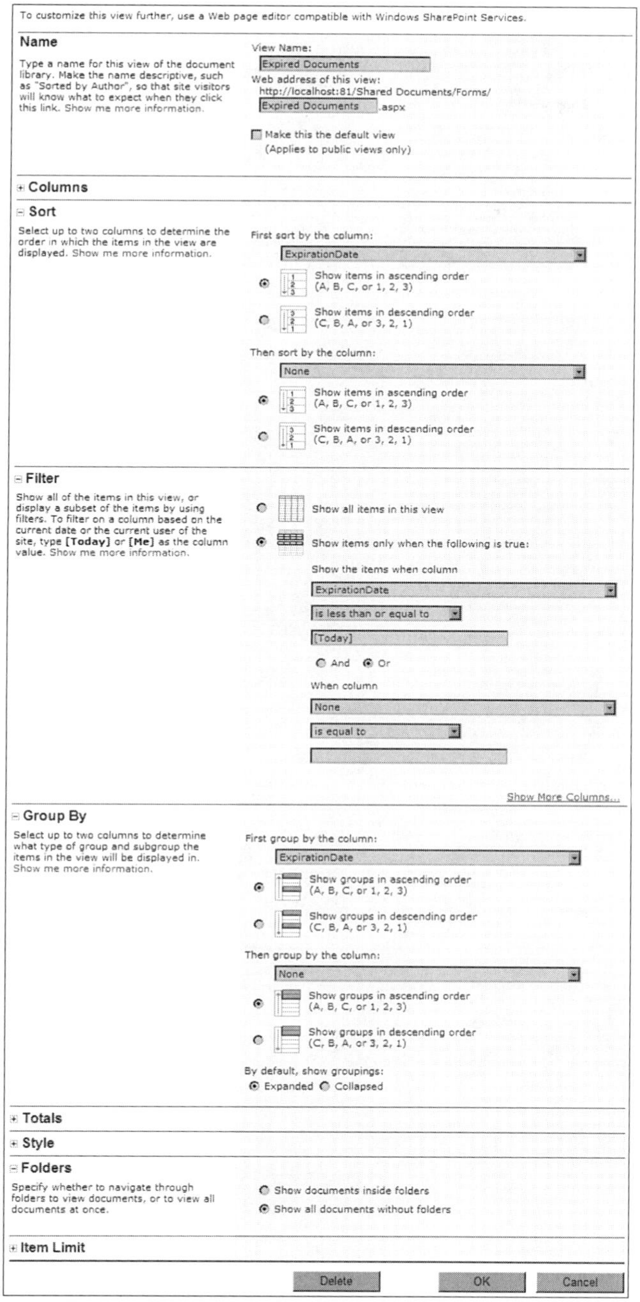

To customize this view further, use a Web page editor compatible with Windows SharePoint Services.

Name

Type a name for this view of the document library. Make the name descriptive, such as "Sorted by Author", so that site visitors will know what to expect when they click this link. Show me more information.

View Name:

Expired Documents

Web address of this view:
http://localhost:81/Shared Documents/Forms/
Expired Documents .aspx

☐ Make this the default view
(Applies to public views only)

⊕ **Columns**

⊟ **Sort**

Select up to two columns to determine the order in which the items in the view are displayed. Show me more information.

First sort by the column:

ExpirationDate

◉ Show items in ascending order
(A, B, C, or 1, 2, 3)

○ Show items in descending order
(C, B, A, or 3, 2, 1)

Then sort by the column:

None

◉ Show items in ascending order
(A, B, C, or 1, 2, 3)

○ Show items in descending order
(C, B, A, or 3, 2, 1)

⊟ **Filter**

Show all of the items in this view, or display a subset of the items by using filters. To filter on a column based on the current date or the current user of the site, type [Today] or [Me] as the column value. Show me more information.

○ Show all items in this view

◉ Show items only when the following is true:

Show the items when column

ExpirationDate

is less than or equal to

[Today]

○ And ◉ Or

When column

None

is equal to

Show More Columns...

⊟ **Group By**

Select up to two columns to determine what type of group and subgroup the items in the view will be displayed in. Show me more information.

First group by the column:

ExpirationDate

◉ Show groups in ascending order
(A, B, C, or 1, 2, 3)

○ Show groups in descending order
(C, B, A, or 3, 2, 1)

Then group by the column:

None

◉ Show groups in ascending order
(A, B, C, or 1, 2, 3)

○ Show groups in descending order
(C, B, A, or 3, 2, 1)

By default, show groupings:
◉ Expanded ○ Collapsed

⊕ **Totals**

⊕ **Style**

⊟ **Folders**

Specify whether to navigate through folders to view documents, or to view all documents at once.

○ Show documents inside folders
◉ Show all documents without folders

⊕ **Item Limit**

[Delete] [OK] [Cancel]

Figure 3.13 Expired Documents view settings.

As we outlined in Chapter 1, "Custom Templates," save the custom document template to your local drive and examine its MANIFEST.XML file. Search for the View element that defines our newly created Expired Documents view. It should look similar to Listing 3.8.

Listing 3.8 MANIFEST.XML Expired Documents View Partial Listing

```
<View Name="{FBB9D2CB-4861-4278-9A03-AF8A8C290C63}" Type="HTML"
Scope="Recursive" DisplayName="Expired Documents" Url="Shared
Documents/Forms/Expired Documents.aspx" BaseViewID="1">
  <ViewFields>
    <FieldRef Name="DocIcon"/>
    <FieldRef Name="LinkFilename"/>
    <FieldRef Name="Last_x0020_Modified"/>
    <FieldRef Name="Editor"/>
    <FieldRef Name="LinkCheckedOutTitle"/>
  </ViewFields>
  <Query>
    <GroupBy Collapse="FALSE">
      <FieldRef Name="ExpirationDate"/>
    </GroupBy>
    <OrderBy>
      <FieldRef Name="ExpirationDate"/>
    </OrderBy>
    <Where>
      <Leq>
        <FieldRef Name="ExpirationDate"/>
        <Value Type="DateTime">
          <Today/>
        </Value>
      </Leq>
    </Where>
  </Query>
  <ViewStyle ID="0"/>
  <RowLimit Paged="TRUE">100</RowLimit>
  <GroupByHeader>
.
.
.
```

From MANIFEST.XML, select the entire `View` definition (1,500 or so lines) for Expired Documents and then copy it to our SCHEMA.XML. It should be inserted into SCHEMA.XML so that the `Views` element is its parent. From a best practice standpoint, it should be inserted as the last `View` definition within `Views`. However, its placement within the `Views` element has no effect on its function.

The `ViewFields` element defines the fields that will be displayed in the view and was generated from the `Columns` section specified in Figure 3.13. The `GroupBy`, `OrderBy`, and `Where` CAML elements map to the `Group By`, `Sort`, and `Filter` sections of the same figure. Furthermore, the `View`'s `Scope` attribute corresponds to the `Folders` section of that same figure.

As mentioned previously, we could have copied the All Documents view definition in SCHEMA.XML and modified the CAML by hand, and we would have achieved the same result. One benefit of harvesting CAML for `View` definitions, `Field` definitions, or just about anything else with a list template is that you can usually skip a significant amount of debugging that you might have to perform if done by hand.

The next step is modifying the recently copied `View` node. You will need to remove the `Name` attribute, add a `WebPartZoneID` reference, and modify the `Url` and `BaseViewID`. These changes are represented in Listing 3.9.

Listing 3.9   Updated `View` after Inserting It into SCHEMA.XML

```
<View BaseViewID="100" Type="HTML" WebPartZoneID="Main"
      Scope="Recursive" DisplayName="Expired Documents"
      Url="Forms/ExpiredDocuments.aspx" >
.
.
.
```

The final configuration piece is to make a copy of ALLITEMS.ASPX and name it ExpiredDocuments.ASPX. This additional file is shown in Figure 3.14.

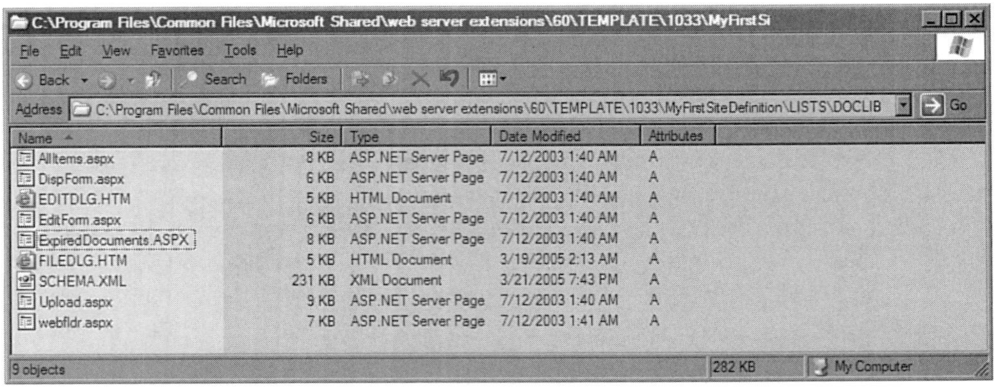

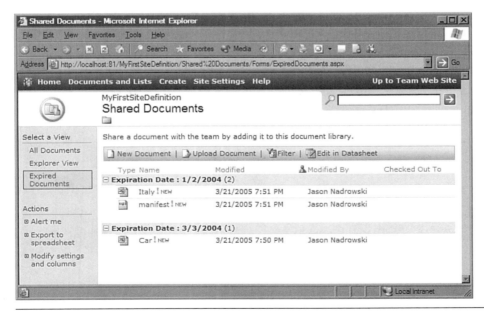

Figure 3.14   ExpiredDocuments.ASPX file added to list definition.

The result of our work is shown in Figure 3.15. We could have added any number of additional views, modified the existing views, or removed some of the views. However, because there are several external references (links) to some of these views, you will need to remove default views—such as All Documents and Explorer views—with care.

Figure 3.15   Expired Documents view.

When we added our view, we selected a `BaseViewID` of 100 so that it was different from the other `BaseViewID` values. Every view must have a unique `BaseViewID`. Furthermore, the `BaseViewID` defines the view's placement order on the left navigation bar shown in Figure 3.15. The view with the lowest `BaseViewID` will be placed at the top, whereas the view with the highest `BaseViewID` will be placed at the bottom of the left navigation bar.

Common `<View>` Child Elements

Table 3.3 enumerates some of the more popular child elements of `View`. In the previous section, we designed a view from SharePoint's web user interface and then harvested its CAML code through a list template. The web user interface only controls `Aggregations`, `Query`, `RowLimit`, and `ViewStyle`. Greater control of views can be achieved with the additional child `View` elements in Table 3.3.

Table 3.3 Common `<View>` Child Elements

Element	Description
Aggregations	Specifies how the view should total or calculate columns in the list.
GroupByFooter	Specifies the footer when the query includes a `GroupBy` and the results are non-null.
GroupByHeader	Defines the header when the query includes a `GroupBy` and the results are non-null.
PagedRecurrenceRowset	Similar to `PagedRowset` except that it applies to an event list with recurring events whose total instances exceed the row limit.
PagedRowset	Executes if more items in the view are returned than those specified by the `RowLimit` element. This will only execute if `RowLimit`'s `Paged` attribute is set to `TRUE`.
Query	Defines the filter, sort, and/or grouping for the view.

(continues)

Table 3.3   Common `<View>` Child Elements (continued)

Element	Description
RowLimit	Defines the maximum number of items to show in a view. If Paged is set to TRUE, the view will render the PagedRowset element, and the user will be allowed to continue on to multiple pages. If Paged is set to FALSE, the view will render the RowLimitExceeded element, and the user will not be able to move on to other pages.
RowLimitExceeded	Executes if more items in the view are returned than those specified by the RowLimit element. This will only execute if RowLimit's Paged attribute is set to FALSE.
Toolbar	Defines the toolbar for the view and is rendered above the view header.
ViewBidiHeader	Defines the header for a view column that supports bidirectional reading.
ViewBody	Defines the rendering of rows in a view.
ViewEmpty	Defines the rendering when no items are returned for a view.
ViewFields	Defines the columns/fields to show in the view.
ViewFooter	Defines the footer of columns/fields to render in the view.
ViewHeader	Defines the header of columns/fields to render in the view.
ViewStyle	Applies one of the predefined styles enumerated in the Style section of the Edit View page (refer to Figure 3.13).

The two most commonly used View child elements are Aggregations and Query. Aggregations specifies how the items of a view should be calculated. Query provides a mechanism for filtering, sorting, and grouping a view.

Aggregations

The Aggregations element specifies how items in the view should be calculated. The results of this calculation are typically shown in a header row. An example of Aggregations use is shown in Listing 3.10. In our example, we are counting the number of times the LinkFilename is used.

Listing 3.10 Aggregations Example in SCHEMA.XML

```
<Aggregations Value="On">
  <FieldRef Name="LinkFilename" Type="COUNT"/>
</Aggregations>
```

As shown in Figure 3.16, we build on Listing 3.8 with Listing 3.10 to count the number of times LinkFilename is used per grouping along with the total number of times for the list. The practical effect is to count the number of items (rows) in the grouping and the number of items in the list. We could have just as easily specified another column instead of LinkFilename.

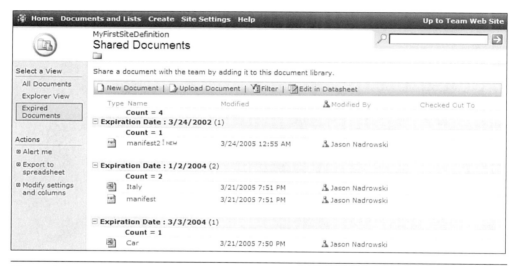

Figure 3.16 Expired Documents view with Aggregations specified.

Although only one column is aggregated in the example, you can aggregate any combination of the columns that are present in the view. Furthermore, each column could have a different aggregation type. Those include average, maximum, minimum, summation, standard deviation, and variation. Obviously, these functions lend themselves better to numeric data types than string data types.

Query

The Query element defines the filtering, sorting, and grouping for a view. The valid child elements for Query include GroupBy, OrderBy, and Where. Although GroupBy and OrderBy will never have descendants past children, there is virtually no limit to the number of descendants that Where can have.

Recall that the query for creating our Expired Documents view is shown in Listing 3.8. In that query, we leveraged GroupBy for grouping, OrderBy for sorting, and Where for filtering. As expected, GroupBy and OrderBy only have child elements, but Where has great-grandchildren descendants. The descendants for Where could exist well beyond great-grandchildren when using a logical AND or a logical OR. All the valid child elements of Where are shown in Table 3.4.

Table 3.4 <Where> Child Elements

Element	Description
And	Logical AND.
DateRangesOverlap	Determines whether a recurring event (beginning of event to end of event) overlaps with a specified date. For example, this could be used to show all events that are going on now.
Eq	Equal to.
Geq	Greater than or equal to.
Gt	Greater than.
IsNotNull	Not Empty/Null.
IsNull	Empty/Null.
Leq	Less than or equal to.
Lt	Less than.
Neg	Not equal to.
Or	Logical OR.

Listing 3.11 details an example Where clause that showcases the level of granularity that can be defined with the And and Or elements. The clause is equivalent to (State='Florida' AND City='Miami') AND (Building-Color='Black' OR BuildingColor='Gray').

Listing 3.11   CAML `Where` Clause Example

```
<Where>
  <And>
    <And>
      <Eq>
        <FieldRef Name="State"/>
        <Value Type="Text">Florida</Value>
      </Eq>
      <Eq>
        <FieldRef Name="City"/>
        <Value Type="Text">Miami</Value>
      </Eq>
    </And>
    <Or>
      <Eq>
        <FieldRef Name="BuildingColor"/>
        <Value Type="Text">Black</Value>
      </Eq>
      <Eq>
        <FieldRef Name=" BuildingColor"/>
        <Value Type="Text">Gray</Value>
      </Eq>
    </Or>
  </And>
</Where>
```

`<Forms>`: Interacting with One Item at a Time

Views are designed to show multiple items from the list. In contrast, forms are designed for just one item. For instance, displaying the properties of an item (DISPFORM.ASPX), editing the properties of an item (EDITFORM.ASPX and EDITDLG.HTM), and the information collected to upload a file to a document library (UPLOAD.ASPX) are all defined within the `Forms` section of SCHEMA.XML. The basic structure of forms within a document library is shown in Listing 3.12.

Listing 3.12   Basic `Forms` Structure in a Document Library

```
<Forms>
  <Form Type="DisplayForm" Url="Forms/DispForm.aspx"
       WebPartZoneID="Main">
    <ListFormOpening />
    <ListFormButtons />
    <ListFormBody />
  </Form>
  <Form Type="EditForm" Url="Forms/EditForm.aspx" WebPartZoneID="Main">
    <ListFormOpening />
    <ListFormButtons />
    <ListFormBody />
    <ListFormClosing />
  <Form Type="NewForm" Url="Forms/Upload.aspx" WebPartZoneID="Main">
    <ListFormOpening />
    <ListFormButtons />
    <ListFormBody />
    <ListFormClosing />
  <Form Type="NewFormDialog" Path="EditDlg.htm">
    <ListFormOpening />
    <ListFormButtons />
    <ListFormBody />
    <ListFormClosing />
</Forms>
```

Table 3.5 details the allowable child elements of `Form`. To be clear, the content in `ListFormOpening`, `ListFormButtons`, `ListFormBody` and `ListFormClosing` is not shown in the listing. The form definitions approximate the length of the view definitions and both weigh-in at about 1,500 lines.

Table 3.5   `<Form>` Child Elements

Element	Description
ListFormOpening	Defines the first section of the form.
ListFormButtons	Defines the toolbars for the form.
ListFormBody	Defines the body of the form.
ListFormClosing	Defines the last section of the form.

`<DefaultDescription>` **Element**

The two remaining top-level elements in SCHEMA.XML are `Default-Description` and `Toolbar`. `DefaultDescription` defines a description for the document library, and `Toolbar` defines a navigation bar. Listing 3.13 details the default description within SCHEMA.XML for a document library.

Listing 3.13　Document Library Description Defined in SCHEMA.XML

```
<DefaultDescription>
  Share a document with the team by adding it to this document library.
</DefaultDescription>
```

The effects of this description are shown in Figure 3.17 immediately above the toolbar.

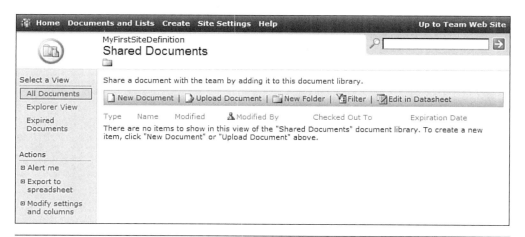

Figure 3.17　Document library using the default description.

Keep in mind that this default description will only be used when the list is created as part of the site definition. When a new list is created in an existing site, the user is prompted for the description (see Figure 3.18). In this scenario, the default description will be blank and will not be pre-populated with the one specified in the site definition.

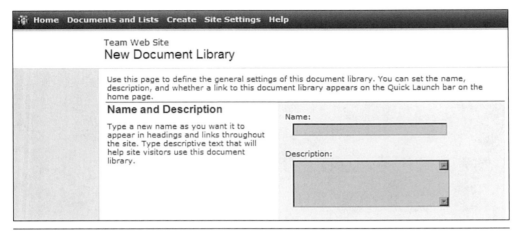

Figure 3. 18   Prompting for description when creating a new document library.

`<Toolbar>` **Element**

The `Toolbar` element defines a block of HTML. Typically this HTML renders a toolbar, but it is not a requirement. In fact, the `Toolbar` element shown in Listing 3.14 does not render a toolbar. It renders the view's Actions items (Alert me, Export to spreadsheet, Modify settings and columns) on the left bar shown in Figure 3.17.

Listing 3.14   `RelatedTasks` Toolbar Defined in SCHEMA.XML

```
<List xmlns:ows="Microsoft SharePoint" Name="Documents"
     Title="Shared Document" Direction="0" Url="Shared Document"
     BaseType="1">
  <MetaData>
.
.
.
    <Toolbar Type="RelatedTasks">
      <HTML>
        <![CDATA[
          <TABLE width=100% cellpadding=0 cellspacing=2
                BORDER=0>
            <TR>
              <TD width=100% ID="L_RelatedTasks">
```

```
      Actions
    </TD>
  </TR>
  <TR>
    <TD class="ms-navline">
      <IMG SRC="/_layouts/images/blank.gif" width=1 height=1
           alt="">
    </TD>
  </TR>
]]></HTML>
<Switch>
  <Expr>
    <GetVar Name="HasPortal"/>
  </Expr>
  <Case Value="TRUE">
```
.
.
.

The `RelatedTasks` toolbar defined in Listing 3.14 is referenced in the ALLITEMS.ASPX page. As shown in Listing 3.15, the `SharePoint:RelatedTasks` server control renders the toolbar's CAML code. Also shown in the listing is the `SharePoint:ViewSelector` server control. This renders a list of links to all the appropriate views defined within SCHEMA.XML.

Listing 3.15   Left Navigation from ALLITEMS.ASPX

```
<TABLE style="padding-top: 8px" class=ms-navframe CELLPADDING=0
      CELLSPACING=0 BORDER=0 width=100%>
  <TR>
    <TD valign=top width=4px>
      <IMG SRC="/_layouts/images/blank.gif" width=1 height=1 alt="">
    </TD>
    <TD valign=top ID=onetidSelectView class=ms-viewselect>
      <TABLE style="margin-left: 3px" width=115px cellpadding=0
            cellspacing=2 BORDER=0>
        <TR>
          <TD width=100% ID="L_SelectView">
            Select a View
          </TD>
```

```
      </TR>
      <TR>
        <TD class="ms-navline">
          <IMG SRC="/_layouts/images/blank.gif" width=1 height=1
               alt="">
        </TD>
      </TR>
    </TABLE>
    <SharePoint:ViewSelector runat="server"/>  
  </TD>
  <TD style="padding-right: 2px;" class=ms-verticaldots>
     
  </TD>
 </TR>
</TABLE>
<TABLE style="padding-top: 8px" class=ms-navframe CELLPADDING=0
CELLSPACING=0 BORDER=0 width=100% height=100%>
  <TR>
    <TD valign=top width=4px>
      <IMG SRC="/_layouts/images/blank.gif" width=1 height=1 alt="">
    </TD>
    <TD valign=top ID=onetidSelectView class=ms-viewselect>
      <SharePoint:RelatedTasks runat="server"/>  
    </TD>
    <TD style="padding-right: 2px;" class=ms-verticaldots>
       
    </TD>
  </TR>
</TABLE>
```

Summary

The major components of a site definition are its list definitions. A list definition specifies a list's fields, views, forms, toolbars, and other specifics. SCHEMA.XML is central to each list definition.

SCHEMA.XML contains the CAML code that defines the list. Furthermore, every ASPX or HTM page used by the list definition must be referenced in SCHEMA.XML. It is the conductor, so to speak, of the list definition.

The major elements of SCHEMA.XML are `List`, `Fields`, `Views`, and `Forms`. `List` is the top-level element within SCHEMA.XML. `Fields`, `Views`, and `Forms` are all children of `List`. `Fields` specifies the various columns (name and type) for a list. `Views` specifies the various ways the list data is presented to the user. `Forms` specifies how data is captured from the user for entry into the list.

CHAPTER 4

Customizing and Implementing Property Types in Windows SharePoint Services

SharePoint is all about user empowerment. One of the best features SharePoint has to empower users is its lists. Users can quickly and easily create a list to hold documents, issues, tasks, announcements, events, and more; the variety of default lists is quite extensive. Every list in SharePoint can have properties. In this chapter, we will discuss a limitation of properties and a way to overcome that limitation.

Ten different property types can be created for any given list. SharePoint offers a wide and varied selection of list properties. Users can create text, date, lookup, hyperlink, and calculated fields, among others. Even though SharePoint gives us so many choices, it always seems like we need something that isn't native to SharePoint. Sure, we can achieve much with something like a text field. Radio buttons give the users a nice way to understand what they are sending to the system. Even a lookup field is fairly robust, until you need to look up data in lists on other sites or other systems. These default elements and others provided in SharePoint are pretty generic and limited.

What about when you need that certain special data or functionality that is ubiquitous throughout several other popular applications in your organization? Perhaps everything in your organization has a job number associated with it. Perhaps your document in SharePoint would benefit from being associated with a particular job number. From the business and user perspective, not being able to implement this custom property type can be a showstopper.

The first several pages of the chapter are dedicated to showing you the principles of customizing a property type to better serve the ever-changing needs of a business organization. This custom property type is then used in an implementation example. The bulk of the chapter guides you through implementing a custom property in a document library. This process is very similar for other lists, as well. Although the example used here focuses exclusively on document libraries, after completing the chapter, you should feel confident to explore this approach with other lists. The beauty of this method is that the patterns applied here can be applied to just about any other situation where a "custom" property type is required.

A Custom Property—Defined

For the purposes of this book, a "custom" property type is a property, other than the ten that are available out of the box, which provides a desired functionality or behavior. One example might be to provide a drop-down lookup populated from a database or web service. The specific business problem will determine the custom property you will need. Let's take a look at a couple examples.

Custom Data Lookups

One very popular modification is a data lookup. Static data could easily be kept in a list on the site and used through a lookup. The problem with lookups is that they are specific to a site and somewhat difficult to maintain. The shelf life of the data stored in the lookup will determine how often it must be updated. The higher the update frequency, the greater the maintenance involved. As a rule of thumb, when the data in a lookup needs to be refreshed many times a day, a real-time lookup is needed. Even though this process can be automated with some custom development, it would still require a significant amount of maintenance to ensure that the batch process completed at the end of each period. Now factor this out by the number of lists that are needed. It quickly becomes obvious that this can be a lot of maintenance. Retrieving data from a foreign system is a common integration problem that SharePoint doesn't address.

Let's look at an example. A database that keeps track of vendors and customers is maintained through an application that has been in service for some time. It would be really nice to just look this data up and bind a customer ID to a list item. The property of a document in a document library would hold the customer ID.

In SharePoint, there is no native way to provide these kinds of lookups. A user would have to cut and paste information into text fields, and no user would be happy about that. Happiness aside, data could be entered incorrectly and thus make the application appear to cause more harm than good. A custom property can provide the one piece of functionality that makes the whole integration happen. When your imagination starts running on data lookups in foreign systems, countless uses come to mind. Let's look at a different type of custom property.

Custom Functionality

Another way to use a custom property is to provide additional functionality. The best way to describe this idea is by example. I worked on a project for policies and procedures where the business user wanted to categorize documents using a tree control. The nodes of the tree control would group together similar policies and procedures. The basic idea was that when a user clicked a node, a list of documents would appear. The custom functionality would be akin to the way Windows Explorer works with a hierarchy of folders in the left pane and files in the right pane.

Picture a web part page with two web parts. The web part on the left would house the tree control, and the web part on the right would display the list of documents. When a user clicks a node of the tree control, a list of documents would appear on the right.

One of the properties of the document library was a tree control. When the tree control was presented to the user in any situation where the properties could be entered or modified, check boxes would appear next to each node. These check boxes could be checked or unchecked, and the value of the node would be saved.

When the user clicked a node in the tree control, the document list web part would dynamically filter list items based on the value of the node selected. This functionality gave the appearance that the documents "lived" in those nodes.

In this case, the data was fairly static. The tree control was maintained in a similar fashion as the other properties. The tree control data (such as the node information) was stored in a database so that it could be used in other systems.

This is just one example of providing functionality within the confines of SharePoint that wouldn't have been possible without a custom property.

Other Custom Property Types

Custom data lookups and custom functionality are not the only uses of a custom property, but they are the most common. Your business need might require some other kind of custom property. The problems are limited only by the creativity of the organization. Hopefully this chapter and the next will show you how to leverage a custom property to solve most of them.

Implementation Design

Microsoft didn't provide a means to create a custom property. Therefore, we must use a type that already exists and modify the behavior of that type in such a way that our application can withstand Microsoft's updates.

The *Single Line of Text* is the most versatile existing type, so we will use that to house the data for the custom type. Everywhere the text field is used, a check will be made to see whether or not it's our custom property. If the field is a custom property, then it will be rendered appropriately, and if it's not, then the system will render the property as it normally would.

It's a fairly straightforward design, though it's a bit more difficult to implement. Before we venture much further, let's cover a major design consideration in the following sidebar.

Warning: Design Considerations

A major caveat to making modifications like these is that Microsoft's shipping code cannot be modified. Shipping code is defined as those files that can be overwritten in a service pack's hot fix and other updates. Microsoft's shipping code includes the site definitions that Microsoft provides out of the box. Several files in the layouts folder are also shipping code.

To give you a visualization of how this situation might affect the application, imagine that production support installs a new service pack without warning, and all the code you've modified is overwritten. There is a way to implement a custom property type (and other customizations) and still be impervious to Microsoft's benevolent updates.

Microsoft enables you to create custom site definitions and has promised not to harass them. When creating a custom site definition, many things can be customized, and they are certainly worth exploration. Because we are focusing on implementing custom properties, we are only going to touch on creating the new site definition and a new list to work with.

There are a few pages in the Layouts/1033 folder to which we will want to add our custom code as well. Keeping in mind Microsoft's update methods, it's easy to see that we will want to copy these few pages into our own folder.

Essentially, we shouldn't edit any files that Microsoft gives us out of the box. The best practice is to make a copy and modify the copy instead. This "copy and modify" method is becoming a mantra—not only for this specific situation, but for almost every source file Microsoft ships.

Several pages are affected by customization like this one. The general areas of interest will be covered, followed by the detailed implementation later in the chapter.

What Is Affected?

There are a few places in SharePoint where the properties of a list make themselves apparent—uploading and editing a document from the web interface and from Word, and creating and modifying properties in a list. In this section, we identify those areas and learn where they exist and how they are used. Armed with this knowledge, we can make short work of implementing a custom property.

Uploading and Modifying a Document

Uploading and modifying a document are handled in two different ASP.NET pages: UPLOAD.ASPX (see Figure 4.1) and EDITFORM.ASPX (see Figure 4.2), respectively. You can navigate to these pages by going to any document library and either uploading a new document or modifying an existing one. If you installed SharePoint in the default location, the documents for the Team site, Blank site, and Document Workspace site definitions are located in C:\Program Files\Common Files\Microsoft Shared\web server extensions\60\TEMPLATE\1033\STS\LISTS\DOCLIB. For simplicity, we will be talking about changes to these site definitions throughout the rest of the chapter. But don't change anything yet! Changes in this location are unsupported by Microsoft for a good reason. These documents affect all lists for all sites using these site definitions. We'll soon see how to make these changes safely.

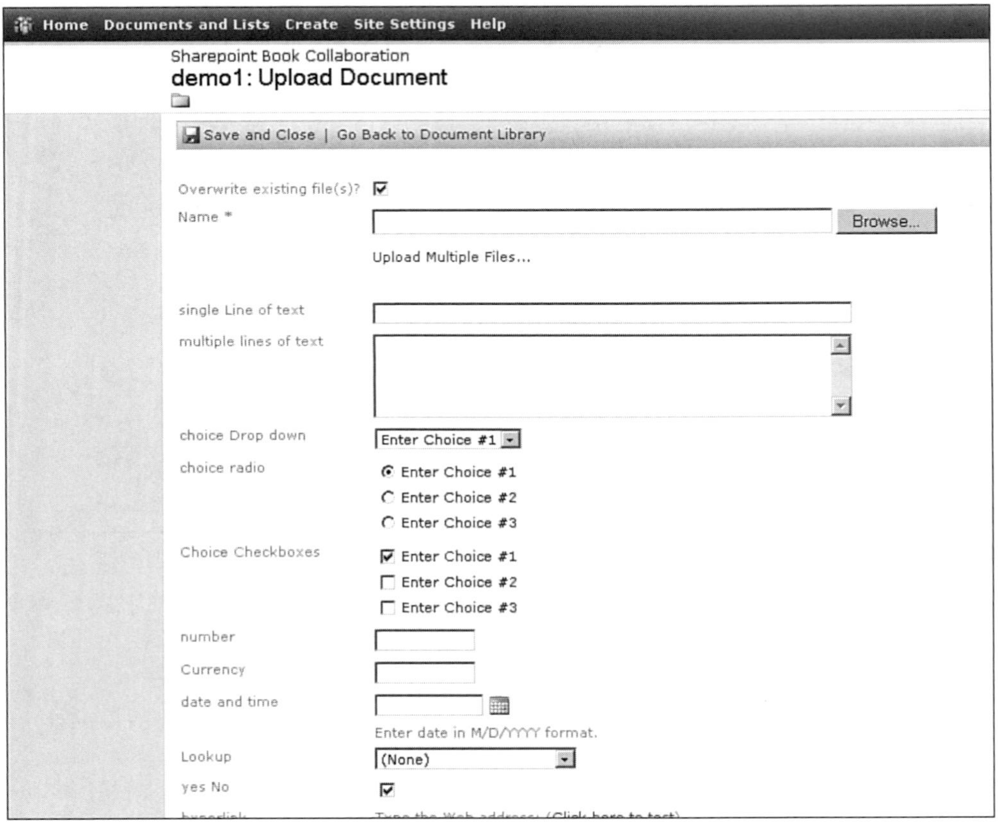

Figure 4.1   Upload.aspx.

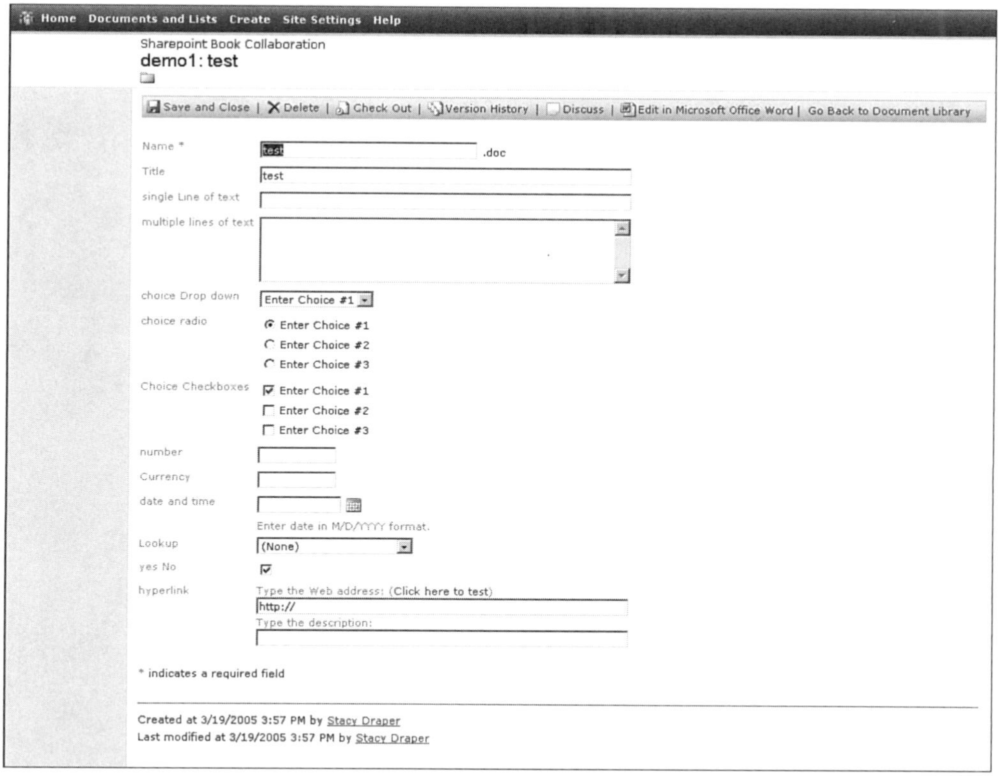

Figure 4.2 EditForm.aspx.

Adding and Editing a Column

One of the greatest things about SharePoint is creating functionality without having to enlist the skills of a developer. Wearing our developer hat, we want to make the site as flexible as possible so that anybody can create new functionality. After the new property has been identified, it almost always becomes immediately apparent that the new property can be used in many places. Let's look at FLDNEW.ASPX and FLDEDIT.ASPX in Figures 4.3 and 4.4, respectively.

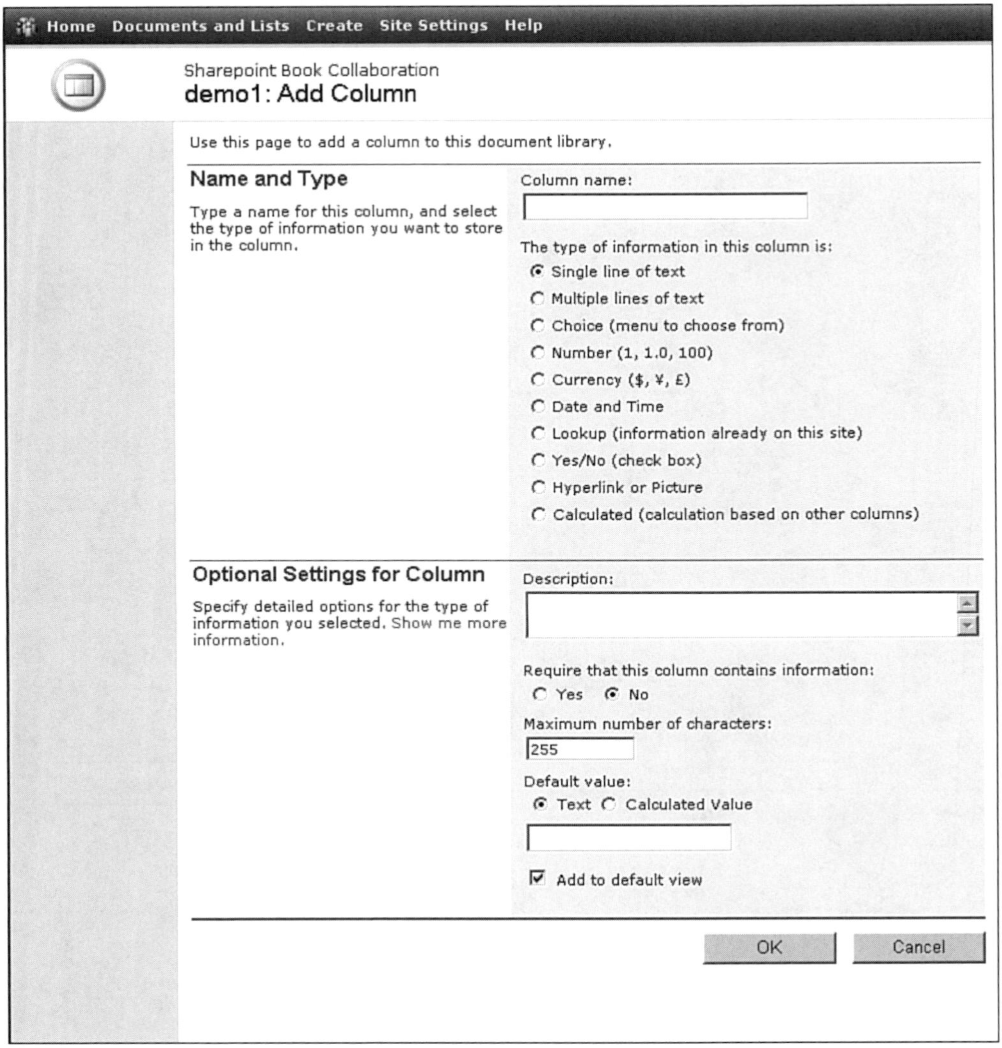

Home   Documents and Lists   Create   Site Settings   Help

Sharepoint Book Collaboration
demo1 : Add Column

Use this page to add a column to this document library.

Name and Type

Type a name for this column, and select the type of information you want to store in the column.

Column name:

The type of information in this column is:

- ⦿ Single line of text
- ○ Multiple lines of text
- ○ Choice (menu to choose from)
- ○ Number (1, 1.0, 100)
- ○ Currency ($, ¥, £)
- ○ Date and Time
- ○ Lookup (information already on this site)
- ○ Yes/No (check box)
- ○ Hyperlink or Picture
- ○ Calculated (calculation based on other columns)

Optional Settings for Column

Specify detailed options for the type of information you selected. Show me more information.

Description:

Require that this column contains information:
- ○ Yes   ⦿ No

Maximum number of characters:

255

Default value:
- ⦿ Text   ○ Calculated Value

☑ Add to default view

OK   Cancel

Figure 4.3   FldNew.aspx.

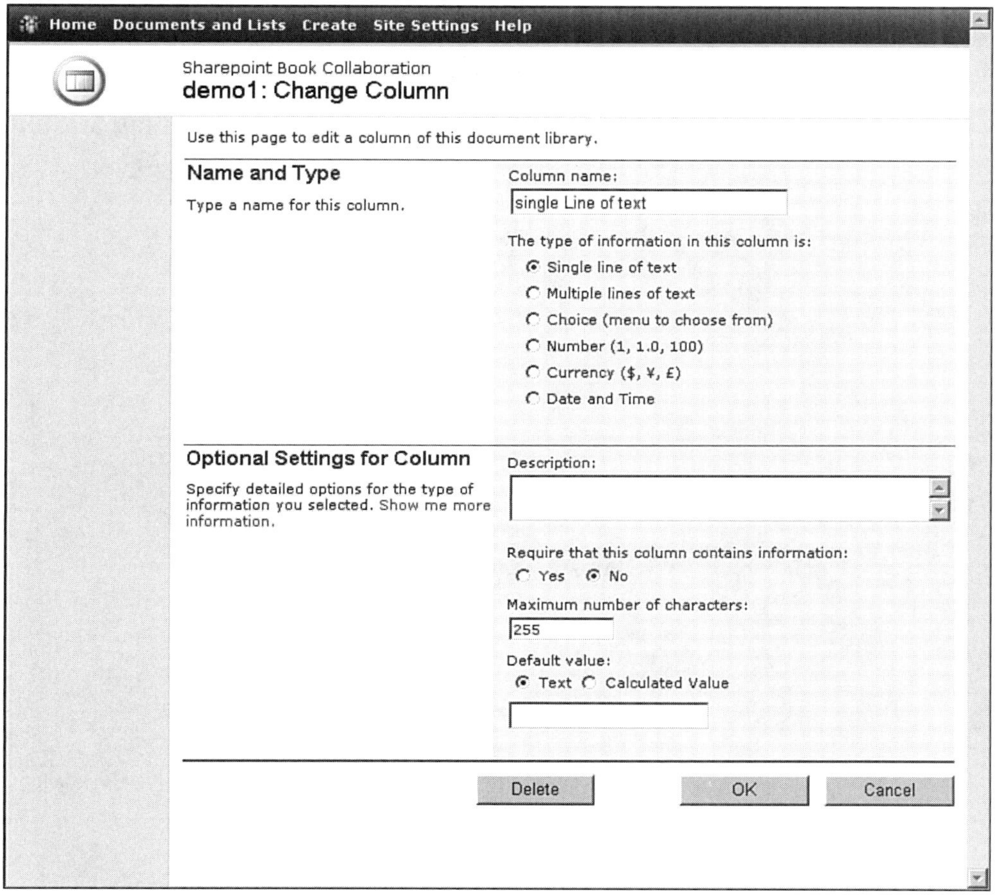

Figure 4.4   FldEdit.aspx.

As you can see, many property types are very generic and have somewhat robust functionality. When we try to integrate them with other applications, however, we find that these fields are extremely limited. The "Name and Type" section is where users select the type of property they want. Ultimately it would be nice to have a radio button for our custom property type. When selected, the optional settings specific to our column appear below. These pages are located at C:\Program Files\Common Files\Microsoft Shared\web server extensions\60\TEMPLATE\LAYOUTS\1033. Again, don't modify anything—these pages must be copied, and then you can make changes to the copies. For now, we are just trying to identify the pieces of the puzzle that can be modified to implement our custom property. Naturally, we'll take a closer look in the implementation example.

Word has a facility to manage the data stored in properties as well. Let's take a look at that next.

Modifying Properties in Microsoft Word

When saving a document to a document library, users are presented with the site name, the library name, and a list of documents in the library. This context helps users understand where they are saving their documents.

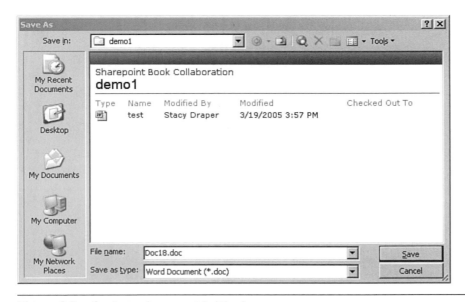

Figure 4.5   Saving a document in Word.

A couple files perform this particular brand of magic—FILEDLG.HTM and SCHEMA.XML are both located at C:\Program Files\Common Files\Microsoft Shared\web server extensions\60\TEMPLATE\1033\STS\LISTS\DOCLIB. Although we won't have to modify these pages, it's nice to know where everything is located.

After the save is committed, the user is presented with the Web File Properties dialog. This dialog also consists of a couple pages, EDIT-DLG.HTM and again SCHEMA.XML, which are located in the same folder mentioned previously. If you ever wanted to try out some CAML but didn't have a place to do it, these three pages can be your first stomping ground!

Here is one of those places where you could go off on a tangent. You could modify EDITDLG.HTM and FILEDLG.HTM for a branding issue or some other standardized customization.

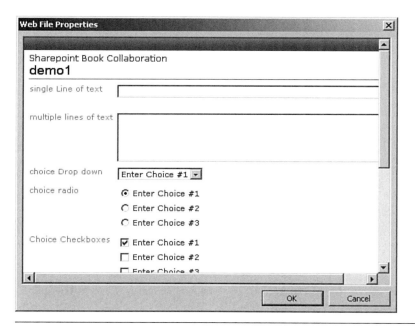

Figure 4.6   Document properties in Microsoft Word.

It is a little-known fact that the properties defined by a document library can be modified in Word. To see this in action, open a document from a document library, select File, and then select Properties, and the same Web File Properties dialog appears.

The depth of what we've covered here has been basic. With the design principles behind us, let's move into implementation and actually make this technique work.

Implementing a Custom Property Type

It seems that on every SharePoint implementation, the customer invariables asks to incorporate some data that is managed by a different system. The second reason is that going through this exercise exposes you to a wide range of technical details. We will only provide as much detail as needed for implementing a custom property type for document libraries. So, for the remainder of this chapter we are going to use an External Data Lookup model as an example of a Custom Property Type. As you are reading, note that you will be exposed to many other starting points to many other problems that should be pretty easy for further exploration on your own. In other words, from this exercise you will be able to recognize and tackle other problems using this as a catalyst.

Author Lookup

Looking at the `pubs` database that ships with SQL Server, we can create an example that demonstrates keeping data in some other store rather than SharePoint. Suppose you wanted to store contracts and other information related to an author. SharePoint is a document repository and serves as a fine tool for this project. It sure would be nice to keep the dynamic data that is stored in SQL Server available to a property when a user adds a document to a document library.

How It Works

There are several different ways that we could make this work. The business requirements will dictate the way that is best for you. In this case, the business requirements dictate a demonstration of how to make a custom property, so we are going to shoot for something simple. An `HtmlSelect` element displaying the authors with the author IDs as values will suffice. In this case, let's assume that our business rule states there will be only one author bound to a document.

If this were an actual business problem, it's only obvious that we would have to enable multiple authors per document. One way would be to use two multi-line select boxes with an arrow button in between to indicate moving an author from one list to another. If there were a large number of authors, it wouldn't make sense to list them all at once. In this case, you might want to perform a search for an author and present the user with a list to choose one or more authors. Whatever you can do in an ASP.NET interface, you can also do in this solution.

Our example is just going to be a select box that is populated with a list of authors. The user will choose one author, and the selected value will be stored in a single line text field. Our example will also demonstrate how to set the text color. Setting the text color will probably never be used in the real world, but the techniques will certainly be used. This will demonstrate how to pass data back to your control and most importantly how to save custom settings for display or functionality.

Creating a Custom Site Definition

A typical example of creating a custom site definition involves copying all the files from an existing definition to a new folder and modifying a couple XML documents. Though some similar concepts have been covered in previous chapters, the basic steps are included here.

Copying an Existing Site

Navigate to C:\Program Files\Common Files\Microsoft Shared\web server extensions\60\TEMPLATE\1033, and you'll see several default site definitions. STS and MPS are at least two, and several have the SPS prefix. The STS folder contains a team site, a document workspace, and a blank site. The MPS folder contains the definitions for meeting workspaces.

To protect yourself from the benevolent updates that Microsoft releases, you cannot modify the shipping code. All you have to do to protect yourself is to copy one of those folders and save it with your own folder name. Creating one from scratch would take an eternity and would be prone to errors. Whenever a new site definition is needed, it's best to just copy one that exists and go from there. The STS has the team site, which is pretty straightforward, so we'll use that one as the foundation for our own.

We'll create a site called CPS, representing Custom Property Site, to demonstrate implementing the custom property. The next thing that needs to be done is to let SharePoint know this site exists.

Copying WEBTEMP.XML

When creating a new site from the user interface, SharePoint presents the user with several sites to choose from. These options are derived from the WEBTEMP.XML file and all WEBTEMP*.XML files in the C:\Program Files\Common Files\Microsoft Shared\web server extensions\60\TEMPLATE\1033\XML folder. Advanced developers will make friends with many files in this folder.

A simple cut and paste with a rename will get us a step closer to where we need to be. We can call our new WEBTEMP.XML file WEBTEMPCPS.XML.

Now that we have our duplicate file, we might assume that we could see the sites listed twice in the template selection page. Because the template names are the same, though, the site templates are not shown.

Customizing WEBTEMP.XML

Let's edit C:\Program Files\Common Files\Microsoft Shared\web server extensions\60\TEMPLATE\1033\XML\WEBTEMPCPS.XML. The first thing we can do is to remove the MPS template node. The `Name` attribute of the `Template` node must match the folder name exactly. Within the WEBTEMPCPS.XML file, let's rename our template from STS to CPS. The `Template` node also has an `ID` field. Microsoft has indicated that the custom site definition should start at 10000 and must not conflict with any of the other WEBTEMP files. Set ours to 10000. The `Title` attribute is what the user who is creating the site will see in the select box. The `imageUrl` is what the user will see when he or she clicks the item. `Description` is always a lot of fun because it helps the user understand what that site template is designed for. These attributes are pretty straightforward, except for the `ID` attribute. The `ID` attribute relates to the `Configurations` section within the ONET.XML file. The ONET.XML file is one of those documents that you can't help but be familiar with if you are going to create your own custom site definitions, because each site definition has its own ONET.XML. So getting back to the `Configuration` node of the WEBTEMPCPS.XML document, let's just have one option for our Custom Property Site. We'll set the `Hidden` attribute to TRUE for the nodes where the `ID` attributes have values 1 and 2. This is one of those few moments where you set something that does exactly what you think it should. Setting the `Hidden` attribute to `true` will cause SharePoint to suppress the option when displaying a list of site templates to choose from. Of course, deleting these two nodes would have had the same effect. Next, let's give our site a better name to avoid getting it confused with the "Team Site" that already exists in CPS. `"Team Site - Custom Property"` sounds great!

This is what your WEBTEMPCPS.XML document should look like.

Listing 4.1   WEBTEMPCPS.XML with New Template Added

```xml
<?xml version="1.0" encoding="utf-8" ?>
<!-- _lcid="1033" _version="11.0.5510" _dal="1" -->
<!-- _LocalBinding -->
<Templates xmlns:ows="Microsoft SharePoint">
  <Template Name="CPS" ID="10000">
    <Configuration ID="0" Title="Team Site - Custom Property"
      Hidden="FALSE" ImageUrl="/_layouts/images/stsprev.png"
      Description="This template creates a site for teams to
      create, organize, and share information quickly and
      easily. It includes a Document Library, and basic lists
      such as Announcements, Events, Contacts, and Quick Links.">
    </Configuration>
    <Configuration ID="1" Title="Blank Site" Hidden="TRUE"
      ImageUrl="/_layouts/images/stsprev.png" Description="This
      template creates a Windows SharePoint Services-enabled Web
      site with a blank home page. You can use a Windows SharePoint
      Services-compatible Web page editor to add interactive lists
      or any other Windows SharePoint Services features.">
    </Configuration>
    <Configuration ID="2" Title="Document Workspace" Hidden="TRUE"
      ImageUrl="/_layouts/images/dwsprev.png" Description="This
      template creates a site for colleagues to work together on
      documents. It provides a document library for storing the
      primary document and supporting files, a Task list for
      assigning to-do items, and a Links list for resources related
      to the document.">
    </Configuration>
  </Template>
</Templates>
```

Creating a Custom Document Library

Creating a custom document library is just about the same, only easier. It's nice to keep original stuff original and modify our own lists. Opening C:\Program Files\Common Files\Microsoft Shared\web server extensions\60\TEMPLATE\1033\CPS\LISTS will reveal all the lists. Simply copy the DOCLIB from our CPS template C:\Program Files\Common

Files\Microsoft Shared\web server extensions\60\TEMPLATE\1033\ CPS\LISTS and paste it in the same folder with the name DOCLIBCPS. This will be the document library that will use the custom property. Now we need to let SharePoint know this thing exists.

Modifying ONET.XML

Open ONET.XML located in C:\Program Files\Common Files\ Microsoft Shared\web server extensions\60\TEMPLATE\1033\CPS\ XML for editing. In the `ListTemplates` node, you will find many `List-Template` elements. Duplicate the `doclib` node and call the new one `doclibcps`. The name must match the folder exactly. The `Type` must be less that 1000. Let's name ours 901.

Listing 4.2   ONET.XML Pointing to Our DOCLIBCPS

```
<ListTemplate Name="doclib" DisplayName="Document Library"
  Type="101" BaseType="1" OnQuickLaunch="TRUE" SecurityBits="11"
  Description="Create a document library when you have a
  collection of documents or other files that you want to share.
  Document libraries support features such as sub-folders, file
  versioning, and check-in/check-out."
  Image="/_layouts/images/itdl.gif"
  DocumentTemplate="101"></ListTemplate>
<ListTemplate Name="doclibcps" DisplayName="Document Library
  cps" Type="901" BaseType="1" OnQuickLaunch="TRUE"
  SecurityBits="11" Description="Document Library with custom
  property" Image="/_layouts/images/itdl.gif"
  DocumentTemplate="101"></ListTemplate>
```

Also in the ONET.XML file, one of the first nodes that we come across is the `<PROJECT>` node. Add an attribute to that called `CustomJSUrl`.

```
CustomJSUrl="/_layouts/[%=System.Threading.Thread.CurrentThread.
➥ CurrentUICulture.LCID%]/CPS/CustomJSLoader.aspx"
```

`CustomJSUrl` creates a custom JavaScript block with an `SRC` attribute that points where `CustomJSUrl` specifies. This script block is included on just about every page and can be used to perform whatever custom functionality you need. This is a very powerful feature, and we will be leveraging it wholeheartedly in this example. OWS.JS is shipping code and cannot be modified. You shouldn't even make a copy of it and use it in your own site definition. Instead, use `CustomJSUrl`.

Creating a New Site Based on a New Site Definition

Of course you must save your WEBTEMPCPS.XML and ONET.XML files, but that's not all. You also must reset IIS. This is easy enough—just open the DOS prompt and execute IISReset. We are now ready to create a site! From just about any Create menu in SharePoint, you can choose to create new "Sites and Workspaces". Choose a name for the title—CPS sounds good for now, as shown in Figure 4.7. As a matter of fact, it sounds so good that we'll reuse it for the Web Site Address field, too.

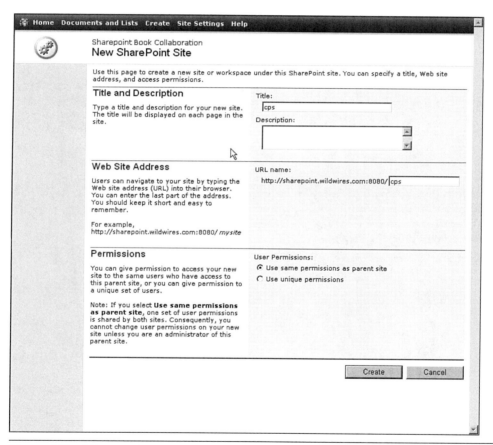

Figure 4.7   Windows SharePoint site creation.

Now on to the Template Selection, where you should see your Team Site - Custom Property site template in the list of templates to choose from (see Figure 4.8).

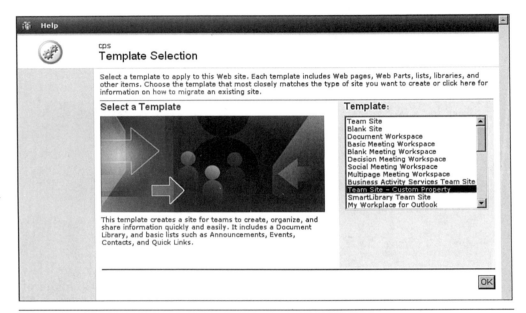

Figure 4.8   Template selection.

If you don't, then something went wrong somewhere.

If SharePoint comes across two identical template names, it will ignore the second one. It's hard to say which one will be the second one. Another common mistake is not resetting IIS. IIS must be reset when any changes are made to WEBTEMP*.XML or ONET.XML. Also ensure that other XML nodes weren't tampered with during our cut and paste adventures. Check the ID of the template when you receive messages that indicate that the template is invalid or cannot be found when trying to create the site. Remember we use all IDs over 10000.

Protecting the Files in the Layouts Folder

One last detail in an effort to fortify our application against Microsoft updates lies in the Layouts folder. The Layouts folder, C:\Program Files\Common Files\Microsoft Shared\web server extensions\60\

TEMPLATE\LAYOUTS, is mapped a virtual directory, _layouts, in all SharePoint sites. Any .NET page can run in this folder.

When you want to add some functionality quickly and easily, the Layouts folder can be your friend. This folder is where we can run our ASP.NET code. By simply adding a folder, we provide some great organization, and voila, you have your very own place to run ASP.NET. Keeping things neat in the Layouts folder provides maintainability and reduced time to market.

Sometimes a change to a page in the Layouts folder is so radical that you don't want any other SharePoint applications to know about it. Because all SharePoint sites share the same pages in the Layouts folder, it seems tempting to change one page and affect all applications. In either case, you shouldn't edit the original file in the Layouts folder. Instead, you should go through the exercise of creating your own Site Definition and pointing to a version of the pages in the Layouts folder.

When a user adds a new column to the document library, you might want to make your custom property available for him or her to choose. On the other hand, you might have a property that you don't want a user to add. It all depends on your needs. Remember to code to the requirements—always develop what is needed rather than what is cool.

To make your custom property available to end users, there are a few pages that you can modify. Most of these pages are in the 1033 folder of the Layouts folder. 1033 represents English. If you have a multilingual application, then you will need to make these changes to each language you support. The only other file that you need to modify is in the document library itself.

If you were to navigate to ALLITEMS.ASPX of a document library and click Modify Settings and Columns, then you would be taken to LISTEDIT.ASPX in the 1033 folder. On the LISTEDIT.ASPX, there are two kinds of links that we are concerned with most—add new column (FLDNEW.ASPX) and each column hyperlink in the list of columns (points to FLDEDIT.ASPX). FLDNEW.ASPX and FLDEDIT.ASPX are the two pages that we must edit.

The first thing we should do is create our own folder in the 1033 folder so that we don't mix our pages up with the Microsoft pages. This is a little more work than just making another page in the same folder, but it will make things clearer for the next person who must modify our application. Create a folder in the 1033 folder and call it CPS. Copy the LISTEDIT.ASPX, FLDNEW.ASPX, and FLDEDIT.ASPX files to the new CPS folder. Naturally, all our relative links are broken. Let's sum those up quickly.

FLDNEW.ASPX and FLDEDIT.ASPX are very straightforward. All that must be done to these pages is to repair the relative links. Only a couple link types break when you move these files: the JavaScript and style sheet references. This is easy enough to fix by putting ../ at the beginning of the path to each style sheet and JavaScript reference.

Listing 4.3   FldNew.aspx and FldEdit.aspx Snippets

```
<script src="../owsbrows.js"></script>
<SharePoint:CssLink DefaultUrl="../styles/ows.css" runat="server"/>
    <SharePoint:Theme runat="server"/>
<script><!--
if (browseris.mac && !browseris.ie5up)
{
    var ms_maccssfpfixup = "../styles/owsmac.css";
    document.write("<link rel='stylesheet' Type='text/css' href='" +
    ms_maccssfpfixup + "'>");
}
//--></script>
<script src="../ows.js"></script>
```

The same fix needs to take place in the LISTEDIT.ASPX page, plus a couple more changes. Because LISTEDIT.ASPX generates several links that reference files located in the Layout folder, we must fix their relative paths as well. Find LSTSETNG.ASPX, ADVSETNG.ASPX (not used, but change it anyways), SAVETMPL.ASPX, SHROPT.ASPX, FORMEDIT.ASPX, VIEWEDIT.ASPX, and VIEWTYPE.ASPX and add ../ to the beginning of each. This will cause the browser to use the pages in the 1033 folder. Of course we could use brute force and just copy the entire Layout folder, but that's not a good practice. We only want to modify as little as possible. One last file that we must edit is the link that gets us to the LISTEDIT.ASPX in the first place—ALLITEMS.ASPX.

ALLITEMS.ASPX resides in the Forms folder of the document library in question. ALLITEMS.ASPX and other dynamically created document library views don't actually contain the link to LISTEDIT.ASPX; instead it contains a toolbar that has the link. The toolbar is in SCHEMA.XML. In SCHEMA.XML, located in C:\Program Files\Common Files\Microsoft Shared\web server extensions\60\TEMPLATE\1033\CPS\LISTS\DOCLIBCPS, find the `Toolbar` node with `Type` attribute set to `RelatedTasks`—it's the last node in the XML document. Next, find the anchor tag for Modify Settings and Columns—it might be easiest just to use the "find" feature of your editing tool to look for LISTEDIT.ASPX and add /cps just before it. This will cause our custom LISTEDIT.ASPX page to open when a user clicks Modify Settings and Columns.

We've just completed the basic steps that are needed when creating a custom property for a document library. When a site is created based on your custom site definition, almost all the plumbing will be in place. We're not out of the woods yet. Leave these files open in your editor, and let's take a look at another reason why you might want to use a custom property so that we can more fully explore the solution.

Controls

We will need several controls to pull this off. The first and most obvious is the user interface that will provide the functionality we are a looking for. For our example, we need to display a list of authors from the `pubs` database, so we'll use a data access component to retrieve this and any other author information we need.

User Control

There are a couple reasons why a custom property must be implemented. One is for functionality, and the other is for the data that it provides. Whatever the situation, you'll probably use a user control for that functionality. The following code is used for providing our custom property:

Listing 4.4 AuthorLookup Class

```
using System;
using System.Data;
using System.Drawing;
using System.Web;
using System.Web.UI.WebControls;
using System.Web.UI.HtmlControls;
using System.Collections;
using SharePointBook; //namespace of our data access component,
                      //defined in the next section
```

```
namespace select{
 public class AuthorLookup : System.Web.UI.UserControl {
  //Global variables for public properties
  private string _DefaultValue = "";
  private string _ElemToSet = "idDefault";
  private string _WhatToReturn = "value";
  private string _Style = "";

  private void Page_Load(object sender, System.EventArgs e) {}

  protected override void Render(System.Web.UI.HtmlTextWriter
➡ writer){
   Authors myExample = new Authors();
   HtmlSelect mySelect = myExample.getAuthors();
   mySelect.Style.Add("color", this.Style);
   if (mySelect.Items.FindByValue(DefaultValue) != null){
    mySelect.Items.FindByValue(DefaultValue).Selected = true;
   }
   switch (WhatToReturn.ToLower()){
    case "value":
     onChangeReturnValue(mySelect);
     break;
    case "both":
     onChangeReturnBoth(mySelect);
     break;
    default:
     onChangeReturnValue(mySelect);
     break;
   }
   this.Controls.Add(mySelect);
   base.Render (writer);
  }

  private void onChangeReturnValue(HtmlSelect mySelect)
  {
   mySelect.Attributes["onchange"] =
    "document.getElementById('" + ElemToSet + "').value = "
    + "this.options[this.selectedIndex].value;";
  }

  private void onChangeReturnBoth(HtmlSelect mySelect){
   mySelect.Attributes["onchange"] =
    "document.getElementById('" + ElemToSet + "').value = "
```

```
      + "this.options[this.selectedIndex].value + '|'"
      + "+ this.options[this.selectedIndex].text ;";
  }

  public string WhatToReturn
  { get {return _WhatToReturn;} set {_WhatToReturn = value;} }

  public string ElemToSet
  { get {return _ElemToSet;} set {_ElemToSet = value;} }

  public string DefaultValue
  { get {return _DefaultValue;} set {_DefaultValue = value;} }

  public string Style
  { get {return _Style;} set {_Style = value;} }

  #region Web Form Designer generated code
  override protected void OnInit(EventArgs e) {
   InitializeComponent();
   base.OnInit(e);
  }

  private void InitializeComponent() {
   this.Load += new System.EventHandler(this.Page_Load);
  }
  #endregion
 }
}
```

Four public properties can be set on the user control. These properties help manage state and functionality.

The assumption is that we are using a select box for our foreign lookup. We've noticed that for select boxes, sometimes you just need the value, and sometimes you need both the value and the text. The What-ToReturn property determines whether the value of the selected item should be returned or both the value and the display. Here we use a | (a pipe character) to delineate between the value and the text.

The assumption with this control is that it will be used on a page in a modal window. The modal window will need to set the HTML element on the parent to a value. The ElemToSet property holds the ID of the element on the parent that needs to be populated.

The `DefaultValue` property holds the item that should be selected in the drop-down list.

The `Style` property is used in this example to set text to red. The significance of this example is to illustrate the idea that data is not the only thing that must be passed around but attribute information as well. Please don't limit yourself to attribute information. Other information or functionality can be passed back in the same way.

Example Data Access Component

The data access functionality has been broken out into a separate class to fetch the specific information we need. In this example we use the `sql-Helper` class of `Microsoft.ApplicationBlocks.Data` for our conduit into the SQL Server.

Listing 4.5   Author Data Access

```
using System;
using System.Data;
using Microsoft.ApplicationBlocks.Data;
using System.Data.SqlClient;
using System.Web;
using System.Web.UI.HtmlControls;

namespace SharePointBook
{
 public class Authors
 {
  public Authors()
  {
  }
  public HtmlSelect getAuthors()
  {
    string strConnection =
"server=localhost\\wildwires;database=pubs;integrated"
    + "security=SSPI";
    System.Web.UI.HtmlControls.HtmlSelect select = new HtmlSelect();
    select.ID ="myDefault";
    select.DataSource = SqlHelper.ExecuteDataset
  (strConnection,"getAuthors", null);
    select.DataTextField = "name";
    select.DataValueField = "au_id";
```

```
  select.DataBind();
  select.Items.Insert(0,"");
  return select;
  }


  public string GetAuthorByID(string AuthorId)
  {
   string returnValue = "No Record Found";
   string strConnection = "server=localhost\\wildwires;
➥ database=pubs;integrated"
    + "security=SSPI";
   SqlParameter[] arParams = new SqlParameter[1];
   arParams[0] = new SqlParameter("@AuthorID", AuthorId);
   System.Data.SqlClient.SqlDataReader objDataReader =
    SqlHelper.ExecuteReader(strConnection, "GetAuthorById",
➥ arParams);
   while (objDataReader.Read() == true)
   {
    returnValue = objDataReader.GetValue(0).ToString();
   }


   return returnValue;
  }
 }
}
```

There are only two methods in this class—GetAuthors and GetAuthor-ByID. GetAuthors returns all the authors through a stored procedure. In its current form, this function only stores the author's key, and that's not really what we want. We would like to display the author's name. This method can be used by a web service to return just the author's name.

Thinking about how the Style property is implemented, let's look at what it would take to get different lists from this same code. If we added a property to our user control, we could pass that value to a generic lookup. Perhaps there is a table that would have a list of queries and a key is passed in. Maybe pass a stored procedure name? This user control could even be made unfriendly by permitting the setting of the database connection information. Nobody would really want to provide users access to database configuration information, so we mentioned this example solely for mental calisthenics. Given a little thought, there is a lot of information that business users might want to store with the document.

Adding a New Column and Modifying Existing Columns in a Document Library Definition

When looking at FLDEDIT.ASPX and FLDNEW.ASPX, we can see that they have many things in common. They look almost identical from the user perspective, and they have just about the same code. In both cases, we have a list of properties to choose from. The user selects one type, and the options change for that type of field. Ultimately, we are shooting for a page that looks similar to Figure 4.9.

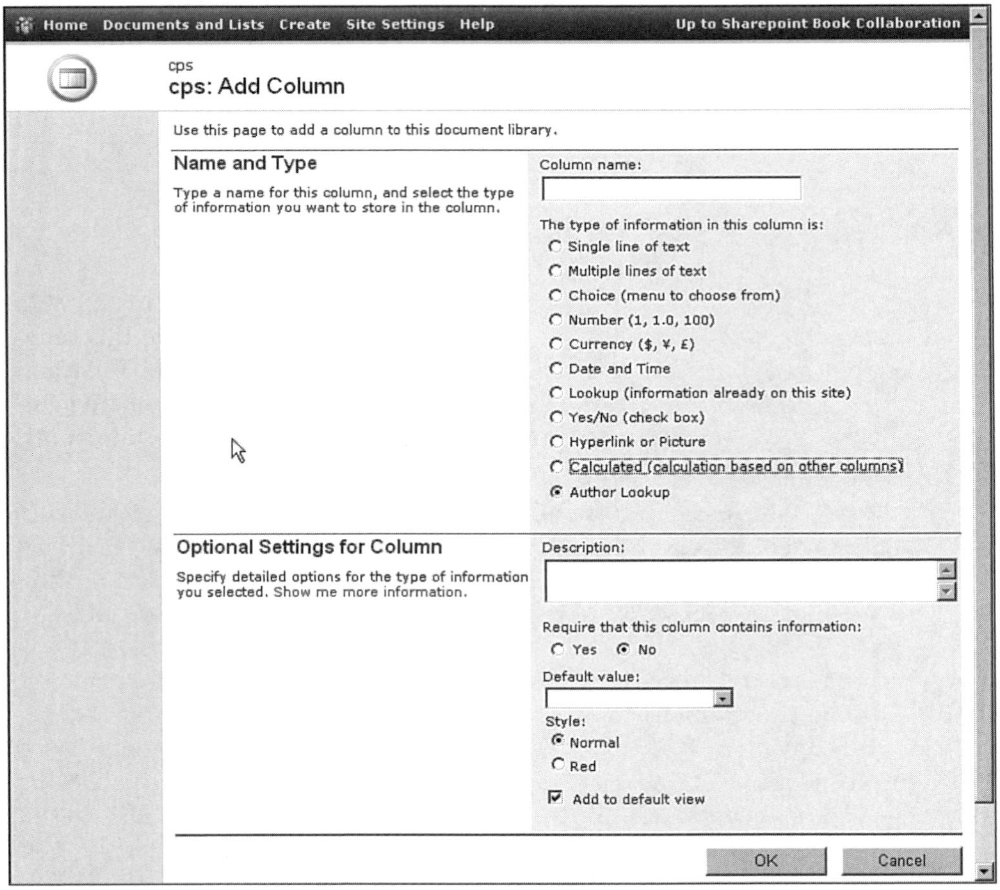

Figure 4.9   Adding a property to a document library.

When the user selects Red, the desired effect is to have the text of the select box turn red—in Figure 4.10, the text Abraham Bennet would become red.

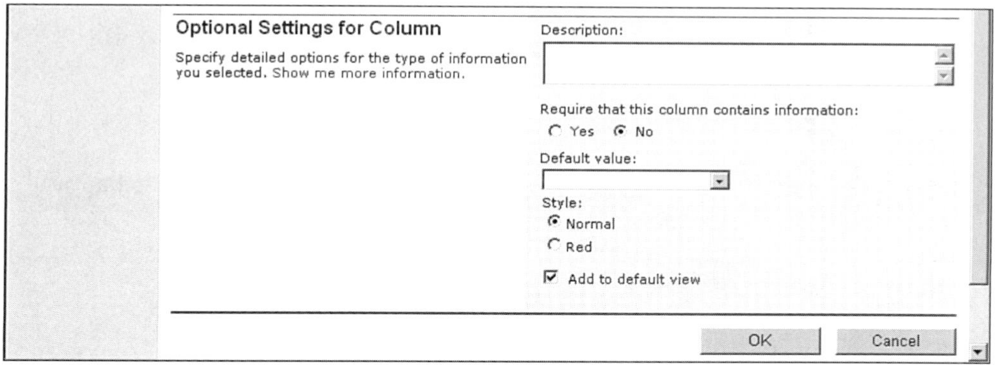

Figure 4.10   Optional settings for column.

First we'll cover what goes on behind the scenes, and then we'll walk through customized line by customized line of how to make this functionality happen. A few things are happening on this page. First and most straightforward is the list of field types and options. These are managed by conditionals. The property types are managed by `if` statements, and the optional settings portion is managed by a `case` statement. The other thing that happens on this page is a lot less obvious. When the user selects the various style settings, a round trip occurs through a JavaScript function called `UpdatePage`. When `UpdatePage` is fired, we need to get our custom setting to the user control. Let's begin by modifying FLD-NEW.ASPX.

FLDNEW.ASPX

Starting from the top of the page and working our way down, the first thing we need to do is register the tag prefix for the user control.

Listing 4.6   FldNew.aspx Snippet

```
<!-- _lcid="1033" _version="11.0.5510" _dal="1" -->
<!-- _LocalBinding -->
<%@ Page language="C#"  ... code removed to save space
<!-- custom Code-->
<%@ Register TagPrefix="uc1" TagName="AuthorLookup"
➥ Src="AuthorLookup.ascx" %>
<!-- end custom code -->
<% SPSite spServer =  ... code removed to save space
```

The next line of customization we come across is a variable declaration.

Listing 4.7   FldNew.aspx Snippet

```
String strLookupList = "";
String strLookupField = "";
String strShowPresence = "";
// custom code
string strALCustomSettings = "";
//end custom code
String strDisplaySize = "";
String strDisplayNameParam = "";
int    iCurrencyLCID = spWeb.CurrencyLocaleID;
```

The variable `strALCustomSettings` represents the custom settings that need to be managed on the page locally. In our case, it will manage the `Style` setting that determines whether the text is red.

The next area helps us manage custom settings and default values in the querystring. This code isn't relevant until the page reloads. This reloading action is caused by the `UpdatePage` JavaScript function, which will be covered momentarily.

Listing 4.8   FldNew.aspx Snippet

```
if ( Request.Url.ToString().IndexOf("LookupListParam") != -1 )
{strLookupList   = Request.QueryString.GetValues
➥ ("LookupListParam")[0] ; }
if ( Request.Url.ToString().IndexOf("LookupFieldParam") != -1 )
```

```
{strLookupField  =  Request.QueryString.GetValues
➥ ("LookupFieldParam")[0]; }
if ( Request.Url.ToString().IndexOf("ShowPresence") != -1 )
{strShowPresence  =  Request.QueryString.GetValues
➥ ("ShowPresence")[0]; }
//custom code
if ( Request.Url.ToString().IndexOf("AuthorLookupParam") != -1 )
{strALCustomSettings  =  Request.QueryString.GetValues
➥ ("AuthorLookupParam")[0] ; }
if ( Request.Url.ToString().IndexOf("Default") != -1 )
{strDefault  =  Request.QueryString.GetValues("Default")[0] ; }
//End Custom Code
if (strFieldType == "")
{
    strFieldType = "Text";
}
```

strDefault is a variable that is already part of FLDNEW.ASPX. We use it here for our custom property type.

The next two modifications are in the same JavaScript function, GetTypeDesc(). The reason behind this is to help make the application uniform and easily portable to other languages.

Listing 4.9   FldNew.aspx Snippet

```
function GetTypeDesc(type)
{
 var L_TypeCounter_Text = "Counter";

 ... code removed to save space.

 var L_TypeComputed_Text = "Computed";
 //custom code
 var L_AuthorLookup_Text = "Author Lookup";
 //end custom code
 var L_TypeUnkown_Text = "Unknown type";
 switch (type)
 {
  case "Text": return L_TypeSingleLine_Text;

  ... code removed to save space.
```

```
  case "URL": return L_TypeURL_Text;
  //custom code
  case "Author Lookup": return L_AuthorLookup_Text;
  //end custom code
  case "Computed": return L_TypeComputed_Text;
 }
 return L_TypeUnkown_Text;
}
```

The next JavaScript function is one that we have alluded to previously.
The `UpdatePage` function is an event handler for the style radio buttons.
The method ultimately forces a round trip by calling the
`document.location.replace` method, replacing the URL with the
same URL plus all the state information we need when the page reloads.

Listing 4.10   FldNew.aspx Snippet

```
function UpdatePage(typeVal) {
 var sArg = "&FieldTypeParam=";
 var sFieldNameArg = "&DisplayNameParam=";
 var sLookup = "Lookup";
 // Custom Code
 var sAuthorLookup = "AuthorLookup";
 // end custom code
 var sUser = "User";
 var sLLArg = "&LookupListParam=";
 var sLLVal = "";
 //Custom Code
 var sALArg = "&AuthorLookupParam=";
 var sALVal = "";
 var sALDArg = "&Default=";
 var sALDVal = "";
 //end custom code
 var sPresArg = "&ShowPresence=";
 var sPresVal = "";
 var sURL = window.location + "";

  ... code removed to save space.

 if (typeVal == sLookup) {
  sLLVal = GetLookupList();
```

```
 if (sLLVal.length != 0)
   sLLVal = sLLArg + sLLVal;
}
//Custom Code
if (typeVal == sAuthorLookup) {
  var tmpElems = document.getElementsByName("CustStyle");
  if (tmpElems != "undefined") {
   for(var i=0;i<tmpElems.length;i++) {
    if (tmpElems[i].checked==true) {
     sALVal = sALArg + tmpElems[i].value;
    }
   }
  }
  var tmpElem = document.getElementById("idDefault");
  if (tmpElem != null){
   sALDVal = sALDArg + document.getElementById("idDefault").value
  }
}
//End Custom Code
if ((typeVal == sUser) || (typeVal == sLookup)) {
 sPresVal = GetShowPresence();
 if (sPresVal.length != 0)
 sPresVal = sPresArg + sPresVal;
}
//Custom Code
var sNewUrl = sURL + sArg + typeVal + sFieldNameArg + nameval +
➡ sDescriptionArg + descval
  + sLLVal + sPresVal + sALVal + sALDVal;
 if (sNewUrl.length > 2040)
  document.location.replace(sURL + sArg + typeVal + sLLVal + sALVal
➡ + sALDVal);
 else
  document.location.replace(sNewUrl);
}
```

The first added line of code creates a constant for the author lookup—fairly simple. The next four lines are variables to help assemble the query string, specifically the custom settings and the default value. The `if` block checks to see whether the radio buttons exist and, if so, acquires the appropriate values and prepares them to be appended to the query string. Depending on the number of customizations you have, you might want to manage this differently. For example, if you offer 25 custom settings, it might not be wise to create a parameter for each. Instead, create a storage system to keep all the customization information in one parameter. Don't forget that you only get a little over 2,000 characters in the URL.

Finally, all the values are appended, and the page is reloaded. Another important thing to note here is that typeVal sets the property type. When UpdatePage is called, the property type is set to "Author-Lookup". A variable on the server side or ASP.NET inline code, str-FieldType, is set by existing functionality. strFieldType is used for several things, including the "Optional Settings for Column" section, which will be covered later more in depth.

There is another function that behaves similarly to this one, called UpdateDateField(). It could be argued that there should be a function specific for custom fields, perhaps called UpdateCustomField(). It just seemed easier and more efficient to hijack UpdatePage(). Our example isn't so different that we couldn't use UpdatePage(), whereas the inner workings of UpdateDateField() are quite a bit different. The point is that if a custom field is more complicated, it might be wise to create a different handler for it.

There are no custom properties in SharePoint, but you can create a text type property and put your own user interface around it. This will accomplish several things—it will provide custom functionality, custom data, or both. The field schema is XML that describes a property. Every property (or field) in document libraries has a field schema. The next thing we will do is to modify the field schema at the time that it is created.

Listing 4.11 FldNew.aspx snippet

```
if (GridWidth < 2)
 {
  alert(L_alert20_Text);
  frm.GridNumRange.focus();
  return false;
 }
}
//custom code
if (Type == "AuthorLookup")
{
 Type = "Text";
 Format = "AuthorLookup";
}
```

```
//end custom code
var Schema = ('<Field ' +
 (Name          ? 'Name="'        + SimpleHTMLEncode(Name)          + '"' : '') +
 (FromBaseType  ? 'FromBaseType="'+ SimpleHTMLEncode(FromBaseType)  + '"' : '') +
 (DisplaySize   ? 'DisplaySize="' + DisplaySize                     + '"' : '') +

  ... code removed to save space.

 (Description   ? 'Description="'  + SimpleHTMLEncode(Description)   + '"' : '') +
 (Required      ? 'Required="'     + SimpleHTMLEncode(Required)      + '"' : '') +
 (NumLines      ? 'NumLines="'     + SimpleHTMLEncode(NumLines)      + '"' : '') +
 (Format        ? 'Format="'       + SimpleHTMLEncode(Format)        + '"' : '') +
 (MaxLength     ? 'MaxLength="'    + MaxLength                       + '"' : '') +
 (Min           ? 'Min="'          + Min                            + '"' : '') +
 (Max           ? 'Max="'          + Max                            + '"' : '') +
```

Just before the field schema gets defined, the `Type` is set back to `Text`, and `Format` is hijacked and set to "`AuthorLookup`". This little ballet keeps SharePoint happy and lets us know what type of field we are working with later on. Any time there is a text field, the format needs to be checked to see whether it's one of the custom types, and if so, it must be rendered accordingly. This model is similar to the one that Microsoft uses for checkboxes and radio buttons.

The next addition is for storing our custom settings. We only have one custom setting: whether or not the text field is red.

Listing 4.12   FldNew.aspx Snippet

```
}else if(Default)
{
 Schema += '<Default>' + SimpleHTMLEncode(Default) + '</Default>';
}
//Custom Code
if (Type == "Text" && Format=="AuthorLookup")
{
 Schema += '<CustomSettings><Style><%=strALCustomSettings%></Style>
➥ </CustomSettings>';
}
//End Custom Code
if (Type == "Calculated")
{
    if (!CheckForIllegals(Formula))
```

The `Default` node and the `CustomSettings` node become child nodes of the `Field` element. Anything you can encode as XML can be stored here. The business requirement might call for a very complicated interface. The interface can be designed by the user, and the settings for that field are stored in the field schema.

This is an opportunity for self-exploration into field schemas because this is where they are created. It's outside the scope of a custom property, but take a look at how the `Calculated` fields are handled and the different choice options. The big take-away here is to understand that we store the custom settings for your field as an XML document in the child node of the `Fields` element.

After all that, we can finally get down to the user interface modifications. The first thing to do is to create the radio button for the custom property type.

Listing 4.13   FldNew.aspx Snippet

```
<TR>
 <TD align="center" nowrap class="ms-authoringcontrols">
 <% if ( strFieldType == "Calculated" ) { %>  ... Code removed to
➥ save space
 </TD>
 <TD  class="ms-authoringcontrols" ... Code removed to save space
 </TD>
</TR>
<!-- Custom Code -->
<TR>
 <TD align="center" nowrap class="ms-authoringcontrols">
 <% if ( strFieldType == "AuthorLookup" ) { %> <INPUT
➥ onClick="UpdatePage('AuthorLookup')" type="radio"
➥ value="AuthorLookup" id=onetidTypeCalculated name="Type"
➥ title="The type of information in this column is : Author Lookup"
➥ CHECKED> <% ; } else { %> <INPUT
➥ onClick="UpdatePage('AuthorLookup')" type="radio"
➥ value="AuthorLookup" id=onetidTypeCalculated name="Type"
➥ title="The type of information in this column is : Author Lookup"
➥ > <% ; } %>
 </TD>
 <TD  class="ms-authoringcontrols"
id="L_onetidTypeAuthorLookup"><LABEL FOR="onetidTypeAuthorLookup">
➥ Author Lookup<!-- --></LABEL></TD>
```

```
</TR>
<!-- end custom code -->
<TR>
 <TD align="center" nowrap class="ms-authoringcontrols"></TD>
 <TD  class="ms-authoringcontrols" ID=align101></TD>
</TR>
```

The easiest way to do this is to copy the bold line (the table row for `Cal-culated`) and change a few things. First, search for `Calculated` and replace it with `AuthorLookup`. The `Title` attribute also needs to be changed to reflect `AuthorLookup`, and finally the parameters that are sent to `UpdatePage()` need to be `AuthorLookup`. There are two HTML elements that are conditionally displayed, so be sure to modify them both. Now, on to the option for the property.

Options
The options are displayed a little differently in that they are done with a `case` statement on the server side. Using cut and paste, it's simple to copy an option that exists and modify it based on the business needs.

Listing 4.14   FldNew.aspx Snippet

```
<%
break;
// custom code
case "AuthorLookup":
%>
 <!-- AuthorLookup -->
 <TR>
  <TD colspan=2></TD>
  <TD class="ms-authoringcontrols" width=10> </TD>
  <TD class="ms-authoringcontrols"
    id=onetidTypeDefaultAuthorLookupValue><label
    ➥ for="idDefault">Default
    value</label>:<FONT size=3> </FONT><BR>
   <TABLE border=0 cellspacing=1>
    <TR>
     <TD class="ms-authoringcontrols">
      <!-- custom code -->
      <input type=hidden name="Default" id="idDefault"
```

```
        value=<%SPEncode.WriteHtmlEncodeWithQuote(Response,
        ➥ strDefault,
        '"');%>>
        <%
        idALookup.DefaultValue = strDefault;
        idALookup.Style = strALCustomSettings;
        %>
        <uc1:AuthorLookup name="ALookup" id="idALookup"
         runat="server"></uc1:AuthorLookup>
       </TD>
      </TR>
      <!-- custom code -->
      <TR>
       <TD class="ms-authoringcontrols">
        <label for="idDefault">Style:</label><BR>
        <input type="radio" name="CustStyle" value="normal"
         id="idCustStyleNormal" onclick="UpdatePage('AuthorLookup')"
         checked><label for="idCustStyleNormal">Normal</label>
         ➥ </input><BR>
        <input type="radio" name="CustStyle" value="red"
         id="idCustStyleRed" onclick="UpdatePage('AuthorLookup')">
         ➥ <label
         for="idCustStyleRed">Red</label></input>
        <script>
         tmpElems = document.getElementsByName("CustStyle")
         for(var i=0;i<tmpElems.length;i++) {
          if (tmpElems[i].value=="<%=strALCustomSettings%>") {
           tmpElems[i].checked = true;
           break;
          }
         }
        </script>
       </TD>
      </TR>
     <!-- end custom code -->
     </TABLE>
    </TD>
   </TR>
<%
break;
case "URL":
%>
 <!-- URL -->
 <TR>
```

The entire `case` section has been added. Again, you can copy a different node and modify it until the desired results have been achieved. The pieces that will be detailed further are bold. The rest is pretty straight-forward.

```
<%
idALookup.DefaultValue = strDefault;
idALookup.Style = strALCustomSettings;
%>
<uc1:AuthorLookup name="ALookup" id="idALookup"
       runat="server"></uc1:AuthorLookup>
```

The user control, for which the code was introduced earlier, is where our custom functionality originates. Here a couple pieces of information are passed to the control. `strDefault` has already been managed for us by existing code on the page. `strALCustomSettings` represents the custom settings that need to be passed to the control. This is too important to just let slip by—understand that whatever custom functionality your control can provide can be passed in this manner. Each option doesn't have to be defined explicitly. The raw data from whatever state management system you come up with can be passed straight through to the user control. The user control is then responsible for referencing your state management system and render accordingly. This concept is intentionally left simple. The complexity should only be driven by the business problems, and the solution should be kept as simple as possible.

That's it for FLDNEW.ASPX—you should now be able to view this page in your browser and create a new property of type author lookup. Now onto FLDEDIT.ASPX, but first let's take a look at some things we'll need.

FLDNEW.ASPX and FLDEDIT.ASPX are just about identical. FLDEDIT.ASPX is a little more complicated than FLDNEW.ASPX simply because FLDEDIT.ASPX must manage existing state. We decided earlier that whenever we come across a text field, we need to look in the `Format` property to see whether it is one of our custom types. To accomplish this, we need to introduce two foreign elements into the mix—`SPCustomField` and FLDTYPESCUSTOM.XML. Neither exists natively in SharePoint.

FLDTYPESCUSTOM.XML

FLDTYPES.XML is considered shipping code, and it shouldn't be modified if you hope to survive a service pack update or hot fix. The neat thing about FLDTYPES.XML is that it contains the definition for all properties. It's nice to understand what goes on in this file, just so that it's easier to figure out solutions to other problems. What must be done in our case is to identify a custom field and what type it is. Following the same model that Microsoft uses, we too will use an XML document to store our custom types. So it only makes sense to create a file called FLDTYPESCUSTOM.XML. This is nothing more than a copy of FLD-TYPES.XML (C:\Program Files\Common Files\Microsoft Shared\web server extensions\60\TEMPLATE\1033\XML) with many things removed. The only nodes we keep are MetaData and the data\rows\row model. The only reason to keep the MetaData element is in case some time in the future you would rather work with the rendering patterns in the same way Microsoft does.

Listing 4.15   FLDTYPESCUSTOM.XML

```
<List>
 <MetaData>
  <Fields>
   <Field Type="Text" Name="TypeName" DisplayName="TypeName" />
   <Field Type="Text" Name="InternalType" DisplayName="InternalType" />
   <Field Type="Text" Name="Sortable" DisplayName="Sortable" />
   <Field Type="Text" Name="Filterable" DisplayName="Filterable" />
   <Field Type="Text" Name="SQLType" DisplayName="SQLType" />
   <Field Type="Text" Name="SQLType2" DisplayName="SQLType2" />
   <RenderPattern Type="Note" Tall="TRUE" Name="HeaderPattern"
     DisplayName="HeaderPattern" />
   <RenderPattern Type="Note" Tall="TRUE" Name="DisplayPattern"
     DisplayName="DisplayPattern" />
   <RenderPattern Type="Note" Tall="TRUE" Name="EditPattern"
     DisplayName="EditPattern" />
   <RenderPattern Type="Note" Tall="TRUE" Name="NewPattern"
     DisplayName="NewPattern" />
   <RenderPattern Type="Note" Tall="TRUE"
     Name="PreviewDisplayPattern"
     DisplayName="PreviewDisplayPattern" />
   <RenderPattern Type="Note" Tall="TRUE" Name="PreviewEditPattern"
     DisplayName="PreviewEditPattern" />
   <RenderPattern Type="Note" Tall="TRUE" Name="PreviewNewPattern"
     DisplayName="PreviewNewPattern" />
   <RenderPattern Type="Note" Tall="TRUE" Name="HeaderBidiPattern"
     DisplayName="HeaderBidiPattern" />
```

```
    <RenderPattern Type="Note" Tall="TRUE" Name="DisplayBidiPattern"
      DisplayName="DisplayBidiPattern" />
    <RenderPattern Type="Note" Tall="TRUE" Name="EditBidiPattern"
      DisplayName="EditBidiPattern" />
    <RenderPattern Type="Note" Tall="TRUE" Name="NewBidiPattern"
      DisplayName="NewBidiPattern" />
   </Fields>
  </MetaData>
  <Data>
   <Rows>
    <Row>
     <Field Name="TypeName" DisplayName="TypeName">AuthorLookup
     ➥ </Field>
    </Row>
   </Rows>
  </Data>
 </List>
```

For each custom field, simply add another `<Row/>` element.

SPFieldCustom

Every other property type in SharePoint is represented by a class. We need, at minimum, a helper class to identify whether or not the field is custom and to gather information about it. The assembly is designed to run at C:\Program Files\Common Files\Microsoft Shared\web server extensions\60\TEMPLATE\LAYOUTS\BIN.

Listing 4.16   `SPCustomField` Helper Class

```
using System;
using System.Xml;
using System.Xml.XPath;
using Microsoft.SharePoint;

namespace SharePointBook
{
 public class SPCustomField
 {
  public SPCustomField() { }
```

```
public bool isCustomField(SPField spField)
{
 string lcid = spField.ParentList.ParentWeb.Locale.LCID.
➥ ToString();
 string strPath = System.Reflection.Assembly.
➥ GetExecutingAssembly().CodeBase;
 int idxMyString = strPath.IndexOf("layouts");
 strPath = strPath.Remove(idxMyString, strPath.Length-idxMyString);
 strPath = strPath + lcid + "/XML/FLDTYPESCUSTOM.xml";
 XmlDocument xmlDocument = new XmlDocument();
 xmlDocument.Load(strPath);
 string strXPath = "//Data/Rows/Row/Field[@Name='TypeName'][. = '"
  + GetAttributeValue(spField, "Format") +"']";
 XmlNode xmlNode = xmlDocument.SelectSingleNode(strXPath);

 return (xmlNode != null);
}

public string GetAttributeValue(SPField spField, string attribute)
{
 string strDocument = spField.SchemaXml;
 string strResult = "";
 XmlDocument xmlDocument = new XmlDocument();
 xmlDocument.LoadXml(strDocument);
 XmlNode xmlNode = xmlDocument.SelectSingleNode
➥ ("//Field[@DisplayName='"
    + spField.Title + "']");
 XmlAttribute xmlAttribute = xmlNode.Attributes[attribute];
 if (xmlAttribute != null){
  strResult = xmlAttribute.Value;
 }
 return strResult;
}

public string GetCustomSetting(SPField spField, string name) {
   string strDocument = spField.SchemaXml;
   string strResult = "";
   XmlDocument xmlDocument = new XmlDocument();
   xmlDocument.LoadXml(strDocument);
   XmlNode xmlNode = xmlDocument.SelectSingleNode
➥ ("//CustomSettings/" + name);
   if (xmlNode !=null){
    strResult = xmlNode.InnerText;
   }
```

```
      return strResult;
  }
 }
}
```

As you can plainly see, no error handling appears in this code; it was written just to explain these points and was kept as simple as possible. There are three methods in this class. The isCustomField takes in an SPField object and determines whether it's a custom type by looking for the Format value in our FLDTYPESCUSTOM.XML file. The GetAttributeValue is probably misleading because it only gets the attributes on the field node, not the children. Finally, we have the GetCustomSettings method, which returns the inner text of a child node of the CustomSettings node.

Your customization needs will drive your storage and retrieval models. This example assumes that everything will be stored in child nodes. It might, however, turn out that child nodes with attributes are required.

Now that we have a way to determine which fields are custom and which are not, we can dig into FLDEDIT.ASPX.

FLDEDIT.ASPX

The fundamental difference between FLDEDIT.ASPX and FLD-NEW.ASPX is that FLDEDIT.ASPX must entertain a preexisting condition. It's a minor difference, and the modifications are generally the same, though some additional code is required for FLDEDIT.ASPX. Instead of trying to compare and contrast the two files, we'll begin from the top on FLDEDIT.ASPX just as we did with FLDNEW.ASPX.

First, we need to register our user control at the top of the page.

Listing 4.17   FldEdit.aspx Snippet

```
<!-- _lcid="1033" _version="11.0.5510" _dal="1" -->
<!-- _LocalBinding -->
<%@ Page language="C#"  ... code removed to save space
<!-- custom Code-->
<%@ Register TagPrefix="uc1" TagName="AuthorLookup"
➥ Src="AuthorLookup.ascx" %>
<!-- end custom code -->
<%
    String strType = "";
```

Near the top of the page, we need to declare a global variable that will represent our SPCustomField class.

Listing 4.18 FldEdit.aspx Snippet

```
<%
//Custom Code
SharePointBook.SPCustomField spCustomField = new
➡ SharePointBook.SPCustomField();
//End Custom Code
SPListCollection spLists = spWeb.Lists;
SPList spList = spLists.GetList(new Guid(Request.QueryString.
➡ GetValues("List")[0]), true);
%>
```

The spCustomField object will be used later to determine whether a text field is actually a custom field and to get the custom type and custom settings. Next, strALCustomSettings needs to be declared to keep track of the custom settings that the user requests.

Listing 4.19 FldEdit.aspx Snippet

```
String strLookupList = "";
String strLookupField = "";
String strShowPresence = "";
// custom code
string strALCustomSettings = "";
//end custom code
String strDisplaySize = "";
String strDisplayNameParam = "";
int     iCurrencyLCID = spWeb.CurrencyLocaleID;
```

strALCustomSettings will ultimately be used to store the custom settings on the server side so that they can be used by the user control. The next modification actually populates that value along with the default value. The assumption is that the query string information is most current. The query string is populated from a post back from UpdatePage().

Listing 4.20   FldEdit.aspx Snippet

```
if ( Request.Url.ToString().IndexOf("LookupFieldParam") != -1 )
{strLookupField  =  Request.QueryString.GetValues
➥ ("LookupFieldParam")[0]; }
if ( Request.Url.ToString().IndexOf("ShowPresence") != -1 )
{strShowPresence  =  Request.QueryString.GetValues
➥ ("ShowPresence")[0]; }
//Custom Code
if ( Request.Url.ToString().IndexOf("Default") != -1 )
{strDefault   =  Request.QueryString.GetValues("Default")[0] ; }
else{strDefault = spField.DefaultValue;}
if ( Request.Url.ToString().IndexOf("AuthorLookupParam") != -1 )
{strALCustomSettings   =  Request.QueryString.GetValues
➥ ("AuthorLookupParam")[0] ; }
else{strALCustomSettings = spCustomField.GetCustomSetting(spField,
➥ "Style");}
//end custom code

if (strFieldType == "")
{
 strFieldType = "Text";
}

if (spField.TypeAsString == strFieldType ||
 (spField.Type == SPFieldType.MultiChoice && strFieldType ==
➥ "Choice"))
{

 strDefaultFormula= spField.DefaultFormula;
 if (strDefaultFormula == null ||
  strDefaultFormula == String.Empty)
 {
  //Custom Code
  if (strFieldTypeParam == ""){
   strDefault = spField.DefaultValue;
  }
  //End Custom Code
 }
 switch(spField.Type)
 {
  case SPFieldType.Text:
  {
```

```
//Custom Code
if (spCustomField.isCustomField(spField))
{
 if (strFieldTypeParam == ""){
  strFieldType  = spCustomField.GetAttributeValue(spField,
  ➥ "Format");
 }
}
else
{
 //Existing code
 SPFieldText field = (SPFieldText)spField;
 iMaxLength = field.MaxLength;
 //End existing code
}
//End Custom Code
 break;
}
case SPFieldType.Calculated:
```

The goal of this long block is to set the default value and the custom settings value. If there is query string information, it should be used.

Next, we look at the `UpdatePage()` method, which causes the post back when the user selects a property type or modifies the configuration information.

Listing 4.21   FldEdit.aspx Snippet

```
function UpdatePage(typeVal) {
 var sArg = "&FieldTypeParam=";
 var sFieldNameArg = "&DisplayNameParam=";
 var sLookup = "Lookup";
 // Custom Code
 var sAuthorLookup = "AuthorLookup";
 // end custom code
 var sUser = "User";
 var sLLArg = "&LookupListParam=";
 var sLLVal = "";
 //Custom Code
 var sALArg = "&AuthorLookupParam=";
 var sALVal = "";
```

```
var sALDArg = "&Default=";
var sALDVal = "";

//end custom code
var sPresArg = "&ShowPresence=";
var sPresVal = "";
var sURL = window.location + "";
var nameval = escapeProperly(document.frmFieldData.DisplayName.
➥ value);
var sDescriptionArg = "&DescriptionParam=";
var descval = escapeProperly(document.frmFieldData.Description.
➥ value);
var dwArgPos = sURL.indexOf(sArg);
if (dwArgPos!=-1) {
 sURL = sURL.substr(0,dwArgPos);
}
if (typeVal == sLookup) {
 sLLVal = GetLookupList();
 if (sLLVal.length != 0)
  sLLVal = sLLArg + sLLVal;
}
//Custom Code
if (typeVal == sAuthorLookup) {
 var tmpElems = document.getElementsByName("CustStyle");
 if (tmpElems != "undefined") {
  for(var i=0;i<tmpElems.length;i++) {
   if (tmpElems[i].checked==true) {
    sALVal = sALArg + tmpElems[i].value;
   }
  }
 }
 var tmpElem = document.getElementById("idDefault");
 if (tmpElem != null){
  sALDVal = sALDArg + document.getElementById("idDefault").value
 }
}
//End Custom Code
if ((typeVal == sUser) || (typeVal == sLookup)) {
 sPresVal = GetShowPresence();
 if (sPresVal.length != 0)
  sPresVal = sPresArg + sPresVal;
}
```

```
var sNewUrl = sURL + sArg + typeVal + sFieldNameArg + nameval +
➥ sDescriptionArg + descval
  + sLLVal + sPresVal + sALVal + sALDVal;
if (sNewUrl.length > 2040)
  document.location.replace(sURL + sArg + typeVal + sLLVal   + sALVal
➥ + sALDVal);
else
  document.location.replace(sNewUrl);
}
```

First, a variable is declared and set to `AuthorLookup`. This variable will be used later to determine what `Type` of property we are dealing with. Next, several variables are initialized to manage the query string information.

Right now there is only one parameter for the custom settings. Given a particular problem, it might be acceptable to have more than one or to keep all values in one delimited string. XML documents sound nice, but they take up a lot of space on the precious query string. Other state management techniques include viewstate, cookies, and session variables to name a few.

A quick note about session variables—first, they must be turned on. Second, all unghosted pages in the site are forced to participate in the session. Normally, if an ASP.NET page doesn't use a session variable, it doesn't have to participate in the session. If there are several unghosted pages on your site, this could cause a huge performance hit. Unghosted pages are those that are stored in the database. When a page is modified in FrontPage 2003 and saved, it is saved to the database and becomes unghosted. It is then processed through the SafeMode parser, which behaves differently in SharePoint than in normal ASP.NET.

The next section of code determines what variables are checked. If this were a little more complicated, or even in this case, it could be argued that we should break out this code or create a new method handler instead of using the already existing one. There are some benefits to this idea, namely that the state management would be easier to deal with and much cleaner.

When looking at `UpdatePage()`, also take a look at `UpdateDate-Field()` and how it works. This should spark some ideas and help you to come up with a solution that works best for the business problem at hand.

After all the variables are set, they are appended and ultimately sent to the location property for the browser.

Just as before, at the last moment we want to set the `Type` to `Text` and set the `Format` to `AuthorLookup`.

Listing 4.22 FldEdit.aspx Snippet

```
//Custom Code
 if (Type == "AuthorLookup")
 {
  Type = "Text";
  Format = "AuthorLookup";
 }
 //End Custom Code
 var Schema = ('<Field ' +
  (Name       ? 'Name="'    + SimpleHTMLEncode(Name)      + '" ' :
➡ '') +
  (FromBaseType ? 'FromBaseType="'+ SimpleHTMLEncode(FromBaseType) +
➡ '" ' : '') +
```

This section of code sets the field schema. The field schema is XML that describes a property in the document library. The following code sets the default value and the custom settings. Take a close look at the custom settings.

Listing 4.23 FldEdit.aspx Snippet

```
}else if(Default)
 {
  Schema += '<Default>' + SimpleHTMLEncode(Default) + '</Default>';
 }
 //Custom Code
 if (Type == "Text"  && Format == "AuthorLookup")
 {
  Schema += '<CustomSettings><Style><%=strALCustomSettings%></Style>
➡ </CustomSettings>';
 }
 //End Custom Code
 if (Type == "Calculated")
 {
  if (!CheckForIllegals(Formula))
```

```
    return false;
if (Formula.charAt(0) != '=')
{
    Formula = "="+Formula;
}
Schema += '<Formula>' + SimpleHTMLEncode(Formula) +'</Formula>';
}
```

The custom settings are a simple bit of XML. Given the situation, this section could become much more complex. The custom settings section is used to store the customized information about your user control.

The user interface is somewhat different from FLDNEW.ASPX. Some types can be converted to others because of the way the data is stored. We have built the custom properties so that they will be interchangeable with anything that a Text type is interchangeable with.

Listing 4.24   FldEdit.aspx Snippet

```
if (spField.Type == SPFieldType.Number ||
  spField.Type == SPFieldType.Currency ||
  spField.Type == SPFieldType.Boolean)
{
%>
 <TR>
  <TD align="center" nowrap class="ms-authoringcontrols">
  <% if ( strFieldType == "Boolean" ) { %> ... Code removed to save
➥ space
  </TD>
  <TD class="ms-authoringcontrols" ... Code removed to save space
...</TD>
 </TR>
<%
}
//Custom Code
if (spField.Type == SPFieldType.Text ||
  spField.Type == SPFieldType.Choice ||
  spField.Type == SPFieldType.Note ||
  spField.Type == SPFieldType.MultiChoice ||
  spField.Type == SPFieldType.DateTime)
{
%>
```

```
<TR>
 <TD align="center" nowrap class="ms-authoringcontrols">
 <% if ( strFieldType == "AuthorLookup" ) { %> <INPUT
➡ onClick="UpdatePage('AuthorLookup')" type="radio"
➡ value="AuthorLookup" id=onetidTypeCalculated name="Type" title=
➡ "The type of information in this column is : Author Lookup"
➡ CHECKED> <% ; } else { %> <INPUT onClick="UpdatePage
➡ ('AuthorLookup')" type="radio" value="AuthorLookup"
➡ id=onetidTypeAuthorLookup name="Type" title="The type of
➡ information in this column is : Author Lookup" > <% ; } %>
 </TD>
 <TD  class="ms-authoringcontrols" id="L_onetidTypeAuthorLookup">
➡ <LABEL FOR="onetidTypeAuthorLookup">Author Lookup<!-- -->
➡ </LABEL></TD>
 </TR>
<%
}//End Custom Code
%>
 <TR>
  <TD align="center" nowrap class="ms-authoringcontrols"></TD>
  <TD  class="ms-authoringcontrols" ID=align101></TD>
 </TR>
</TABLE>
```

If you look at the preceding snippet of code in context, you can see how the various properties are rendered. The code in bold is our author lookup radio button. When creating a new custom property type, it is easiest just to copy and paste a new row from an existing row. Modify the new section of code to handle your property type.

Listing 4.25   FldEdit.aspx Snippet

```
<%
break;
//Custom Code
case "AuthorLookup":
%>
 <!-- AuthorLookup -->
 <TR>
  <TD colspan=2></TD>
  <TD class="ms-authoringcontrols" width=10> </TD>
```

```
<TD class="ms-authoringcontrols"
➡ id=onetidTypeDefaultAuthorLookupValue>
➡ <label for="idDefault">Default value</label>:
➡ <FONT size=3> </FONT><BR>
  <TABLE border=0 cellspacing=1>
   <TR>
    <TD class="ms-authoringcontrols">
     <input type=hidden name="Default" id="idDefault"
     ➡ value=<%SPEncode.WriteHtmlEncodeWithQuote(Response,
     ➡ strDefault, '"');%>>
     <%
     idALookup.DefaultValue = strDefault;
     idALookup.Style = strALCustomSettings;
     %>
     <uc1:AuthorLookup name="ALookup" id="idALookup" runat="server"/>
    </TD>
   </TR>
   <!-- custom code -->
   <TR>
    <TD class="ms-authoringcontrols">
     <label for="idDefault">Style:</label><BR>
     <input type="radio" name="CustStyle" value="normal"
     ➡ id="idCustStyleNormal" onclick="UpdatePage('AuthorLookup')"
     ➡ checked><label for="idCustStyleNormal">Normal</label>
     ➡ </input><BR>
     <input type="radio" name="CustStyle" value="red"
     ➡ id="idCustStyleRed" onclick="UpdatePage('AuthorLookup')">
     ➡ <label for="idCustStyleRed">Red</label></input>
     <script>
      tmpElems = document.getElementsByName("CustStyle")
      for(var i=0;i<tmpElems.length;i++) {
       if (tmpElems[i].value=="<%=strALCustomSettings%>") {
        tmpElems[i].checked = true;
        break;
       }
      }
     </script>
    </TD>
   </TR>
   <!-- end custom code -->
  </TABLE>
 </TD>
</TR>
```

```
<%
break;
//end custom code
case "URL":
%>
 <!-- URL -->
 <TR>
  <TD colspan=2></TD>
```

An entire new `case` was added to handle the options for `AuthorLookup` type. The items in bold are what's really different between other rows. As a developer, you can gain a lot of flexibility from this technique. User controls can be added as well as plain HTML elements. Think of this as a normal web part page.

Now the user can edit a field that he or she has previously created.

LISTEDIT.ASPX

Revisiting LISTEDIT.ASPX, we can see that there is a column of type `Text`, which should be the Author Lookup. The `SPCustomField` class `GetAttributeValue` method can be used to fix this problem. First, declare the object at the top of the page.

Listing 4.26   Listedit.aspx Snippet

```
SharePointBook.SPCustomField spCustomField = new
➡ SharePointBook.SPCustomField();
string[] strLists = Request.QueryString.GetValues("List");
```

The next step is to find out what kind of custom property this is; remember that there can be more than one.

Listing 4.27   Listedit.aspx Snippet

```
switch (spField.Type)
{
 case SPFieldType.Text:
  //Custom Code
  switch (spCustomField.GetAttributeValue(spField,"Format"))
```

```
{
  case "AuthorLookup":
%>
  <TD class=ms-propertysheet>Author Lookup</TD>
<%
  break;
  default:
%>
  <TD class=ms-propertysheet>Single line of text</TD>
<%
  break;
  }
  //End Custom Code
break;
case SPFieldType.Note:
```

This will fix the display problems and indicate to the user the correct property type. Even though it's really a text type, we can use the Format attribute to override the single line of text functionality and present something else.

Modifying the FLDNEW.ASPX, FLDEDIT.ASPX, and LIST-EDIT.ASPX files and adding a few support features is all that is needed to create and maintain a custom property type. But that doesn't do much good if you can't use it. Incorporating a custom property when a user uploads or modifies a document through the web browser or Microsoft Word is the next step in this process.

Uploading and Modifying a Document in the Web Interface and in Microsoft Word

When a user modifies properties through the web, he or she will see an interface that looks like Figure 4.11.

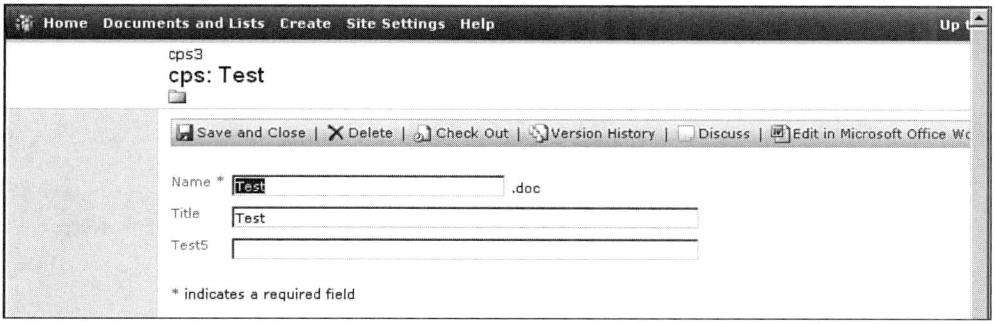

Figure 4.11 Modifying properties of a document.

"Test5" is the author lookup field and is represented as a single line of text. To understand how to modify this field, it's important to understand how the fields are rendered.

How Fields Are Rendered

Before taking the jump to entering or modifying properties, we need to take a closer look at how the HTML is rendered on the page. Viewing the HTML source and searching for one of your fields will reveal a script block. I have a field called "test5", and one of my script blocks looks like this: `<SCRIPT>fld = new TextField(frm,"test5","test5","test");` `fld.cchMaxLength = "255";fld.cchDisplaySize = "";fld.IMEM-` `ode="";fld.BuildUI();</SCRIPT>`. This script block is rendered by JavaScript on the client. Remember the OWS.JS file? One of its jobs is to render the properties in HTML. To go over the script block, there is a new field that is created, and the length and display size are set. IMEMode (Input Method Editor) enables users to enter and edit foreign character sets such as Chinese, French, or Korean characters. And finally, BuildUI puts it all together and adds it to a form object. The code in the OWS.JS is JavaScript and heavily uses the object-oriented features of the language. For the more adventurous, meandering through the OWS.JS file and understanding how it works would be time well spent. Keep in mind, though, that the content of the OWS.JS file should never be tampered with. The important thing to understand is that the fields are rendered on the client.

Code could be added to the bottom of the page to render the custom properties, and then the fields would be out of order. So code could be written that would render all the properties appropriately. But that's a lot of work, and it would have to be added to the EDITFORM.ASPX and UPLOAD.ASPX files, and editing properties in Word would still render the properties as single line of text properties.

Because we have the `CustomJSUrl` feature, we can add our own JavaScript file. Find the custom elements and replace them with our custom functionality. A very simple example like the one demonstrated here could put the select box right inline with the properties. Because custom fields are very complicated, we'll provide a button to open a modal window. Upon closing the window, we will set a display and internal value. The display value ensures the use of a proper selection and will not be stored. The internal value represents a key from a third-party system. In this case, it's the `pubs` database. In the real world, this information can be a key from any number of places such as PeopleSoft, Oracle Financials, or a homegrown application. We are shooting for a screen that looks like Figure 4.12.

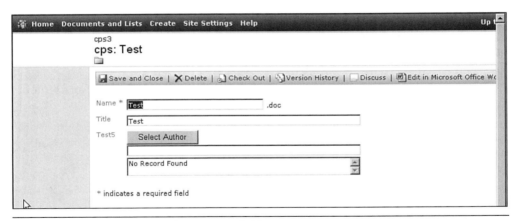

Figure 4.12   Upload/Edit with custom field.

When the user clicks Select Author, a modal dialog window opens as in Figure 4.13.

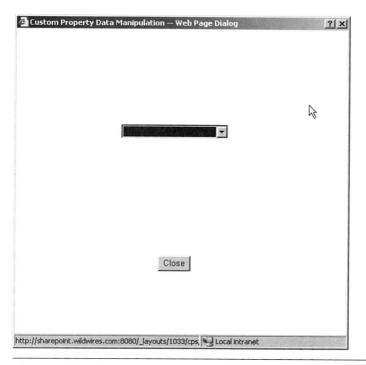

Figure 4.13   Custom property data manipulation page.

Though it is fairly plain, the point still sings out. There is an element that will facilitate our custom property. This example has been of just one simple HTML element. This could be an entire worksheet or a way to search on several pieces of information to find a particular customer number. After the user selects an author and closes the window, the information is passed back to the parent window, and the fields are populated accordingly (see Figure 4.14). Notice there is no cancel button in the modal window (refer to Figure 4.13). In a real application, you should probably have one. To keep things simple, the cancel button has been left out.

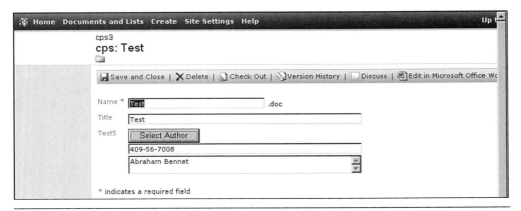

Figure 4.14   Results populated for user convenience.

In Figure 4.14, just below the Select Author button is the ID for Abraham Bennet. User interfaces are nice when they all behave the same way. This technique will work the same for the web and for Word.

How is all this done? JavaScript. Make friends with JavaScript if you haven't already. Microsoft has leveraged as much object-oriented programming as JavaScript has to offer. There is a particular problem with the way JavaScript files are included—let's see how to overcome this next peculiarity.

JavaScript Loader

Loading a custom JavaScript block is a nice feature. The file referenced in CustomJSUrl is loaded for any page that can benefit from custom JavaScript. Remember, OWS.JS is shipping code and cannot be modified. This custom JavaScript enables developers to add their own functionality. However, something terrible happens when the JavaScript file is included—context is lost for the included file. Earlier we added an attribute to the project node:

```
CustomJSUrl="/_layouts/[%=System.Threading.Thread.CurrentThread.
➥ CurrentUICulture.LCID%]/CPS/CustomJSLoader.aspx"
```

If we take out the preceding slash from the address, then the context is fine for the web and for Word because the JavaScript isn't included at all. Interestingly enough, JavaScript does have access to the correct context. The CUSTOMJSLOADER.ASPX file gets the context from JavaScript and passes on that information in the form of a parameter on a URL.

Listing 4.28   CustomJSLoader.aspx Snippet

```
<%@ Page language="C#"      %>
<%@ Register Tagprefix="SharePoint"
➥ Namespace="Microsoft.SharePoint.WebControls"
➥ Assembly="Microsoft.SharePoint, Version=11.0.0.0, Culture=neutral,
➥ PublicKeyToken=71e9bce111e9429c" %>
<%@ Register Tagprefix="Utilities"
➥ Namespace="Microsoft.SharePoint.Utilities"
➥ Assembly="Microsoft.SharePoint, Version=11.0.0.0, Culture=neutral,
➥ PublicKeyToken=71e9bce111e9429c" %>
<%@ Import Namespace="Microsoft.SharePoint" %>
<%@ Register Tagprefix="WebPartPages"
➥ Namespace="Microsoft.SharePoint.WebPartPages"
➥ Assembly="Microsoft.SharePoint, Version=11.0.0.0, Culture=neutral,
➥ PublicKeyToken=71e9bce111e9429c" %>
for (i=0;document.getElementsByTagName('script').length-1>=i;i++){
 if (document.getElementsByTagName('SCRIPT')[i].src == '<%=
➥ Request.ServerVariables["PATH_INFO"]%>'){
  document.getElementsByTagName('SCRIPT')[i].src =
➥ '/_layouts/<%=System.Threading.Thread.CurrentThread.
➥ CurrentUICulture.LCID%>/CPS/Custom_JS.aspx?context=' +
➥ escape(unescape(window.location));
       }
}
```

PATH_INFO contains the path and page name of the page we are on. By looping through all the SCRIPT tags, we can find the SCRIPT block whose src is the same as PATH_INFO. This will yield the index of the script block that loaded CUSTOMJSLOADER.ASPX in the first place. After we find the index of the SCRIPT block, we will replace the source with our URL and parameter information that point to a JavaScript file that does the heavy lifting.

Unescaping and escaping can seem a little silly at first, but it is necessary. Parameter information in the URL is already escaped. If there wasn't an unescape first, then we would be escaping already escaped code, which turns out to be a mess.

Another point to note is that it seems like this code could be placed directly into the CustomJSUrl attribute. The folks at Microsoft realized that the CustomJSUrl attribute is meant for a URL, so they designed the system so that this attribute is URL-encoded when rendered. When the single quotes and double quotes become encoded, the JavaScript no longer functions properly.

The appendix includes a complete listing of the CUSTOM_JS.ASPX file that is used; for now, let's just jump right into the heart of it. The concept is to replace an existing HTML element through JavaScript. For this purpose, we will use the `outerHTML` property of the existing element.

Listing 4.29   Custom_JS.aspx Snippet

```
for(var i=0; i<=CustomFieldList.length-1; i++){
 if (CustomFieldList[i][1] == 'AuthorLookup'){
  tmpElem = document.getElementById(this.frm.stFieldPrefix +
➡ CustomFieldList[i][0]);
  if (tmpElem != null){
   var idDisp = "disp" + this.frm.stFieldPrefix +
➡ CustomFieldList[i][0];
   tmpElem.readOnly = true;
   tmpElem.onfocus = "document.getElementById('btn" + tmpElem.name +
➡ "').focus();document.getElementById('btn" + tmpElem.name +
➡ "').select();";
   strButton = "<INPUT tabindex= \"" + tmpElem.tabIndex + "\"
➡ id=\"btn" + tmpElem.name + "\" name=\"btn" + tmpElem.name + "\"
➡ TYPE=\"BUTTON\" VALUE=\"Select Author\" ONCLICK=\"showModal('" +
➡ tmpElem.name + "','" + CustomFieldList[i][0] + "');\">";
   strDisplay = "<textarea readonly class= \"" + tmpElem.className +
➡ "\"id=\"" + idDisp + "\" name=\"" + idDisp + "\"></textarea>";
   tmpElem.outerHTML = strButton + '<BR>' + tmpElem.outerHTML +
➡ '<BR>' + strDisplay;
  }
 }
}
```

A two-dimensional array, which we'll explore how to define in just a few pages, contains the internal name of the field and the field type. For each field type, there would be a separate `if` block. For the purposes of our example, we just have the one custom type, `AuthorLookup`.

Notice `this.frm.stFieldPrefix`. `frm` is a form object that we can use for our purposes and is actually defined in OWS.JS. `stFieldPrefix` is a prefix that is a constant and is prepended to each HTML element. `tmpElem` then becomes the HTML element in question. Whatever you can do in HTML, you can accomplish here. For example, the user should be able to get focus on the field. This might be a desired effect or not. If the business requires it, the interface could be changed quite radically. We went for a generic solution to solve most business problems, and the button and modal window is a fairly versatile technique. The point is that a fairly creative solution can be created. Finally, we set the `outerHTML` of the `tmpElem` with new and old HTML. This is important because the form validation will use this HTML later on, which brings up another reason why it's better to use this technique rather than a new web part. By leveraging all the existing functionality of the page, we don't have to worry about double clicks, form validation, or anything that is acquired for free from the page. Now let's look at where the `Custom-FieldList` variable comes from.

The `CustomFieldList` is actually created from the server side and is rendered as a JavaScript array. This is one of the reasons why the context is so important. Because of the way the SharePoint object model works, it's important to know the site, the web, and the list in which you are interested. Suffice it to say that the `URL` and `list` variables are created early on, and we won't end this discussion without covering them in detail. Just know that the `URL` and `list` variables contain the necessary information and enable the code to execute as designed.

Listing 4.30   Custom_JS.aspx Snippet

```
function getCustomFieldList(){
 <%
 if (loadCPS){
 try{
  SharePointBook.SPCustomField spCustomField = new SharePointBook.
➥ SPCustomField();
  int count = 0;
  string strOutput = "";

  SPSite siteCollection = new SPSite(url);
  SPWeb spWeb = siteCollection.OpenWeb();
  SPList spList = spWeb.Lists[list];
  SPFieldCollection spFields = spList.Fields;
   foreach (SPField f in spFields) {
    if (f.Type.ToString() == "Text"){
     if(spCustomField.isCustomField(f)){
      strOutput += "CustomFields [" + count + "] = new Array(2);";
```

```
    strOutput += "CustomFields [" + count + "][0] = '" +
    ➥ f.InternalName + "';";
    strOutput += "CustomFields [" + count + "][1] = '" +
    ➥ spCustomField.GetAttributeValue(f,"Format") + "';";
    count++;
   }
  }
 }
 if (strOutput !=""){
  strOutput = "CustomFields = new Array(" + count + ");" +
  ➥ strOutput;
  strOutput += "return CustomFields;";
 }
 else{
  strOutput = "return null;";
 }
 Response.Write (strOutput);
 }
 catch (Exception e){
  Response.Write ("alert('!"+e.Message+"');");
 }
}
%>
return null;
}
```

One of the first things we do is to get the siteCollection, open the web and the list, and fetch the list of fields from the fields collection. We iterate through the list of fields, constructing a string that will be rendered to the client. There is some additional logic shown that will properly render the JavaScript code, but the important thing to realize is that the iteration through the fields collection ultimately creates a JavaScript array. The next thing to examine is the url and list variable initialization.

If the correct context were available, we wouldn't need a loader facility. But because it's not, it creates an interesting problem to solve. The first thing we need to do is break out all the parameters that were once available in the query string.

Listing 4.31 Custom_JS.aspx Snippet

```
string myContext = Request.QueryString["Context"];
int idxQuery = myContext.IndexOf('?');
Hashtable hash = new Hashtable();
if (idxQuery>0) {
 for (int i=0;i<param.Length;i++){
  if (param[i].IndexOf('=')>0) {
   nameValue = param[i].Split('=');
   hash.Add(nameValue[0], nameValue[1]);
  }
 }
}
```

This code is a simple way to create a `hashtable` of name-value pairs so that we can simply use the parameters from the previous `url`.

It's pretty obvious from the web what the `url` is, but from Microsoft Word, nothing can be seen. Going to the IIS logs can help you solve a problem like this. There you can see the parameter information, the path info, and a myriad of other information. From there it is pretty easy to determine what Word was doing through the web. When the user attempts to save a file from Word to a `url`, Word will display a list of files at that `url`. After the user has chosen to save the file in that location, another modal dialog window appears with the list of properties. Both modal dialogs load `CustomJSUrl`. Looking at the information in IIS logs, it is easy to determine that Word passes the parameters `location` and `dialogview`. The `dialogview` that we are most interested in is "`Save-Form`". "`SaveForm`" causes the list of properties to show.

Listing 4.32 Custom_JS.aspx Snippet

```
dialogview = hash.ContainsKey("dialogview") ? hash["dialogview"].
➥ ToString() : "";
location = hash.ContainsKey("location") ? hash["location"].
➥ ToString() : "" ;

if (dialogview == "SaveForm"){
 location = location.Remove(location.ToLower().IndexOf("/"),
➥ location.Length -location.ToLower().IndexOf("/"));
 url = myContext.Remove(myContext.ToLower().LastIndexOf
```

```
➡ ("/_vti_bin/owssvr.dll"), myContext.Length - myContext.ToLower().
➡ LastIndexOf
➡ ("/_vti_bin/owssvr.dll")) + "/" + location;
list = location;
 loadCPS = true;
}

if (myContext.ToLower().IndexOf("/forms/editform.aspx") > 0){
 url = myContext.Remove(myContext.ToLower().LastIndexOf
➡ ("/forms/editform.aspx"), myContext.Length -
➡ myContext.ToLower().LastIndexOf("/forms/editform.aspx") );
 list = url.Substring(url.LastIndexOf('/') + 1).ToString();
 loadCPS = true;
}

if (myContext.ToLower().IndexOf("/forms/upload.aspx") > 0){
 url = myContext.Remove(myContext.ToLower().LastIndexOf
➡ ("/forms/upload.aspx"), myContext.Length - myContext.ToLower().
➡ LastIndexOf("/forms/upload.aspx"));
 list = url.Substring(url.LastIndexOf('/') + 1).ToString();
 loadCPS = true;
}
```

All three `if` blocks are dedicated to setting the value for `url`, `list`, and `loadCPS`. As we alluded to before, `url` and `list` are variables that help reconstruct the context. The `loadCPS` variable is a Boolean that will be used to allow or disallow code from running. Because the script block is loaded on just about every page, it's important to run code only when it is necessary. The first `if` block is dedicated to Word activity. The last two are used in the web application. To ensure uniqueness, the Forms folder and the filename were included. Although this code could be consolidated, we've repeated it here for clarity.

The display value is not stored, so SharePoint doesn't have any way to give us that data. If it's needed, then it must be fetched from the client side. Remember, that's where all this rendering magic takes place—putting a JavaScript web service to good use by fetching the data as needed. Much documentation is available on the web about the subject; we'll only be covering what it takes to make this example clear.

Author Lookup Web Service Calls

There are several pieces to the puzzle when it comes to JavaScript web services. First, a `div` tag must be rendered with a behavior pointing to webservice.htc. This file can be downloaded from Microsoft.com and is advertised as unsupported. The webservice.htc is a substantial file and takes some time to load. When loaded, an event is fired and a handler called. That handler can begin to load the Web Service Definition Language (WSDL). When the WSDL is done loading, yet another handler is fired. At this point, everything is finally ready for web service calls. In this last handler, which we'll call `serviceAvailable()`, the web service requests that fetch the author's name can be fired. A final event handler to handle the result, `handleWebServiceResult()`, will populate the values. The following is a look at the code out of context. The entire CUSTOM_JS.ASPX file is in the appendix.

Listing 4.33   Custom_JS.aspx Snippet

```
var newText = document.createElement("<div onserviceavailable=
➥ \"serviceAvailable();\" onreadystatechange=\"doneloading();
➥ \" id=\"divWebServiceCaller\" style=\"behavior:url
➥ (<%=url%>/_layouts/1033/CPS/webservice.htc)\"></div>");
document.body.appendChild(newText);

function doneloading(){
 if (document.getElementById("divWebServiceCaller").
➥ readyState=="complete"){
  loadWebServices();
 }
}

function loadWebServices() {
 document.getElementById("divWebServiceCaller").useService
➥ ("http://<%=host%>/_vti_bin/getAuthor.asmx?wsdl","GetAuthor");
}

function serviceAvailable() {
 var CustomFieldList = getCustomFieldList();
 if (CustomFieldList != null){
  for(var i=0; i<=CustomFieldList.length-1; i++){
```

```
 tmpElem = document.getElementById(this.frm.stFieldPrefix +
➥ CustomFieldList[i][0]);
 if (tmpElem != null){
  if (CustomFieldList[i][1] == 'AuthorLookup'){
   var idDisp = "disp" + this.frm.stFieldPrefix +
   ➥ CustomFieldList[i][0];
   var idCall = document.getElementById("divWebServiceCaller").
   ➥ GetAuthor.callService(handleWebServiceResult, "ById",
   ➥ tmpElem.value);
   hash.add (idCall, document.getElementById(idDisp));
  }
 }
 }
}
}

function handleWebServiceResult(res) {
 if (!res.error) {
  var tmpElem = hash.get(res.id)
  tmpElem.value = res.value;
 }
 else {
  alert("Unsuccessful call. Error is " + res.errorDetail.string);
 }
}
```

When `serviceAvailable()` is finally called, the array of custom fields is
iterated through, just as before. For each iteration, the display field
object and `idCall` are added to a hash table. The `idCall` is a return
value from the web service call. This way, when a call back is made and
`handleWebServiceResult()` is called, there is an easy way to figure out
which call back is being answered. `res.id` is the same as the `callID` that
we received earlier. Simply by looking up the `callID` in the hash table,
we can set the value of the `tmpElem`, which is the `textarea` tag that displays the display value. What about that hash table? It's not very monu-
mental.

Listing 4.34   Custom_JS.aspx Snippet

```
function hashtable() {
 this.add = mAdd;
 this.get = mGet;
}

function mAdd(name, value) {
 this[name] = value;
}

function mGet(strKeyName) {
 return(this[strKeyName]);
}

var hash = new hashtable();
```

That's basically it. Because JavaScript is not strongly typed, anything can be stored as the value, including the HTML element object. The "Caller ID" is used as the key. The Caller ID is simply a consecutive auto number.

The rest is housekeeping, which is fundamentally everything. The code is listed in the appendix in its entirety. We've seen how to call a web service, but we haven't seen the web service itself.

GETAUTHOR.ASMX

GETAUTHOR.ASMX is the web service that is called from JavaScript to get the author's name. GETAUTHOR.ASMX is a gross representation of what that web service would look like. A call is made to our data services to get the name based on the ID passed in, and it returns the author's name.

Listing 4.35   GetAuthor.asmx

```
using System;
using System.Collections;
using System.ComponentModel;
using System.Data;
using System.Diagnostics;
```

```
using System.Web;
using System.Web.Services;
using SharePointBook;

namespace select
{
 public class getAuthor : System.Web.Services.WebService {
  public getAuthor() {
   InitializeComponent();
  }
  #region Component Designer generated code

  //Required by the Web Services Designer
  private IContainer components = null;

  private void InitializeComponent(){}
  protected override void Dispose( bool disposing ){
   if(disposing && components != null){
   components.Dispose();
   }
   base.Dispose(disposing);
  }
  #endregion

  [WebMethod]
  public string ById(string AuthorId){
   Authors myExample = new Authors();
   return myExample.GetAuthorByID(AuthorId);
  }
 }
}
```

It's easy to imagine all the different calls that might be made. But remember there's a performance hit for each web service call, even if it's only a burden for the client. On a properties page, it's not likely that you will have hundreds or even tens of custom properties that require a lookup that will use a web service; in all actuality, there will only be a few, so this burden is considered acceptable.

You might assume that a web service, which is a page with an .ASMX extension, would live in the Layouts folder. Not true. Web services are meant to be run from the ISAPI folder. Some changes can be made to the web.config file in the Layouts folder, but web services are meant to be run from the ISAPI folder, C:\Program Files\Common Files\Microsoft Shared\web server extensions\60\ISAPI, in SharePoint. You must make a special preparation before you can run the web service.

Running a Web Service in SharePoint

Typically, a web service will return the WSDL by simply adding ?WSDL to the end of the url. Extra steps are needed to run a web service because of the enhanced security model used by Windows SharePoint Service. The first thing you should do is to create static .WSDL and .DISCO files. Using the command prompt provided by Visual Studio, navigate the file system to where the web service is. In the command prompt, enter

```
Disco http://server_name:Port/path/GetAuthor.asmx
```

Two files will be created—GetAuthor.disco and GetAuthor.wsdl—and they both need editing. First, they both need to be converted to ASP.NET pages. Open GetAuthor.disco and replace

```
<?xml version="1.0" encoding="utf-8"?>
```

with

```
<%@ Page Language="C#" Inherits="System.Web.UI.Page"%> <%@ Assembly
➥ Name="Microsoft.SharePoint, Microsoft.SharePoint, Version=
➥ 11.0.0.0, Culture=neutral, PublicKeyToken=71e9bce111e9429c" %>
➥ <%@ Import Namespace="Microsoft.SharePoint.Utilities" %> <%@
➥ Import Namespace="Microsoft.SharePoint" %>
<% Response.ContentType = "text/xml"; %>
```

Replace this line

```
<contractRef ref="http://server_name:Port/Path/GetAuthor.asmx?wsdl"
➥ docRef="http://server_name:New_Port/Project_Name/Service1.asmx"
➥ xmlns="http://schemas.xmlsoap.org/disco/scl/" />
```

with

```
<contractRef ref=<% SPEncode.WriteHtmlEncodeWithQuote(Response,
➥ SPWeb.OriginalBaseUrl(Request)
 + "?wsdl", '"'); %> docRef=<% SPEncode.WriteHtmlEncodeWithQuote
➥ (Response,
 SPWeb.OriginalBaseUrl(Request), '"'); %> xmlns="http://schemas.
➥ xmlsoap.org/disco/scl/" />
```

Finally, replace

```
<soap address="http://server_name: Port/Path/GetAuthor.asmx"
➥ xmlns:q1="http://tempuri.org/" binding="q1:Service1Soap"
➥ xmlns="http://schemas.xmlsoap.org/disco/soap/" />
```

with

```
<soap address=<% SPEncode.WriteHtmlEncodeWithQuote(Response,
➥ SPWeb.OriginalBaseUrl(Request), '"'); %> xmlns:q1=
➥ "http://tempuri.org/" binding="q1:Service1Soap" xmlns=
➥ "http://schemas.xmlsoap.org/disco/soap/" />
```

And save the file as *GetAuthor*Disco.aspx, where GetAuthor is the name of your web service. Next, open GetAuthor.wsdl and replace

```
<?xml version="1.0" encoding="utf-8"?>
```

with

```
<%@ Page Language="C#" Inherits="System.Web.UI.Page"%> <%@ Assembly
➥ Name="Microsoft.SharePoint, Microsoft.SharePoint, Version=
➥ 11.0.0.0, Culture=neutral, PublicKeyToken=71e9bce111e9429c" %>
➥ <%@ Import Namespace="Microsoft.SharePoint.Utilities" %> <%@
➥ Import Namespace="Microsoft.SharePoint" %>
<% Response.ContentType = "text/xml"; %>
```

Next, find the soap tag

```
<soap:address location="http://server_name:Port/Path/GetAuthor.asmx" />
```

and replace it with

```
<soap:address location=<% SPEncode.WriteHtmlEncodeWithQuote
➥ (Response, SPWeb.OriginalBaseUrl(Request), '"'); %> />
```

And save the file as *GetAuthor*Wsdl.aspx. Ok, that was kind of boring, but after these two files are in place, you don't have to modify them much. The .WSDL file needs more love than the .DISCO file. The .DISCO file won't change often, but the .WSDL file will change every time you change a method signature or add a method. Other than that, it's pretty static. Now it's just a matter of putting them where they go. Copy the two .ASPX pages you just made, GETAUTHORWSDL.ASPX and GETAUTHORWSDL.ASPX, and the GETAUTHOR.ASMX file to C:\Program Files\Common Files\Microsoft Shared\web server extensions\60\ISAPI. Copy the .DLL to the bin folder of C:\Program Files\Common Files\Microsoft Shared\web server extensions\60\ISAPI as well.

The data access class needs to be added to the bin folder as well. This class could be added to the global assembly cache and called from there, but for simplicity in this example we just put it in the *bin* folder as well.

CUSTOMPROPERTYDATAMANIPULATION.ASPX

For each type of custom property, there should be an .ASPX page that will be opened in the modal window. CUSTOMPROPERTYDATA MANIPULATION.ASPX represents any page that would be used to present the custom property types to the user. A better name would indicate the property that is being used.

When the user clicks the Author Lookup button, a modal dialog is opened, and CUSTOMPROPERTYDATAMANIPULATION.ASPX is rendered. This page presents our user control to the user along with a button to close the window. In a real-world situation, you would probably have a cancel button, and your custom property type would be a little more complicated.

A quick note about Word and its modal windows is that Word caches the pages. In development, it can be quite frustrating to delete the cache from the browser every time you make a change. A common cure for caching involves the following lines of code:

Listing 4.36   Snippet to Prevent Caching

```
Response.Cache.SetNoServerCaching();
Response.Cache.SetCacheability(System.Web.HttpCacheability.NoCache);
Response.Cache.SetNoStore();
Response.Cache.SetExpires(new DateTime(1900, 1, 1, 0, 0, 0, 0));
```

This code will keep the page from caching in most cases except for when you get a syntax error. In that case, you need to delete the cache from Internet Explorer. The heart of this technique is retrieving the custom field schema from SharePoint and passing information to the user control. Using the same techniques as before, we will pass the context information and field of interest in the query string when the user clicks the Select Author button.

Listing 4.37   CustomPropertyDataManipulation.aspx

```
<%
string url = Request.QueryString["URL"];
string list = url.Substring(url.LastIndexOf('/') + 1).ToString();
string strField = Request.QueryString["InternalFieldName"];

SPSite siteCollection = new SPSite(url);
SPWeb spWeb = siteCollection.OpenWeb();
SPList spList = spWeb.Lists[list];

SPFieldCollection spFields = spList.Fields;
SPField spField = spFields.GetFieldByInternalName(strField);

SharePointBook.SPCustomField spCustomField = new SharePointBook.
➥ SPCustomField();
AuthorLookup1.Style = spCustomField.GetCustomSetting(spField,
➥ "Style").ToString();
AuthorLookup1.DefaultValue = Request.QueryString["defaultValue"];
%>
<TD><uc1:AuthorLookup id="AuthorLookup1" ElemToSet="myOutput"
➥ WhatToReturn="both" runat="server"></uc1:AuthorLookup></TD>
```

The `url` is parsed to retrieve the `siteCollection` and the library. The `strField` is populated from the query string as well. With that information, we can look up the custom properties of the field and pass the information to the user control.

We've used setting the text to red as an example of how to pass specific information to the user control. Anything could be passed back to the user control. , though, not just style settings. A key could be passed to indicate what kind of data to return and from where. Perhaps there are several lookups that would be valuable, such as a query on publishers or books, or a query from some other database all together.

Summary

Custom properties are useful when integrating third-party applications. Although much custom code must be implemented, when in place, one or many custom properties can be used. We've touched on many internal facets pertaining to the inner workings of SharePoint. Although we have focused specifically on document libraries, these same techniques can be used in other Lists as well. This example was chosen for this book because it forces exposure to many different features inside SharePoint. Let's take a quick recap of what we've covered.

- A custom property is a property that doesn't ship with SharePoint that fulfills a business need.
- As a rule of thumb, never customize code Microsoft gives us; instead, make a copy and edit the copy.
- A new site definition should always be created for any custom site modifications, for supportability but also for organization and sanity.
- FLDEDIT.ASPX, FLDNEW.ASPX, and LISTEDIT.ASPX are used for creating and maintaining a custom property. Granted, we specifically looked at a document library, but don't forget that these same pages are used in other lists as well.
- We've seen JavaScript, user controls, ASP.NET, web services, and Data Access Blocks, which we already assumed you had experience with, and it's good to know that SharePoint uses those things that developers already know.
- In this chapter and a few places throughout this book, we've discussed `CustomJSUrl`. This single attribute can be a valuable tool—it makes the integration of a custom property into Word possible.
- We've created a web service that will run in the SharePoint environment. There are a handful of web services you should take the time to explore, but writing your own can also come in handy.

CHAPTER 5

Global Customizations

Up to this point, we have discussed customizations that are selectively applied to sites. In this chapter, we talk about customizations that are globally applied to every site. We discuss customizing themes, automated emails, document icons, and online help.

Themes

Themes provide a quick way for users to customize their site's look. Behind the scenes, all that is happening is the application of predefined style sheets.

There are two basic types of themes: SharePoint themes and Front-Page themes. SharePoint themes exist as physical content and configuration files on the SharePoint server. These are referenced dynamically in the site's ASPX pages through a SharePoint web control. On the other hand, FrontPage themes originate on the web designer's computer. When a FrontPage theme is applied, the CSS and image files are copied from the client's computer into the SharePoint site. The site's web pages, therefore, become unghosted.

Because FrontPage themes are configured at the web developer's computer rather than at the server level, it is outside the scope of this chapter to go beyond summarizing their functionality. Briefly, each FrontPage theme is packaged within a separate ELM file. These ELM files aggregate several other CSS and image files together. Changes to the theme necessitate unpacking the ELM file, adding, modifying, or deleting the appropriate files, and then repacking them. See Microsoft Support Q295409 article "Unpacking and repacking files in themes in FrontPage" for more detailed information.

As far as the SharePoint server is concerned, a FrontPage theme represents several individual files that are copied to each SharePoint site. Thus, if a FrontPage developer modifies a theme, it is not reflected on a

SharePoint site using the old theme unless the developer reapplies the new theme and saves the changes to the site. Separate copies of these theme files exist for each modified site and are stored in the SharePoint database. This implementation makes it exceedingly difficult to make changes to the FrontPage theme across all sites currently using it. In this situation, the web developer must connect to every site using the theme, modify the theme, and then save changes. Managing consistent changes to FrontPage themes in even a small company becomes intolerable.

SharePoint Themes

The general properties of all SharePoint themes are specified within SPTHEMES.XML. The theme's title, description, preview image, and path to its definition are contained within this file. As such, there is an obvious parallel to WEBTEMP.XML.

As shown in Figure 5.1, SPTHEMES.XML is located in the C:\Program Files\Common Files\Microsoft Shared\web server extensions\60\TEMPLATE\LAYOUTS\1033 folder. The various theme definitions are found as subfolders of C:\Program Files\Common Files\Microsoft Shared\web server extensions\60\TEMPLATE\THEMES.

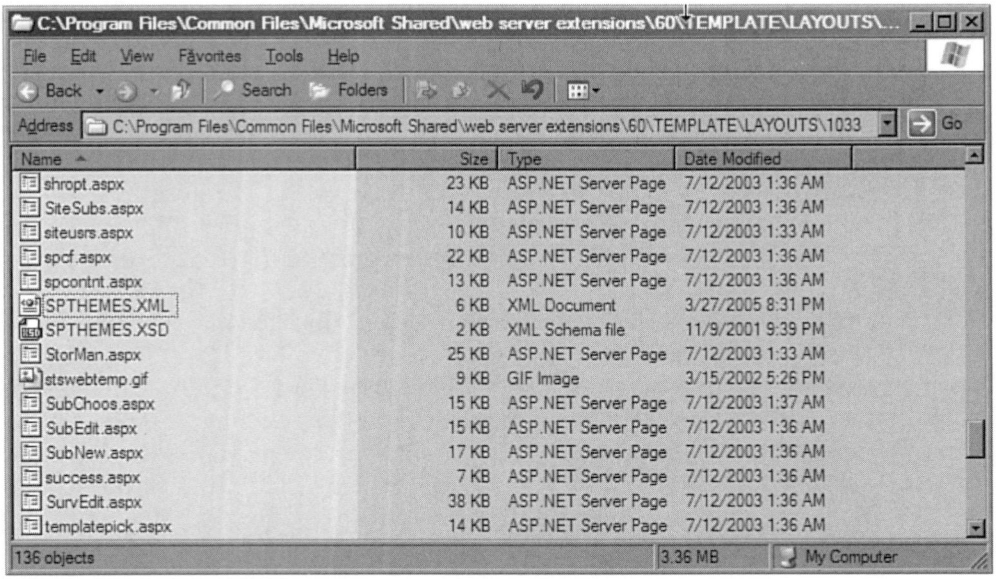

Figure 5.1   Layouts/1033 folder with SPTHEMES.XML highlighted.

Although you could modify the existing theme definitions, it is highly recommended to create a new one instead. To that end, let us walk through an example of creating a new theme. This new theme will be entitled My First Theme. First, modify SPTHEMES.XML so that the bolded `Templates` node shown in Listing 5.1 is added to the bottom.

Listing 5.1   SPTHEMES.XML with My First Theme Added

```
.
.
.

<Templates>
  <TemplateID>spring</TemplateID>
  <DisplayName>Spring</DisplayName>
  <Description>Description</Description>
  <Thumbnail>../images/thspring.png</Thumbnail>
  <Preview>../images/thspring.gif</Preview>
</Templates>
<Templates>
  <TemplateID>water</TemplateID>
  <DisplayName>Water</DisplayName>
  <Description>Description</Description>
  <Thumbnail>../images/thwater.png</Thumbnail>
  <Preview>../images/thwater.gif</Preview>
</Templates>
<Templates>
  <TemplateID>myfirsttheme</TemplateID>
  <DisplayName>My First Theme</DisplayName>
  <Description>Description</Description>
  <Thumbnail>../images/thspring.png</Thumbnail>
  <Preview>../images/thspring.gif</Preview>
</Templates>
</SPThemes>
```

The placement of the `Templates` nodes within SPTHEMES.XML determines their order in the selection list shown in Figure 5.2. We could have maintained the alphabetical structure of this list by placing the bolded My First Theme `Templates` node between the Journal and Papyrus theme nodes.

As shown in Listing 5.1, each `Templates` node in SPTHEMES.XML contains a title (`DisplayName`), description (`Description`), images

(Thumbnail and Preview), and path to its definition (TemplateID). Addressing the path to the definition and the definition itself is the next step in the process of adding a theme.

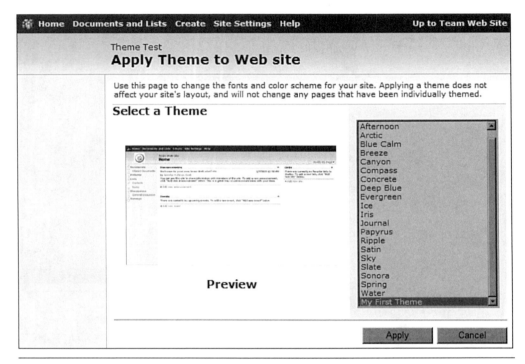

Figure 5.2   Applying My First Theme.

Now that we have specified a *myfirsttheme* folder in SPTHEMES.XML, we must honor our statement. As with site definitions, the preferred way to create a new theme is to copy an old one and modify it as appropriate. Therefore, make a copy of the SPRING folder and rename it MyFirstTheme.

The resulting MyFirstTheme theme, along with all the other theme definitions, is shown in Figure 5.3. However, you are under no obligation to base your theme off the SPRING theme as we did. You could have based it on any of the other themes.

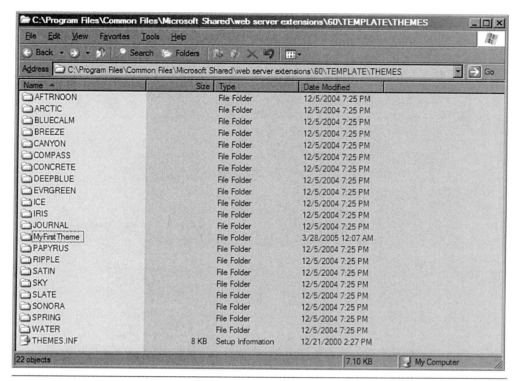

Figure 5.3   Themes folder.

Next, rename the SPRING.INF file to MYFIRSTTHEME.INF. This is done so that it matches the `TemplateID` specified in SPTHEMES.XML and consequently the folder name. The modified INF filename and the files that define the theme are shown in Figure 5.4.

If we were creating a new theme, we would modify the CSS and images as desired. We also would have specified a new preview image in SPTHEMES.XML to reflect our changes in the theme definition.

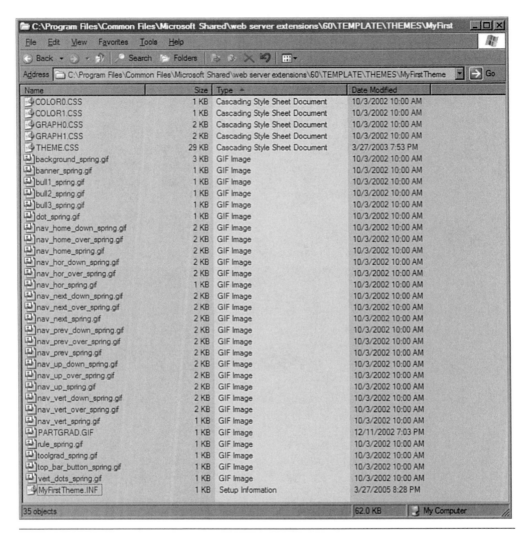

Figure 5.4   MyFirstTheme folder with a matching MYFIRSTTHEME.INF file.

The final change requires us to update the title in the renamed INF file. The updated text of MyFirstTheme.INF is bolded in Listing 5.2.

Listing 5.2   MyFirstTheme.INF

```
[info]
title=My First Theme
codepage=65001
version=3.00
format=2.00
readonly=true
refcount=0

[titles]
1031=Frühling
.
.
.
```

After executing an IISReset, your new theme will be fully installed within SharePoint. However, if you receive an error similar to Figure 5.5, you have probably forgotten to update the name of the INF file to match the `TemplateID` value.

After your site encounters this error, you will not be able to rename the INF file, execute an IISReset, and then apply the theme again. You will continue to receive the same error. To overcome this issue, you must delete the site that encountered the error, create it anew, and then apply the theme after correctly renaming the INF file.

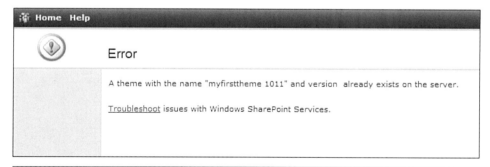

Figure 5.5   Error applying theme.

Customizing Email Alerts

Alerts are a way that users keep informed about changes to document libraries, lists, search results, and virtually all SharePoint content without having to check each site manually on a periodic basis. Through email, SharePoint alerts the users to changes. Figure 5.6 shows a typical alert message. SharePoint generated this message when a user deleted a file from a document library. Alert messages can be customized through NOTIFSITEHDR.XML, NOTIFLISTHDR.XML, NOTIFITEM. XML, and NOTIFSITEFTR.XML, which can be found in the C:\Program Files\Common Files\Microsoft Shared\web server extensions\60\TEMPLATE\1033\XML folder.

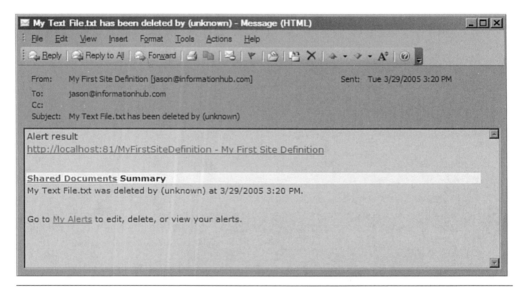

Figure 5.6 Default styled alert email.

The summation of these four XML files defines the HTML email message sent for the alert. Listing 5.3 details the HTML email of Figure 5.6. As shown in the bolded comments of Listing 5.3, SharePoint renders the NOTIFSITEHDR.XML first and then appends it with NOTIFLISTHDR.XML, NOTIFITEM.XML, and finally NOTIFSITEFTR. XML.

Listing 5.3   HTML Source of Figure 5.6

```html
<!--[ Begin Source: "NotifSiteHdr.xml" ]-->
<HTML dir=ltr>
<HEAD>
 <TITLE></TITLE>
 <STYLE type="text/css"><!--
   .ms-notif-descriptiontext {
     color: black;
     font-family: verdana;
     font-size: 8pt;
   }
   .ms-notif-subsmanageheader {
     background-color: #F2F2F2;
     font-family: verdana;
     font-size: 8pt;
     text-align: left;
     text-decoration: none;
     font-weight: bold;
     vertical-align: top;
   }
   .ms-notif-titlearea {
     font-family: verdana;
     font-size: 9pt;
   }
   .ms-notif-pagetitle {
     color: black;
     font-family: arial;
     font-size: 14pt;
     font-weight: normal;
   }
   .ms-notif-sectionline {
     background-color: #2254b1;
   }
 --></STYLE>
</HEAD>
<BODY marginheight="0" marginwidth="0" topmargin="0" leftmargin="0"
      text="#000000"
  link="#1B55FB" vlink="#BB1CFF" alink="#FF1C2C">
 <TABLE height="100%" width="100%" cellpadding="0" cellspacing="0"
        border="0">
   <TR>
    <TD valign="top">
```

```
<TABLE width="100%">
 <TR><TD class="ms-notif-titlearea" colspan="2" height="1">
   Alert result
 </TD></TR>
 <TR><TD class="ms-notif-titlearea" colspan="2" height="1">
  <A href="http://localhost:81/MyFirstSiteDefinition">
  http://localhost:81/MyFirstSiteDefinition - My First Site
  Definition
  </A>
 </TD></TR>
<!--[ Begin Source: "NotifListHdr.xml" ]-->
 <TR><TD> </TD></TR>
 <TR><TD class="ms-notif-subsmanageheader" colspan="2" height="1">
  <A href=
    "http://localhost:81/MyFirstSiteDefinition/
    ➥ Shared%20Documents">
  Shared Documents
  </A>
  Summary</TD>
 </TR>
<!--[ Begin Source: "NotifItem.xml" ]-->
  <TR>
  <TD class="ms-notif-descriptiontext">
  My Text File.txt was deleted by (unknown) at 3/29/2005
  ➥ 3:20 PM.
  </TD></TR>
<!--[ Begin Source: "NotifSiteFtr.xml" ]-->
  <TR><TD> </TD></TR>
  <TR><TD class="ms-notif-descriptiontext" colspan="2" height="1">
  Go to
  <A href=
"http://localhost:81/MyFirstSiteDefinition/_layouts/1033/
➥ MySubs.aspx">
    My Alerts
  </A> to edit, delete, or view your alerts.
  </TD></TR>
   </TABLE>
  </TD>
 </TR>
 </TABLE>
</BODY>
</HTML>
```

In general, NOTIFSITEHDR.XML defines high-level information about the email. It defines the email subject, HTML styles, opening HTML body tag, and information on the site where the alert originated. NOTIFLISTHDR.XML provides information on the list where the alert originated. NOTIFITEM.XML provides information on the specific list or library item that generated the alert. Finally, NOTIFSITEFTR.XML provides a link to the site's administrative page that manages alerts and closes the HTML tags opened in NOTIFSITEHDR.XML. In actuality, you could have consolidated the code of all four files into one file.

Listing 5.4 details a portion of our modified NOTIFSITEHDR.XML file. The CAML code shown in this file is representative of the code in the other XML files. Microsoft first tends to define variables, through setVar, that will be used in later sections and then generates the email's HTML message. As stated before, this is simply what Microsoft did. You are not required to follow this pattern. However, from a best practice standpoint, it is preferred if you follow their lead.

Listing 5.4 Partial Listing of NOTIFSITEHDR.XML

```xml
<xml>
  <SetVar Name="NotifyTitle" Scope="Request">
    <Switch>
      <Expr>
        <GetVar Name="AlertFrequency"/>
      </Expr>
      <Case Value="0">
        <HTML>Alert result</HTML>
      </Case>
      <Case Value="1">
        <HTML>Daily Summary</HTML>
      </Case>
      <Case Value="2">
        <HTML>Weekly Summary</HTML>
      </Case>
    </Switch>
  </SetVar>
  <SetVar Name="Subject" Scope="Request">
    <HTML><![CDATA[SharePoint Alert:  ]]></HTML>
    <IfEqual>
      <Expr1>
        <GetVar Name="AlertFrequency"/>
```

```
    </Expr1>
    <Expr2>
      <HTML>0</HTML>
    </Expr2>
    <Then>
      <Switch>
        <Expr>
          <GetVar Name="EventType"/>
        </Expr>
        <Default>
          <GetVar Name="ItemName"/>
          <HTML> has been changed by </HTML>
          <GetVar Name="ModifiedBy"/>
        </Default>
        <Case Value="1">
          <GetVar Name="ItemName"/>
          <HTML> has been added by </HTML>
          <GetVar Name="ModifiedBy"/>
        </Case>
        <Case Value="2">
          <GetVar Name="ItemName"/>
          <HTML> has been modified by </HTML>
          <GetVar Name="ModifiedBy"/>
        </Case>
.
.
.

      </Switch>
    </Then>
    <Else>
      <GetVar Name="SiteName"/>
      <HTML><![CDATA[ ]]></HTML>
      <GetVar Name="NotifyTitle"/>
    </Else>
  </IfEqual>
</SetVar>
<HTML>
  <![CDATA[
    <!--[ Begin Source: "NotifSiteHdr.xml" ]-->
    <HTML dir=ltr>
      <HEAD>
        <TITLE></TITLE>
        <STYLE type="text/css"><!--
          .ms-notif-descriptiontext {
              color: black;
```

```
                font-family:
    ]]>
  </HTML>
.
.
.
```

In Listing 5.4, two variables are instantiated through `SetVar`— `NotifyTitle` and `Subject`. The resulting `NotifyTitle` value is reused (which is always preferable to recalculating) several times throughout NOTIFSITEHDR.XML with the aid of `GetVar`. The `Subject` variable is a special variable that SharePoint will read to specify the email's subject. It is not referenced with `GetVar` in any of the XML files.

The only modification we have made to NOTIFSITEHDR.XML in Listing 5.4 was to insert the "SharePoint Alert:" into the `Subject` variable's definition. Thus the new subject will now be prefixed with "Share-Point Alert:" for all subsequent alerts. An email with the updated subject is shown in Figure 5.7.

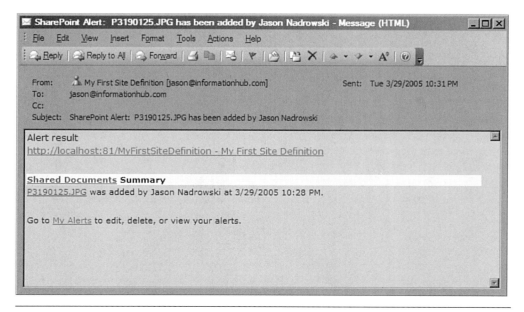

Figure 5.7   Alert email with modified subject.

The remainder of the file generates its portion of the HTML email. It should be noted that you can access several predefined variables through `GetVar`. These variables are summarized in Table 5.1.

Table 5.1   Predefined Variables Accessible within the Alert XML Files

Variable Name	Description
AlertFrequency	Specifies how frequently the user chose to be alerted. Valid integer values include: 0 (immediate), 1 (daily), and 2 (weekly).
EventType	Specifies the event type that triggered this alert. Valid integer values include: 1 (item added), 2 (item modified), 4 (item deleted), 16 (discussion added), 32 (discussion modified), 64 (discussion deleted), 128 (discussion closed), and 256 (discussion activated).
ItemName	Specifies the item's name.
ItemUrl	Specifies the item's absolute URL.
ListName	Specifies the list's title.
ListUrl	Specifies the list's absolute URL.
ModifiedBy	Specifies the person who last modified the item.
MySubsUrl	Specifies the site's alerts administration page.
SiteLanguage	Specifies the site's LCID.
SiteName	Specifies the site's title.
SiteUrl	Specifies the site's absolute URL.
TimeLastModified	Specifies the item's modification time.

Keep in mind that the SharePoint Timer Service will need to be recycled before any changes to the notification XML files are reflected in alert emails. Executing IISReset has no affect on the alert subsystem. Remember, it is the SharePoint Timer Service that sends the alert emails.

Customizing the Site Collection Retention Warning Email

If configured by the SharePoint administrator, site collection retention warnings are sent to site collection owners whose sites have not been accessed for a predefined length of time. These emails should prompt owners to delete unused content, thereby conserving SharePoint server hard disk space.

The customization of retention warnings is a bit simpler than alerts. There is only one file—DEADWEB.XML—and the available CAML is significantly restricted. An example retention warning email is shown in Figure 5.8.

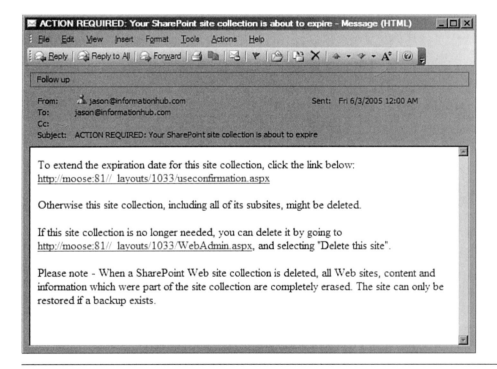

Figure 5.8   Inactive site collection email.

DEADWEB.XML is located in C:\Program Files\Common Files\Microsoft Shared\web server extensions\60\TEMPLATE\1033\ XML. Its default contents are shown in Listing 5.5.

Listing 5.5 DEADWEB.XML

```xml
<?xml version="1.0" encoding="utf-8" ?>
<!-- _lcid="1033" _version="11.0.5510" _dal="1" -->
<!-- _LocalBinding -->
<Email>
  <Confirmation>
    <ConfirmationSubject>
      Confirm SharePoint Web site in use
    </ConfirmationSubject>
    <ConfirmationBody>
      <![CDATA[Please follow the link below to your SharePoint Web
              site to confirm that it is still in use.
              <br><a href="|0">|0</a><br><br>
              If the site is not being used, please go to
              <a href="|1">|1</a>,
              and select "Delete This Site" to remove the Web site.
              <br><br>
              You will receive reminders of this until you confirm
              the site is in use, or delete it.]]>
    </ConfirmationBody>
  </Confirmation>
  <AutoDeleteWarning>
    <AutoDeleteSubject>
      ACTION REQUIRED: Your SharePoint site collection is about to
      expire
    </AutoDeleteSubject>
    <AutoDeleteBody>
      <![CDATA[To extend the expiration date for this site
              collection, click the link below:
              <br><a href="|0">|0</a><br><br>
              Otherwise this site collection, including all of its
              subsites, might be deleted.<br><br>
              If this site collection is no longer needed, you can
              delete it by going to <a href="|1">|1</a>, and
              selecting "Delete this site".<br><br>
              Please note - When a SharePoint Web site collection is
              deleted, all Web sites, content and information which
              were part of the site collection are
              completely erased.
              The site can only be restored if a backup exists.]]>
    </AutoDeleteBody>
  </AutoDeleteWarning>
</Email>
```

DEADWEB.XML is divided between two `xml` elements: `Confirmation` and `AutoDeleteWarning`. `AutoDeleteWarning` defines the email when the site will be deleted automatically ("Automatically delete the site collection if use is not confirmed" is checked in Figure 5.9). `Confirmation` defines the email when the site will not be automatically deleted ("Automatically delete the site collection if use is not confirmed" is not checked).

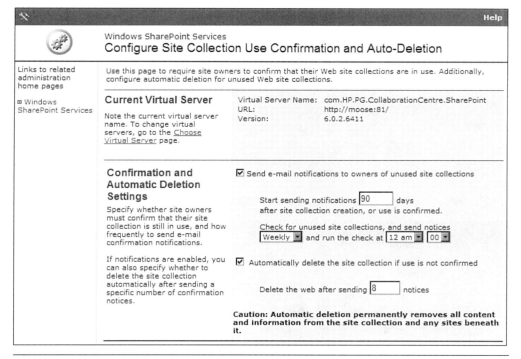

Figure 5.9   Confirmation and Auto-Deletion Settings.

`Confirmation` and `AutoDeleteWarning` subject and body tags in Listing 5.5 are self-explanatory. The interesting references are `|0` and `|1`. These reference the use confirmation and site collection deletion full URLs, respectively. In our example, they were translated to http://moose:81//_layouts/1033/useconfirmation.aspx and http://moose:81//_layouts/1033/WebAdmin.aspx.

Modifying the Document Library's File Type Behaviors

SharePoint can display an icon for each document in the library. This document icon is based on that document's file extension. Icons provide a quick way for users to scan the document library to zero in on the file for which they are searching. Figure 5.10 shows a document library with several different file types and their associated icons.

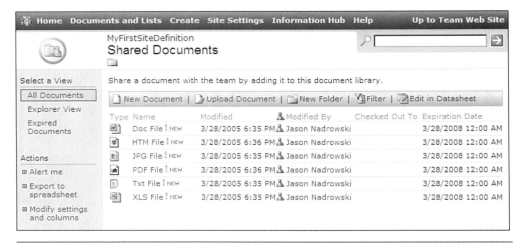

Figure 5.10   Shared Documents without PDF icon.

One noticeably incorrect icon in Figure 5.10 is the PDF icon. In actuality, this isn't a SharePoint error. SharePoint simply does not define an icon for Adobe or any other vendor's file types. When an undefined file type is encountered, SharePoint displays its default icon (ICGEN.GIF).

As with everything else in SharePoint, document icons can be customized. We can therefore configure SharePoint to display the PDF icon for PDF documents or any other file extension rather easily.

Adding a PDF Icon

Document type mappings to document icons are defined within DOCI-CON.XML, which is found in C:\Program Files\Common Files\Microsoft Shared\web server extensions\60\TEMPLATE\XML. Mapping a document icon to a file extension is as simple as adding a single line to the XML file. As shown in Listing 5.6, we added an additional `Mapping` element to DOCICON.XML so that it would show a PDF icon for a PDF document.

Listing 5.6 DOCICON.XML Extension

```
<DocIcons>
.
.
.

  <ByExtension>
.
.
.

    <Mapping Key="one" Value="icone.gif"
            EditText="Microsoft Office OneNote"
            OpenControl="SharePoint.OpenDocuments"/>
    <Mapping Key="pdf" Value="pdf.gif" />
    <Mapping Key="png" Value="icpng.gif"/>
    <Mapping Key="pot" Value="icpot.gif"
            EditText="Microsoft Office PowerPoint"
            OpenControl="SharePoint.OpenDocuments"/>
    <Mapping Key="ppt" Value="icppt.gif"
            EditText="Microsoft Office PowerPoint"
            OpenControl="SharePoint.OpenDocuments"/>.
.
.
.
```

`Mapping`'s `Key` attribute specifies the file extension, while the `Value` attribute specifies the icon to display. Because the image is retrieved from the _layouts/images virtual folder, our PDF icon must be copied to the C:\Program Files\Common Files\Microsoft Shared\web server extensions\60\TEMPLATE\IMAGES folder.

PDF.GIF is deployed with Adobe Acrobat Professional. Assuming you have installed Acrobat Professional on your computer, you should find the image in one of the folders under C:\Program Files\Adobe. Alternatively, there are several resources on the Internet where you can download the PDF.GIF icon. After performing an IISReset, the PDF icon will appear next to PDF documents in the document library. This is shown in Figure 5.11.

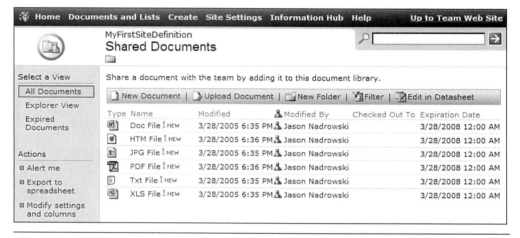

Figure 5.11   Shared Documents with PDF icon.

DOCICON.XML: Beyond File Extensions and Icons

DOCICON.XML defines more than the mapping of an icon to an extension. It also associates a file's meta name to an icon and defines how to open, edit, and render files. This rich functionality is summarized in Table 5.2.

Table 5.2   `<Mapping>` Attributes

Attribute	Required	Type	Description
AcceptHeader	No	Text	Specifies the client application to use to open this document type. If the specified client application does not exist on the user's computer, SharePoint can render the contents of the document as HTML. See the `Microsoft.HtmlTrans.Interface` namespace for more information.
EditText	No	Text	Specifies a friendly name for the application that will edit the document.
HandlerUrl	No	Text	Specifies a server URL that will convert the document's content to HTML when the user does not have the specified client application installed.
Key	Yes	Text	Specifies the file extension if in the `ByExtension` section or the `ProgID` if in the `ByProgID` section.
OpenControl	No	Text	Specifies the ActiveX control to use to open the document for editing.
Value	No	Text	Specifies the icon's filename. The icon must exist within the C:\Program Files\Common Files\Microsoft Shared\Web Server Extensions\60\Template\Images folder or sub-tree.

In the previous section, we discussed how to associate an icon with an extension. However, SharePoint provides an additional way to associate icons with files. This additional way is through examination of a file's `meta` tags.

Listing 5.7 details the top portion of a Microsoft Office document saved as an HTML file. As you can see, there is quite a bit of embedded information that tells us that this file was authored by Microsoft Word. The most official of these hints is the bolded `meta` tag that has a `name` attribute of `ProgID`. SharePoint uses the `content` attribute of this tag to associate an icon with the file. The icon determined from the `meta` tag

takes precedence over an icon determined from the document extension.

Listing 5.7   MyFile.HTM with a `meta` Tag Linking It to Microsoft Word

```html
<html xmlns:o="urn:schemas-microsoft-com:office:office"
xmlns:w="urn:schemas-microsoft-com:office:word"
xmlns="http://www.w3.org/TR/REC-html40">

<head>
<meta http-equiv=Content-Type content="text/html; charset=
➥ windows-1252">
<meta name=ProgId content=Word.Document>
.
.
.
```

From Listing 5.8, you can see that a file's behaviors (icons, opening, editing, and rendering) are defined through its `meta` tag or extension. The
bolded elements in the listing define a Word document's behaviors for
both `meta` tag and extension.

Listing 5.8   DOCICON.XML `ProgID` and Extension

```xml
<DocIcons>
  <ByProgID>
    <Mapping Key="Excel.Sheet" Value="ichtmxls.gif"
             EditText="Microsoft Office Excel"
             OpenControl="SharePoint.OpenDocuments"/>
    <Mapping Key="FrontPage.Editor.Document" Value="ichtmfp.gif"
             EditText="Microsoft Office FrontPage"
             OpenControl="SharePoint.OpenDocuments"/>
    <Mapping Key="PowerPoint.Slide" Value="ichtmppt.gif"
             EditText="Microsoft Office PowerPoint"
             OpenControl="SharePoint.OpenDocuments"/>
    <Mapping Key="Publisher.Document" Value="ichtmpub.gif"
             EditText="Microsoft Office Publisher"
             OpenControl="SharePoint.OpenDocuments"/>
    <Mapping Key="SharePoint.WebPartPage.Document"
             Value="icsmrtpg.gif"
```

```
            EditText="Microsoft Office FrontPage"
            OpenControl="SharePoint.OpenDocuments"/>
    <Mapping Key="Word.Document" Value="ichtmdoc.gif"
            EditText="Microsoft Office Word"
            OpenControl="SharePoint.OpenDocuments"/>
    <Mapping Key="XDocs.Document" Value="icxddoc.gif"
            EditText="Microsoft Office InfoPath"
            OpenControl="SharePoint.OpenXMLDocuments"/>
    <Mapping Key="InfoPath.Document" Value="icxddoc.gif"
            EditText="Microsoft Office InfoPath"
            OpenControl="SharePoint.OpenXMLDocuments"/>
</ByProgID>
<ByExtension>
  <Mapping Key="asax" Value="icasax.gif"/>
  <Mapping Key="ascx" Value="icascx.gif"/>
  <Mapping Key="asmx" Value="icasmx.gif"/>
  <Mapping Key="asp" Value="icasp.gif"/>
  <Mapping Key="aspx" Value="icaspx.gif"/>
  <Mapping Key="bmp" Value="icbmp.gif"/>
  <Mapping Key="cat" Value="iccat.gif"/>
  <Mapping Key="chm" Value="icchm.gif"/>
  <Mapping Key="config" Value="icconfig.gif"/>
  <Mapping Key="css" Value="iccss.gif"/>
  <Mapping Key="db" Value="icdb.gif"/>
  <Mapping Key="dib" Value="icdib.gif"/>
  <Mapping Key="disc" Value="icdisc.gif"/>
  <Mapping Key="doc" Value="icdoc.gif"
            EditText="Microsoft Office Word"
            OpenControl="SharePoint.OpenDocuments"/>
.
.
.
```

When associating a file's meta tag with an icon, SharePoint matches the file's content attribute with the DOCICON.XML's Key attribute. Because our example has a content attribute valued as Word.Document, the icon with a Key of Word.Document will be selected. This is shown in Figure 5.12 with the file Word Saved As HTM. Notice that the ICHTM-DOC.GIF icon is displayed instead of the icon associated with HTM files. As stated previously, an icon determined from the meta tag takes precedence over an icon determined from the document extension.

🏠 Home Documents and Lists Create Site Settings Information Hub Help				Up to Team Web Site	

MyFirstSiteDefinition
Shared Documents

Select a View	Share a document with the team by adding it to this document library.				
All Documents	New Document | Upload Document | New Folder | Filter | Edit in Datasheet				
Explorer View	Type Name	Modified	Modified By	Checked Out To	Expiration Date
Expired Documents	📄 Doc File ! NEW	3/28/2005 6:35 PM	👤 Jason Nadrowski		3/28/2008 12:00 AM
	📄 HTM File ! NEW	3/28/2005 6:36 PM	👤 Jason Nadrowski		3/28/2008 12:00 AM
Actions	📄 JPG File ! NEW	3/28/2005 6:35 PM	👤 Jason Nadrowski		3/28/2008 12:00 AM
⊞ Alert me	📄 PDF File ! NEW	3/28/2005 6:36 PM	👤 Jason Nadrowski		3/28/2008 12:00 AM
⊞ Export to spreadsheet	📄 Txt File ! NEW	3/29/2005 12:16 AM	👤 Jason Nadrowski		3/28/2008 12:00 AM
	📄 Word Saved As HTM ! NEW	3/29/2005 12:21 AM	👤 Jason Nadrowski		3/29/2008 12:00 AM
⊞ Modify settings and columns	📄 Word Saved As XML ! NEW	3/29/2005 12:21 AM	👤 Jason Nadrowski		3/29/2008 12:00 AM
	📄 XLS File ! NEW	3/28/2005 6:35 PM	👤 Jason Nadrowski		3/28/2008 12:00 AM

Figure 5.12   Shared Documents with `meta` tag associated icons.

One of the features afforded to Microsoft Office documents is that they have an Edit in Microsoft Office FrontPage/Excel/PowerPoint/Word selection from the drop-down menu. This feature, shown in Figure 5.13, is customized from DOCICON.XML.

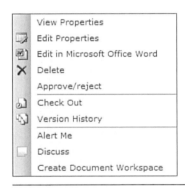

Figure 5.13   Document library drop-down menu.

The `Mapping` element's `EditText` helps to specify the text to display in the menu. In Listing 5.8, we see that the text is Microsoft Office Word. As shown in Figure 5.13, SharePoint prepends "Edit in" to that text. It therefore displays "Edit in Microsoft Office Word" in the menu. More extensive changes, such as those explained in Chapter 2, "Site

Definitions," and shown in Figure 2.6, can be accomplished through JavaScript manipulation.

We further see in Listing 5.8 that the `OpenControl` specifies a value of `SharePoint.OpenDocuments`. This value references a Microsoft ActiveX control that is used to open the document. `SharePoint.Open-Documents` is authored by Microsoft and can only open Microsoft Office documents. It cannot open Acrobat (PDF) or other types of documents.

You could build your own ActiveX control to extend the functionality of `SharePoint.OpenDocuments`. It could provide more integration with SharePoint and non-Office applications. The supporting SharePoint web pages would need to be edited to support this upgraded ActiveX control and facilitate its download to the user's computer. Furthermore, client applications integrated with this ActiveX control would need to support WebDAV for them to save their edits.

Another alternative is to use the site definition's `CustomJSUrl` directly. JavaScript could enable the direct modification of the menu and the creation of a simpler implementation that did not need to duplicate all the `SharePoint.OpenDocuments` methods.

Customizing Help

SharePoint's online help (see Figure 5.14) replicates the functionality of a CHM file. It offers context-sensitive help and provides a CHM-like user interface. Unfortunately, it lacks the capacity to do keyword searches. Unlike a CHM file, SharePoint's online help system is easily extensible. As such, this extensibility lends itself to implementing a keyword system of your own or just about anything else.

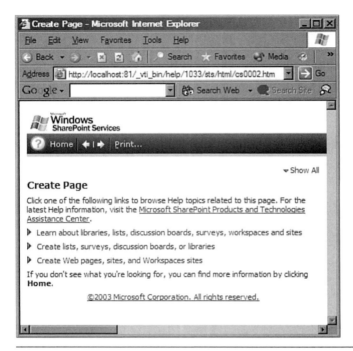

Figure 5.14   SharePoint Help for the Create Page.

Every online help page is in fact an HTML page. Modifying the content is as simple as modifying an HTML file. Adding additional content is also just as easy.

Underpinning this system are STS.XML and client-side JavaScript. STS.XML provides a mapping of predefined keys to URLs. The JavaScript on SharePoint web pages uses those predefined keys to look up appropriate help. This is how clicking Help on the Documents and Lists page will return specific help for documents and lists, while clicking Help on the Create page will return specific help for the creation of Lists, Libraries, and Web Pages.

Help File Basics

SharePoint maps the physical folder C:\Program Files\Common Files\Microsoft Shared\web server extensions\60\ISAPI\HELP to the virtual folder http://<servername:port>/_vti_bin/help. These folders contain help for Windows SharePoint Services and SharePoint Portal Server. The folder hierarchy is detailed in Table 5.3, while an example of the virtual mapping is shown in Figure 5.14.

Table 5.3   C:\Program Files\Common Files\Microsoft Shared\web server extensions \60\ISAPI\HELP and http://<servername:port>/_vti_bin/help Child Folders

Folder	Description
1033\SPS\HTML	SharePoint Portal Server HTML, CSS, and JavaScript Help files.
1033\SPS\Images	SharePoint Portal Server Image Help files.
1033\STS\HTML	Windows SharePoint Services HTML, CSS, and JavaScript Help files.
1033\STS\Images	Windows SharePoint Services Image Help files.

It should be noted that there are more than HTML and image files in the help folders. The HTML help folders also hold JavaScript and CSS files. For example, CS0002.HTM, listed in Listing 5.9, references one CSS and two JavaScript files.

Listing 5.9   CS0002.HTM (Create Page Help) `<Head>` Partial Listing

```
<html dir="ltr" xmlns:msxsl="urn:schemas-microsoft-com:xslt">
<head>
  <META http-equiv="Content-Type" content="text/html; charset=utf-8">
  <META HTTP-EQUIV="assetid" CONTENT="SP01041974">
  <title>Create Page</title>
  <link rel="stylesheet" type="text/css" href="ont.css">
  <script type="text/javascript" language="Javascript"
          src= "sExpCollapse.js"></script>
  <script type="text/javascript" language="JavaScript"
          src="backgo.js"></script>
  <SCRIPT>
    var strShow = 'Show';
    var strHide = 'Hide';

    function go(url)
    {
      navigate(url);
    }
  </SCRIPT>
  .
  .
  .
```

Because all the help files reference a CSS, formatting changes to the help files can be made easily. Changing the text formatting, background color, or just about any other style changes only requires a simple change to the CSS file.

The commonness of resources among pages also exists for JavaScript code. Perhaps the most used JavaScript function is `ToggleDiv`, which is defined in SEXPCOLLAPSE.JS and was referenced in Listing 5.9. It expands and collapses high-level topics so the user is not overwhelmed with choices. For instance, the function in the Create page help shown in Figure 5.14 is used to expand and collapse the three subtopics—(1) *Learn about libraries, lists, discussion boards, surveys, workspaces and sites*; (2) *Create lists, surveys, discussion boards, or libraries*; and (3) *Create Web pages, sites, and Workspaces sites*. Microsoft cleverly refers to these expandable lists as expandos.

In Listing 5.10, we examine the first expando in the Create page's online help. Clicking on the topic executes `ToggleDiv` with the `id` of the `div` to expand or collapse.

Listing 5.10   CS0002.HTM (Create Page Help) Partial Listing

```
<p>
  Click one of the following links to browse Help topics related to
  this page. For the latest Help information, visit the
  <a TARGET="_blank"
  href="http://go.microsoft.com/fwlink/?linkid=13080&amp;clcid=
➡ 0x409">
    Microsoft SharePoint Products and Technologies Assistance Center
  </a>.
</p>
<p>
  <a class="DropDown" href="javascript:ToggleDiv
➡ ('divExpCollAsst_1')">
    <img src="../images/blueup.gif" border="0"
         id="divExpCollAsst_1_img">
    Learn about libraries, lists, discussion boards, surveys,
    workspaces and sites
  </a>
</p>
<div class="ACECollapsed" border="0" id="divExpCollAsst_1">
```

```
<ul>
  <li>
    <a href="wscLists.htm" id="SP01009462" lcid=" ">
      About lists
    </a>
  </li>
  <li>
    <a href="wscDocLi.htm" id="SP01009463" lcid=" ">
      About libraries
    </a>
  </li>
.
.
.
```

Customizing Help Files and Context-Sensitive Help (STS.XML)

It almost goes without saying that a future service pack might update the help files. Thus, your modifications to the online help system could be overwritten and lost. In fact, WSS SP2 updated one of these help files—WSAPSUBC.HTM. Therefore, it is recommended that the entire help system be copied and accessed from another folder when customizations are desired.

Let's walk through an example of modifying the Windows Share-Point Services help. The first step is to make a copy of the STS folder in C:\Program Files\Common Files\Microsoft Shared\Web Server Extensions\60\ISAPI\HELP\1033. Name the newly copied folder STS-2005.

Next, we modify CS0002.HTM to replace the text Microsoft Share-Point Products and Technologies Assistance Center (refer to Figure 5.14) with Microsoft's SharePoint site (see Figure 5.15). As shown in Listing 5.11, change the URL and text. The resulting web page is displayed in Figure 5.15.

Listing 5.11   Modified CS0002.HTM (Create Page Help) Partial Listing

```
<p>
  Click one of the following links to browse Help topics related to
  this page. For the latest information, visit
  <a href="http://www.microsoft.com/SharePoint">
    Microsoft's SharePoint site
  </a>
</p>
```

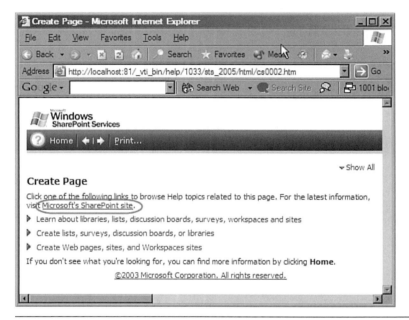

Figure 5.15   SharePoint Create Page Help with updated link.

To capture the image for Figure 5.15, we manually navigated to the STS_2005/HTML virtual folder. Now the question is how to link help pages to our SharePoint pages. The answer is through the mapping interface that SharePoint provides.

These mappings exist in the C:\Program Files\Common Files\Microsoft Shared\web server extensions\60\TEMPLATE\XML\ HELP folder. SPSMAP.XML defines the default mappings for Share-Point Portal Server help, and STS.XML defines the default mappings for Windows SharePoint Services help. However, we want to define custom mappings in our own file.

SharePoint constructs a dictionary of mappings for all files in the C:\Program Files\Common Files\Microsoft Shared\web server extensions\60\TEMPLATE\XML\HELP folder. The custom files are parsed in alphabetical order, and then the SharePoint default files (SPSMAP.XML and STS.XML) are parsed. Thus, if A.XML, B.XML, and STS.XML all have the same mappings defined, the values in A.XML will take precedence over the other files.

To create our custom mapping file, we copied STS.XML and renamed it STS_2005.XML. Next, we changed the STS path to STS_2005. This change ensures that our modified HTML files will be used instead of the SharePoint default help files. Listing 5.12 details the new STS_2005.XML. It consists of a series of `key` and `url` mappings. The mapping for the `CreatePage` is also included in the snippet.

Listing 5.12   STS_2005.XML (Modified Version of STS.XML)

```
<?xml version='1.0'?>
<helpmaps>
  <helpmap>
    <key>helphome</key>
    <url>sts_2005/html/wstoc.htm</url>
  </helpmap>
  <helpmap>
    <key>NavBarHelpHome</key>
    <url>sts_2005/html/wstoc.htm</url>
  </helpmap>
  .
  .
  .

  <helpmap>
    <key>CreatePage</key>
    <url>sts_2005/html/cs0002.htm</url>
  </helpmap>
  .
  .
  .
```

Now you must be asking, how are the keys embedded within CRE-ATE.ASPX and other web pages? The answer is JavaScript functionality. You might recall the navigation bar defined in ONET.XML. In case you don't, it is shown in Listing 5.13. It defines the Url for Help as executing the HelpWindowKey function with a key of NavBarHelpHome. As defined in Listing 5.12, this will map to STS_2005/HTML/WSTOC.HTM. In essence, clicking on the navigation bar's Help link will launch the help table of contents.

Listing 5.13   Default ONET.XML Top Navigation Bar

```
<Project Title="Team Web Site" ListDir="Lists"
        xmlns:ows="Microsoft SharePoint">
  <NavBars>
    <NavBar Name="SharePoint Top Navbar"
            Separator="   "
            Body="&lt;a ID='onettopnavbar#LABEL_ID#' href='#URL#'
            accesskey='J'&gt;#LABEL#&lt;/a&gt;"
            ID="1002">
      <NavBarLink Name="Documents and Lists"
                  Url="_layouts/[%=System.Threading.Thread.
                  CurrentThread.CurrentUICulture.LCID%]/
                  viewlsts.aspx">
      </NavBarLink>
      <NavBarLink Name="Create"
                  Url="_layouts/[%=System.Threading.Thread.
                  CurrentThread.CurrentUICulture.LCID%]/
                  create.aspx">
      </NavBarLink>
      <NavBarLink Name="Site Settings"
                  Url="_layouts/[%=System.Threading.Thread.
                  CurrentThread.CurrentUICulture.LCID%]/
                  settings.aspx">
      </NavBarLink>
      <NavBarLink Name="Help"
                  Url='javascript:HelpWindowKey("NavBarHelpHome")'>
      </NavBarLink>
    </NavBar>
```

.
.
.

However, the navigation bar's `NavBarHelpHome` key can be overridden within a web page. For instance, the CREATE.ASPX page that has been the focus in this section uses this navigation bar but overrides the default value through the `navBarHelpOverrideKey` JavaScript variable. The override through JavaScript is shown in Listing 5.14 and specifies that the `CreatePage` key should be used in lieu of any default key.

Listing 5.14　　CREATE.ASPX Overriding the `NavBarHelpHome` Key

```
<BODY marginwidth=0 marginheight=0 scroll="yes">
  <script>
    var navBarHelpOverrideKey = "CreatePage";
  </script> .
  .
  .
```

Of course the Help link on the top navigation bar doesn't hold exclusivity when launching help. You could call the `HelpWindowKey` function from any place on the page. You would pass the desired key as a parameter to the `HelpWindowKey` function.

After executing an IISReset, our new help system will be used instead of the SharePoint online help system.

As mentioned previously, the STS_2005.XML file trumps the same keys defined in STS.XML. This is why the `CreatePage` key will be mapped to the `url` defined in STS_2005.XML rather than STS.XML.

One interesting aspect of these mappings happens when a specified key cannot be found. In that case, the `helphome` key is used in its place. Just as with other keys, the custom mapping files take precedence over SharePoint's default STS.XML and SPSMAP.XML.

Now that you understand the help system, any deficiencies it might have in your enterprise can be remedied. Just remember to avoid making direct changes to SharePoint's default help files because your good work might be erased with the next service pack.

Summary

In this chapter, we discussed customizing themes, automated emails, document icons, and online help. A theme is a package of CSS files and CSS referenced resources (graphic files). Two types of themes can be applied to SharePoint sites: FrontPage and SharePoint themes. Front-Page themes exist on the FrontPage developer's computer and are copied to the SharePoint site when the developer saves SharePoint site modifications through FrontPage. SharePoint themes exist on the SharePoint server and are applied through the SharePoint web user interface.

SharePoint and FrontPage themes can be added, deleted, or modified. Our emphasis in this chapter was on SharePoint themes. Each SharePoint theme exists within its own folder. The folder contains a series of CSS, CSS referenced graphic files, and an INF file. The INF file contains several control parameters for the theme.

SharePoint enables the customization of alerts and site collection retention warnings. Alert emails are sent to users who request to be alerted about changes to SharePoint content such as additions to document libraries or modification of list items. Alert emails use CAML code to generate their dynamic output, whereas site collection retention warnings use a proprietary syntax. Both emails use XML files as the basis for their generation. Thus, customizing these XML files enables the customization of the emails.

SharePoint provides default document icons for file types originating from or supported by Microsoft. Noticeably absent are icons for file types from other vendors—such as Adobe Acrobat or Macromedia Flash files. DOCICON.XML defines the mapping of a file extension to a graphics file. Therefore, modifying DOCICON.XML appropriately and copying the referenced graphic files to the SharePoint server enables the customization of SharePoint's document icons.

SharePoint's online help system exists as a collection of HTML files, XML files, and client-side JavaScript. STS.XML and SPSMAP.XML provide a dictionary of keywords that map to HTML files. SharePoint web pages reference help through these keywords. The client-side JavaScript looks up these keywords and directs the user to the appropriate HTML help page.

Custom_JS.ASPX

The following code is Custom_JS.aspx, which is used in Chapter 4. Custom_JS.aspx provides the necessary functionality to call the web service to retrieve the author information.

```
<!-- _lcid="1033" _version="11.0.5510" _dal="1" -->
<%@ Page language="C#"      %>
<%@ Register Tagprefix="SharePoint" Namespace=
➥ "Microsoft.SharePoint.WebControls" Assembly=
➥ "Microsoft.SharePoint, Version=11.0.0.0, Culture=
➥ neutral, PublicKeyToken=71e9bce111e9429c" %>
<%@ Register Tagprefix="Utilities" Namespace=
➥ "Microsoft.SharePoint.Utilities" Assembly=
➥ "Microsoft.SharePoint, Version=11.0.0.0, Culture=
➥ neutral, PublicKeyToken=71e9bce111e9429c" %>
<%@ Import Namespace="Microsoft.SharePoint" %>
<%@ Register Tagprefix="WebPartPages" Namespace=
➥ "Microsoft.SharePoint.WebPartPages" Assembly=
➥ "Microsoft.SharePoint, Version=11.0.0.0, Culture=
➥ neutral, PublicKeyToken=71e9bce111e9429c" %>
<%
bool loadCPS = false;
string host = Request.ServerVariables["HTTP_HOST"];
string myContext = Request.QueryString["Context"];
string url = "";
string list = "";
string dialogview = "";
string location = "";
int idxQuery = myContext.IndexOf('?');
Hashtable hash = new Hashtable();
string[] nameValue;
string[] param = myContext.Substring(idxQuery + 1).
➥ Split('&');
```

```
if (idxQuery>0) {
    for (int i=0;i<param.Length;i++){
        if (param[i].IndexOf('=')>0) {
            nameValue = param[i].Split('=');
            hash.Add(nameValue[0], nameValue[1]);
        }
    }
}


dialogview = hash.ContainsKey("dialogview") ? hash
➥ ["dialogview"].ToString() : "";
location = hash.ContainsKey("location") ? hash
➥ ["location"].ToString() : "" ;

if (dialogview == "SaveForm"){
    location = location.Remove(location.ToLower().
➥ IndexOf("/"), location.Length -location.ToLower().
➥ IndexOf("/"));
    url = myContext.Remove(myContext.ToLower().
    ➥ LastIndexOf("/_vti_bin/owssvr.dll"),
    ➥ myContext.Length - myContext.ToLower().
    ➥ LastIndexOf("/_vti_bin/owssvr.dll")) + "/" +
    ➥ location;
    list = location;
    loadCPS = true;
}


if (myContext.ToLower().IndexOf("/forms/editform.aspx")
➥ > 0){
    url = myContext.Remove(myContext.ToLower().
    ➥ LastIndexOf("/forms/editform.aspx"), myContext.
    ➥ Length - myContext.ToLower().LastIndexOf
    ➥ ("/forms/editform.aspx") );
    list = url.Substring(url.LastIndexOf('/') +
    ➥ 1).ToString();
    loadCPS = true;
}


if (myContext.ToLower().IndexOf("/forms/upload.aspx")
➥ > 0){
    url = myContext.Remove(myContext.ToLower().
    ➥ LastIndexOf("/forms/upload.aspx"), myContext.
    ➥ Length - myContext.ToLower().LastIndexOf
    ➥ ("/forms/upload.aspx"));
```

```
        list = url.Substring(url.LastIndexOf('/') + 1).
        ➥ ToString();
        loadCPS = true;
    }


%>
function getPageName(){
    var sPath = window.location.pathname;
    var sPage = sPath.substring(sPath.lastIndexOf('/')
    ➥ + 1);
    return sPage;
}

if (<%=loadCPS.ToString().ToLower()%>){
    // global variables - don't initialize if we don't
    // need them
    var url = '<%=Server.UrlEncode(url)%>'
    var count = 0;
    var hash = new hashtable();

    if(typeof window.attachEvent != 'undefined'){
        window.attachEvent('onload',
        ➥ doCustomFieldsDataEntry);
        if (window.onload !=null){
            window.attachEvent('onload',
            ➥ window.onload);
        }
    }
}

function showModal(elemName, strField){
    var retValue = window.showModalDialog('/_layouts/
    ➥ 1033/cps/CustomPropertyDataManipulation.
    ➥ aspx?URL=' + url + '&DefaultValue=' + document.
    ➥ getElementById(elemName).value +
    ➥ '&DefaultDisplay=' + document.getElementById
    ➥ ('disp' + elemName).value +
    ➥ '&InternalFieldName=' + strField + '','','');
    document.getElementById(elemName).value =
    ➥ retValue[0];
    document.getElementById('disp' + elemName).value =
    ➥ retValue[1];
}
```

```
function doCustomFieldsDataEntry(){
    var CustomFieldList = getCustomFieldList();
    var strButton ="";
    var tmpElem;

    if (CustomFieldList != null){
    var newText = document.createElement("<div
 ➥ onserviceavailable=\"serviceAvailable();\"
 ➥ onreadystatechange=\"doneloading();\"
 ➥ id=\"divWebServiceCaller\" style=\"behavior:url
 ➥ (<%=url%>/_layouts/1033/CPS/webservice.htc)
 ➥ \"></div>");
    document.body.appendChild(newText);
        for(var i=0; i<=CustomFieldList.length-1; i++){
            if (CustomFieldList[i][1] ==
         ➥ 'AuthorLookup'){
                tmpElem = document.getElementById
                 ➥ (this.frm.stFieldPrefix +
                 ➥ CustomFieldList[i][0]);
                if (tmpElem != null){
                    var idDisp = "disp" + this.frm.
                     ➥ stFieldPrefix + CustomFieldList
                     ➥ [i][0];
                    tmpElem.readOnly = true;
                    tmpElem.onfocus = "document.
                     ➥ getElementById('btn' +
                     ➥ tmpElem.name + "').focus();
                     ➥ document.getElementById('btn' +
                     ➥ tmpElem.name + "').select();";
                    strButton = "<INPUT tabindex= \"" +
                     ➥ tmpElem.tabIndex + "\" id=\"btn"
                     ➥ + tmpElem.name + "\"  name=\"btn"
                     ➥ + tmpElem.name + "\" TYPE=\"BUTTON\"
                     ➥ VALUE=\"Select Author\"
                     ➥ ONCLICK=\"showModal('" +
                     ➥ tmpElem.name + "','" +
                     ➥ CustomFieldList[i][0] + "');\">";
                    strDisplay = "<textarea readonly
                     ➥ class= \"" + tmpElem.className +
                     ➥ "\"id=\"" + idDisp  + "\" name=\""
                     ➥ + idDisp + "\"></textarea>";
                    tmpElem.outerHTML = strButton +
                     ➥ '<BR>' + tmpElem.outerHTML +
```

```
                            ➥ '<BR>' + strDisplay;
                    }
                }
            }
        }
    }

    function serviceAvailable() {
        var CustomFieldList = getCustomFieldList();
        if (CustomFieldList != null){
            for(var i=0; i<=CustomFieldList.length-1; i++){
                tmpElem = document.getElementById(this.frm.
                ➥ stFieldPrefix + CustomFieldList[i][0]);
                if (tmpElem != null){
                    if (CustomFieldList[i][1] ==
                    ➥ 'AuthorLookup'){
                        var idDisp = "disp" + this.frm.
                        ➥ stFieldPrefix + CustomFieldList
                        ➥ [i][0];
                        var idCall = document.getElementById
                        ➥ ("divWebServiceCaller").
                        ➥ GetAuthor.callService
                        ➥ (handleWebServiceResult, "ById",
                        ➥ tmpElem.value);
                        hash.add (idCall, document.
                        ➥ getElementById(idDisp));

                    }
                }
            }
        }
    }

    function handleWebServiceResult(res) {
        if (!res.error) {
            var tmpElem = hash.get(res.id)
            tmpElem.value = res.value;
        }
      else {
            alert("Unsuccessful call. Error is " +
            ➥ res.errorDetail.string);
        }
    }
```

```
function doneloading(){
   if (document.getElementById("divWebServiceCaller").
   ➥ readyState=="complete"){
      loadWebServices();
   }
}

function getCustomFieldList(){
   <%
      if (loadCPS){
      try{
         SharePointBook.SPCustomField spCustomField
         ➥ = new SharePointBook.SPCustomField();
         int count = 0;
         string strOutput = "";

         SPSite siteCollection = new SPSite(url);
         SPWeb spWeb = siteCollection.OpenWeb();
         SPList spList = spWeb.Lists[list];
         SPFieldCollection spFields = spList.Fields;
            foreach (SPField f in spFields)      {
               if (f.Type.ToString() == "Text"){
                  if(spCustomField.
                  ➥ isCustomField(f)){
                     strOutput += "CustomFields
                     ➥ [" + count + "] = new
                     ➥ Array(2);";
                     strOutput += "CustomFields
                     ➥ [" + count + "][0] = '" +
                     ➥ f.InternalName + "';";
                     strOutput += "CustomFields
                     ➥ [" + count + "][1] = '" +
                     ➥ spCustomField.
                     ➥ GetAttributeValue
                     ➥ (f,"Format") + "';";
                     count++;
                  }
               }
            }
            if (strOutput !="")
            {
               strOutput = "CustomFields = new Array
               ➥ (" + count + ");" + strOutput;
```

```
                strOutput += "return CustomFields;";
            }
            else
            {
                strOutput = "return null;";
            }
            Response.Write (strOutput);
        }
        catch (Exception e)
        {
            Response.Write ("alert('!"+e.Message+"');");
        }
    }
    %>
return null;
}

function hashtable() {
    this.add = mAdd;
    this.get = mGet;
}

function mAdd(name, value) {
        this[name] = value;
}

function mGet(strKeyName) {
    return(this[strKeyName]);
}

function loadWebServices() {
    document.getElementById("divWebServiceCaller").
    ➥ useService("http://<%=host%>/_vti_bin/getAuthor.
    ➥ asmx?wsdl","GetAuthor");
}
```

Index

M

THIS BOOK IS SAFARI ENABLED

INCLUDES FREE 45-DAY ACCESS TO THE ONLINE EDITION

The Safari® Enabled icon on the cover of your favorite technology book means the book is available through Safari Bookshelf. When you buy this book, you get free access to the online edition for 45 days.

Safari Bookshelf is an electronic reference library that lets you easily search thousands of technical books, find code samples, download chapters, and access technical information whenever and wherever you need it.

TO GAIN 45-DAY SAFARI ENABLED ACCESS TO THIS BOOK:

- Go to **http://www.awprofessional.com/safarienabled**
- Complete the brief registration form
- Enter the coupon code found in the front of this book on the "Copyright" page

If you have difficulty registering on Safari Bookshelf or accessing the online edition, please e-mail customer-service@safaribooksonline.com.

Addison
Wesley